A Note on the Author

BRIGID KEENAN is an author and journalist. She has worked as an editor on *Nova* magazine, the *Observer* and the *Sunday Times*. She has published two fashion histories as well as *Travels in Kashmir*, *Damascus* and the bestselling *Diplomatic Baggage*, and is a founding board member of the Palestine Festival of Literature. She lives in Pimlico and Somerset.

Packing Up

Further Adventures of a Trailing Spouse

BRIGID KEENAN

BLOOMSBURY

LONDON · OXFORD · NEW YORK · NEW DELHI · SYDNEY

Bloomsbury Paperbacks
An imprint of Bloomsbury Publishing Plc

50 Bedford Square
London
WC1B 3DP
UK

1385 Broadway
New York
NY 10018
USA

www.bloomsbury.com

BLOOMSBURY and the Diana logo are trademarks of Bloomsbury Publishing Plc

First published in Great Britain 2014
This paperback edition first published in 2015

British Library Cataloguing-in-Publication Data
A catalogue record for this book is available from the British Library.

ISBN: HB: 978-1-4088-4690-2
PB: 978-1-4088-4692-6
ePub: 978-1-4088-4691-9

2 4 6 8 10 9 7 5 3 1

Typeset by Hewer Text UK Ltd, Edinburgh
Printed and bound in Great Britain by CPI Group (UK) Ltd, Croydon CR0 4YY

MIX
Paper from
responsible sources
FSC® C020471

To find out more about our authors and books visit www.bloomsbury.com.
Here you will find extracts, author interviews, details of forthcoming events
and the option to sign up for our newsletters.

For my family, especially Malachy,
Maisie, Jackson and Iolo

Contents

Preface

Packing Up can be read by itself but it's also a sequel to a book I wrote ten years ago about the trials and tribulations of being married to a diplomat and becoming what is known as a trailing spouse, i.e., someone saintly who sacrifices their own career in order to accompany someone else round the world while they do theirs.

This book is about what happened next – it finds AW and I still travelling and trying to settle into strange places, but making other kinds of journeys too, emotional ones: becoming grandparents, getting older, and facing the black hole of retirement. While I was writing it I noticed that lots of other older women seemed to be publishing their memoirs and said to my daughter Claudia, 'If books written by young women are called chick lit, what do you think older women's should be called?' After some thought, she suggested decreplit. Here is my own contribution to decreplit: it could never have been achieved without my family. My thanks, as ever, go first to my dear AW for dragging me round the world in his wake, forcing me to open my eyes to its wonders, and for making me laugh (when I am not crying), and then to our beloved daughters Hester and Claudia, who have been the best travelling companions I could have wished for. Thank you all for so gamely allowing me to write about you.

This book is for them, and it is for Malachy, Maisie, Jackson and Iolo, the next generation, the lights of my life – may their lives be as lucky as mine has been. It is for all trailing partners who get to see the world but sometimes feel homesick and lonely; it is for the friends I have made along the way, especially Cynthia, who so wanted to read this book, and it is for all my gallant, exhausted, fellow grannies.

Finally, even though the events I write about in *Packing Up* were jotted down in my diary soon after they took place, that is no guarantee that other people saw them in the same way as I did, so I apologise in advance to anyone who remembers things differently from me.

Prologue

Prophecies and minor miracles

It must have been about halfway through our posting to Kazakhstan that AW, my diplomat husband, told me he had been to see a fortune-teller. I was completely taken aback because this seemed so out of character. (I had forgotten that he had consulted the *I Ching*, a Chinese book that predicts your future, before we came to Kazakhstan, and our destiny had come out under the heading PIT OF BLOOD, which was still a lingering worry.) And then I was filled with utter fury, imagining him discussing our intimate family details with a total stranger; I think I would have felt better if he had had an affair with her instead.

AW kept trying to tell me that Olga was a renowned fortune-teller, and that the Kazakhstani Minister of Defence never made a move without consulting her, but I went off in a sulk, and then of course (what person wouldn't have?) I had to come crawling back because I was secretly longing to know what she had told him. I can't reveal everything she said, but according to AW (who, by the way, swore he didn't tell her *anything* about us in advance) she predicted that within three years both our daughters would be married and one of them would have a baby. This was obviously completely impossible: Hester, our eldest, was just completing her

3

training as a lawyer, and though she did have a boyfriend, marriage wasn't even a pale patch, let alone a glimmer, on the horizon; while Claudia, the younger one, was at London University and had just broken off with her German boyfriend. So, as I said mockingly to AW, his fortune-teller's prophecies about our children were about as likely to happen as pigs breaking the sound barrier. In the end, of course, it all turned out exactly as Olga said it would and before scoffing at anyone ever again, I should try to keep in mind that I am not too good at predictions myself. I am the clever dick who, long ago when they were building it, swore that the Channel Tunnel was doomed to failure because no one would dare go into it, certainly not me; also the one who, back in the day, forecast that videos would never catch on (who on earth would spend eight pounds or more buying a film that they would only look at once?) and worst of all, I am the person who once refused an invitation to tea with the Beatles because no one had ever heard of them, and it was at a weekend and I couldn't be bothered.

Olga told AW that I was a writer and had just finished a book (true) which was about to be published (also true) and that it would do reasonably well (which turned out to be true, too). As for AW himself, she predicted that he would spend a good many more years in the ex-Soviet Union. 'Not if I have anything to do with it,' I said crossly – which was rather pointless as I never have had anything to do with these postings of AW's.

I was fashion editor on the *Sunday Times* when I married him in 1973. He was working overseas in development aid then, and I gave up my wonderful job for love, and have travelled with him to his overseas assignments (this is the seventh) over the four decades since. The story of all this, and how AW rose from being a humble economist weighing rice grains in the middle of nowhere in Nepal, to the top rung as an EU Ambassador (at this moment to Kazakhstan, Kyrgystan and Tajikistan in Central Asia) and how our little family coped with it all (or didn't), is told in *Diplomatic Baggage*, the book that the fortune-teller was referring to. (Speaking of which, quite recently AW and I were at a dinner given by an Iranian couple in London when, halfway through the meal, our charming hostess leaned towards AW and said, 'I am so sorry I have not yet read your wife's book, *Diplomatic Garbage.*' AW nearly did the nose trick with his food trying to contain his mirth. At the same dinner I overheard one of the other women guests say to our host, who was a very nice but not particularly exciting elderly gentleman, 'You know, you are the most divinely attractive man I have ever met.' My jaw dropped: I've never been good at flirting and now I see why, I just couldn't have brazened that out.)

We spent four years in Kazakhstan. AW loved it immediately (could that possibly have had anything to do with the thirty or so utterly gorgeous women working in his office? He says no, it was the landscape). I hated it, and the length of our posting stretched ahead like an eternity of term-time at boarding school or a prison sentence. This nomadic way of life is an emotional roller-coaster ride for us trailing spouses (as we are known by our husbands' employers): we spend the first months in each new posting crying with homesickness and loneliness and hating our husbands for taking us there, and then the last year sobbing again because we don't want to leave. People with normal lives can't begin to understand what it's like to be sent (in my case) from England to Brussels to Trinidad to Barbados, to India to West Africa to Syria to Brussels to Kazakhstan. Nothing links these postings of ours, there is no continuity: it's like being reincarnated eight times in one life. You arrive in each new place all naked (as it were) and friendless and vulnerable, you gradually build up a little world of people and interests around yourself and then, bingo, you are suddenly sent off to the other side of the world to start all over again. Kazakhstan was my worst so far because a) it was so far away and I missed my daughters so much, b) I didn't speak Russian or Kazakh, c) our house was outside the town so I couldn't wander around the streets looking in shop windows, d) I arrived in the snow and ice and bitter cold of a Central Asian midwinter, and e) our last posting was pre-revolution Syria, which, in spite of its repressive government, was the most fascinating place on earth. (The nearest interesting old building to us in Kazakhstan was a ten-hour drive away.)

Then there is the question of friends. When you have your children with you this is easy: you meet other mums dropping off their kids at the school gates. But when your offspring are older and have gone home to be educated – as they often have to because there is nowhere appropriate in your posting (this has been a source of grievance in our family for more than twenty years) – you find them by joining the local international women's club, or whatever it is called, where you are. The miracle is that there always seems to be one, and that's where I met my friends in Kazakhstan.

Finding something to do is the next and biggest hurdle – otherwise you begin to feel like a large dog cooped up in the house all day while your owner is at work: there have been times when, hearing AW returning from the office in the evening, I have had the urge to run downstairs barking and jumping up and down trying to lick his face.

Diplomatic wives are not allowed to work professionally in our husbands' postings, but we can do voluntary work, so teaching, doctoring and nursing are good careers for a trailing spouse, but the best I have come across so far is hairdressing.

One of the wives in Kazakhstan was one: she brought a dryer and a backwash basin with her when she came, and opened a salon for friends at home – she met all the other wives, had lots to do and made some money on the side. Perfect. I've tried various things: in the Gambia I found a Chinese factory to make dressing gowns I designed in batik cloth, I sold these to friends (and, just before – annoyingly – we were moved on, to Liberty's in London); in Barbados I helped with fund-raising for disabled children (we raised USD $1 million); in Syria I wrote a book about the old city of Damascus. Writing is usually too solitary to be much comfort in foreign parts, but this book involved exploring the alleyways of the old town and finding houses for my co-author Tim Beddow to photograph, so it was ideal.

In India I volunteered to help in the DCWA (Diplomatic and Commonwealth Wives Association) medical clinic and had high hopes of a career there, but I only lasted a day. Two men came in on my first morning; neither of them spoke a word of English but the older one was rolling his eyes to indicate pain and pointing to a place on the back of his neck. I couldn't see anything there, but desperate to help, I put a big plaster on it. He seemed pleased – but then the younger one came up to me, turned around and held up his hair to reveal a huge pus-filled boil in the same place on *his* neck and I realised the older man had only come along to help with communications. I couldn't find any more big plasters so I peeled the one off the older man and put it on the younger one. They went off quite happily, but I crept off home at the end of the day, ashamed of my poor medical skills, and never went back.

In Kazakhstan I filled my first year writing *Diplomatic Baggage*, and then I found a new hobby cleaning and stitching up the dirty, torn, old Central Asian embroideries you could sometimes find in the backs of shops or in heaps at craft fairs. I became slightly obsessed with this; I love mending things.

We modern trailing spouses are so spoiled compared to women of previous generations – like my mother, married to an Indian Army officer – who didn't have telephones, airplanes, email, TV or the Internet and couldn't easily keep in touch with their families, let alone see them, for years at a time. But neither did they have that 'Oh God-what-should-I-be-doing-with-my-life?' angst that can affect us today because they didn't have careers to give up in the first place. They just got on with it, painting and sketching and writing about their experiences in books with gallant titles like *Uphill Steps in India* or *My Lonely Summer in Kashmir*, and some of them became as well known – or more so – as the men they were married to: Lady Macartney's account of living in Central Asia in the early twentieth century continues to sell; Isabel Burton's *The Inner Life of Syria, Palestine and the Holy Land* is still available (she was married to the adventurer and scholar, Richard Burton, who famously instructed her to 'pay, pack and follow' when he was suddenly recalled to London from Syria in 1871). There are others in our own times: Deborah Moggach, for instance, who wrote the first of her wonderful novels when her husband was posted to Pakistan or, in a different field, Ann Paludan, who became a world expert on Chinese sculpture because her husband was posted to Beijing. But of all the trailing spouses who gained fame they wouldn't have if they had stayed at home, Julia Child, the author of the kitchen bible, *Mastering the Art of French Cooking*, is the queen: when her husband was posted from the US to Paris, she went with him and, to fill her time, she took cookery lessons – for which women all over the world, including me, will be forever grateful. (At first she did a course in making hats; luckily she gave that up or we might have had *Mastering the Art of French Fascinators* instead.)

In Kazakhstan we settled down with Nina, our cook, and Ira, our maid (you are allowed 'staff' when you become an Ambassador), plus Yuri, our handyman/gardener/driver – all Russians, as apparently Kazakhs don't like doing those kinds of jobs – in a pleasant Residence on a hill looking out over the city of Almaty across the vast steppe beyond to snow-capped mountains on the horizon. Almaty was once the capital of Kazakhstan but has recently been supplanted by Astana, a much more difficult place on the edge of Siberia, where the temperature is plus forty in summer and minus forty in winter and the mosquitoes are the size of bats. Thank goodness we did not have to go and live *there*.

We inherited Nina from our predecessor, and understood that before she became a cook she was a nursery school teacher. Towards the end of AW's posting in Kazakhstan she invited us to visit her in her dacha in the country, just outside Almaty. To our surprise, when we drove there, we had to enter a restricted military zone, so we asked Nina why her house was in an army area. 'Because of my job before,' she replied. Her job before? As a nursery school teacher? We were puzzled, but then she went on to tell us that before she was a teacher, back in the days of the Soviet Union, she worked in a munitions factory making weapons of mass destruction, bombs in particular. We were astonished, and ever since I have had fantasies involving Nina making a *Bombe Surprise* for a diplomatic party that really would astonish everyone.

I loved my outings with Nina to buy food at the Green Market, in spite of the fact that the disgusting horsemeat counter dominated the meat section (horsemeat sausage full of lumps of yellow fat is the main delicacy in Kaz). I once had to have my picture taken to go with an article on Kazakh food which I'd written for a magazine in England. 'Let's have lots of local colour in it,' said the editor. So I posed for the photographer in front of this stall, and then worried that I looked so awful that morning that readers would probably not be able to tell the difference between me and a dead horse.

One day, looking around the market, I noticed a shelf of assorted jam jars with no labels, filled with some kind of gooey white stuff. I asked Nina, who had learned a bit of English by then, what on earth it was.

'Dog fat,' she stated calmly.

'Dog fat!' I shrieked. 'Oh God! Do you *eat* it?'

'No, is for cold,' said Nina, making chest-massaging movements, which I took to mean you rubbed it on your chest if you had a cold. Even so – dog fat, aargh.

Soon after this AW and I were invited to dinner by a French couple. The first course was a pâté of some sort. 'This is delicious,' I murmured to our hostess.

'Thank you,' she said. 'It is my new discovery: rabbits' livers.' There was a sudden silence, everyone stopped abruptly, mid-chew – my mind raced round whether they came from the local market – perhaps still inside the rabbits? (yuk) or imported from France, cleaned and vacuum-packed (not so bad) – and then all our jaws reluctantly started up again, while we tried not to catch each other's eye.

Another evening we were invited to dinner by the Japanese Ambassador and his wife. It was a truly wonderful meal of about ten different, exquisite, tiny courses with accompanying wines. The accompanying wines seemed to undo the normal editing section of my brain so that when we came to leave I couldn't rein in my enthusiasm. 'That was the most delicious meal I have had since I came to Kazakhstan,' I gushed, clutching the Ambassador's wife's hand and gazing earnestly into her eyes. 'No! It was the best meal I have ever had in my life – no! I think it was the best meal ever cooked by anyone since the dawn of civilisation . . .'

'We must go home now,' said AW, pulling my arm gently but firmly.

These two dinners were given by foreigners. Kazakhs were always boasting about their reputation as hosts. 'Here in Kazakhstan we are world famous for our hospitality,' they liked to say, but we were only ever asked to one private Kazakh party in the whole of our four years there – it went on for hours and hours and I was on a table with only Russian or Kazakh speakers, so perhaps the lack of invitations was a blessing in disguise. We celebrated our daughter Claudia's twenty-fourth birthday in a new restaurant in Almaty. The cabaret was an Uzbek strongman bending iron bars and doing acrobatics, which was quite entertaining, but the finale to his act was being used as a human target – literally: people were invited to throw darts at his chest. In my memory the darts had pompoms on them, but I think I may have got that confused with bullfighting because there was the same sort of cruel vibe. It was quite shocking and probably left Claudia, not to mention the rest of us, scarred for life.

One good thing about Kazakhstan is that, a bit like Belgium, it is not too difficult to get from there to other, really fascinating places – like Samarkand and Bukhara in Uzbekistan – which otherwise we would have never visited.

The first time AW and I went to Uzbekistan by train (it took about twelve hours overnight) it was May and there was a heatwave. The radiators in the train were on, so we were sweltering in our compartment. As the evening progressed, our neighbours in other carriages, getting drunker as the hours passed, took to poking their heads round our door to have a look at us foreigners. We told one, who seemed to speak a bit of English, that we were desperately hot, and he offered to go and talk to the sleeping-car conductor about turning off the heating, or at least opening a window. A few minutes later he came back looking extremely agitated.

'My God!' he said. 'I shock, I shock' – you could tell that he really was. 'I see conductor and tea boy – how you say? Doing homosexual. I shock.'

He then disappeared, leaving us feeling distinctly uneasy and worried about the tea boy (who must have been about seventeen) for the rest of the journey, if not the rest of our lives. The only thing that distracted us a bit was seeing what AW thought was a meteorite fall to earth in a blaze of light in the pitch-black sky. You get an idea of the vastness of Kazakhstan, and how few people live there, by the fact that as the night train crosses the country you see almost no glimmers of human habitation out on the dark steppe.

Even without the tea boy, this trip was already tense. I had been in England briefly, visiting our daughters, and by chance had been summoned for a mammogram whilst there. I thought no more about it, but just as I was stepping on to the plane to go back to Kazakhstan my mobile rang: it was my doctor saying she wanted me to come in for another check as they'd seen something suspicious on the scan. I explained that I was on my way to an un-cancellable holiday with my husband in Uzbekistan, and that I couldn't turn back anyway as my luggage was on board. She said okay, but made me promise to come home immediately it was over. On the plane they played Elton John singing 'Goodbye England's Rose' and I wondered if this was a bad omen – but then I decided that since my blood is mostly Irish it didn't apply.

AW had hired a driver to bring our car down from Almaty to the railway station in Shimkent, on the border, so that we would be able to visit all kinds of places off the beaten track – and I prayed not to have cancer in every mosque and obscure shrine the length and breadth of Uzbekistan, even crawling three times under a fallen holy tree. This was a bit of a gamble, actually, because it is a fertility ritual, but I just hoped that whoever was in charge up there would understand and make it work for illness instead. It seemed to. When I got back to London two weeks later, whatever it was they'd seen on the mammogram had vanished, and I felt as if I had been given my life back.

There was another miracle on this holiday, or an example of Fate in action, or maybe just a coincidence. When we drove into Bukhara for the very first time, AW got lost, so we stopped and asked a young boy if he could help us find our hotel. (Knowing AW, just asking someone for directions was a miracle in the first place.) The boy jumped into the car to help us and then asked if he could be our guide. 'No,' said AW firmly, 'we just want to be on our own, but meet us at the hotel for lunch tomorrow.'

The boy met us every day after that. His name was Tolibjon, he was sixteen, well mannered and intelligent, and we became friends – but not so much that we agreed to his request to help him get to London to learn English. In fact we were quite fierce about *not* helping him. Three days later, we left Bukhara and more or less put the encounter out of our minds. Months passed, we were driving into Bukhara again and who was *the very first person* we should see as we entered the city, but Tolibjon. (I looked up the population of Bukhara later and discovered this was a one-in-more-than-a-quarter-of-a-million chance.) This time we exchanged email addresses before we left and, later in the year, when we returned to Uzbekistan with our family on holiday, we met up with him in Tashkent. He had worked so hard on his English, found out all about language schools in London, and was so eager and so pleasant, that we were finally persuaded we should help him study in England. He arrived in London not long afterwards, aged seventeen, all alone, and learned the language so quickly and so fluently that when he telephones I can never tell which well-spoken British friend he is. He went on to do a degree in law and we were all at his graduation cheering him on for he has become part of our family. He works for one of the top British investment banks now and his life is a million miles from what it would have been if he had not been standing on the pavement that second time we drove into Bukhara. Don't tell me there isn't a guiding hand there somewhere.

On that last family visit to Uzbekistan, Tolibjon told us about a textile market that tourists don't know, not far from Samarkand (I have to keep the place a secret because it is where the local traders buy the *suzanis* and embroideries they sell to the shops, and if I give the game away they won't be able to earn a living). The market happens early on Sunday mornings and AW promised we could pop in there on our way to visit Shahrisabz, the birthplace of Tamerlane.

At first we couldn't see anyone selling textiles, only cabbages and carrots, but then we were directed to a rather scruffy, trestle-tabled version of Aladdin's cave at the back where there were dozens of women selling all kinds of fabulous embroideries. AW groaned and said he'd go and wait by the restaurant. Mad with excitement, I plunged into the market with my slightly reluctant cousin Frances and started bargaining and buying stuff. Soon more and more women turned up, all shrieking and yelling and shoving, and pushing their embroideries into our faces and fighting each other for our attention. Soon a riot broke out – I mean, a real riot. The police were called and we foreigners were taken to a room near the restaurant and locked in. But this didn't stop the market women. It had become a sort of hilarious game. They besieged the room, feverishly trying to push textiles down the chimney, under the door, through gaps in the windows.

In the end we were ordered to leave. We had a police escort fighting back the crowd as we got to the car, and even as AW pulled away, the women were still trying to open the doors and push their embroideries in.

Driving off, my family treated me as though I was Imelda Marcos. AW said, 'I can't believe it; your *shopping* caused a riot, the *police* had to be called,' and they all vowed they would never go near a market – or a shop or anywhere selling anything – with me again.

'I only wanted a few embroideries,' I muttered, but I felt embarrassed, and guilty. The women had been so desperate to earn a few dollars and I was so lucky to have dollars to spend.

Restaurant menus reunited us. I know it's childish to giggle at menu translations (and just imagine how any of us would manage in Uzbek) but we did come across some funny ones on our travels in Uzbekistan: 'Beef language with fungus sauce'; 'Pizza with complications'; and a dish that was, strangely, 'Peopled by mushrooms'. I once saw 'fried ice cream' on a menu in India and have been baffled ever since; and AW and I still smile when we remember the newspaper headline in Nepal that read, KING WARNS AGAINST PLAYING WITH THE FUNDAMENTALS.

Language is so odd, you only have to leave out one letter and everything changes. I texted Louise, a friend, the other day and realised afterwards that I had missed out the i and had written 'Dear Louse'.

In Delhi I once heard someone refer to the Silky Road instead of the Silk Road, which left me with a mental image of people lolling about indolently on embroidered cushions, smoking opium and watching belly dancers, instead of the exhausted traders, burdened camel caravans and cold mountain passes I used to imagine.

In Kazakhstan, as in all Russian-speaking countries, the H in English words is pronounced G, so it's Garry Potter, or Genry the Eighth, or alchogol. We wondered if Father Christmas there says 'Go Go Go!' instead of 'Ho Ho Ho!' AW has his own secret theory that maybe Gogol, the great Russian writer, was really called Hohol.

Comings and goings

At weekends in Kazakhstan, AW and I would often go on excursions into the steppe or the mountains with our eccentric archaeologist friends Renato and Jean Marc, to look at ancient burial sites, or just picnic in beautiful surroundings.

Not long after one of these outings, AW asked me to look at an itchy place on his shoulder. I put on my glasses and examined the spot, but all I could see was a small black mole. A couple of mornings later, when AW was shaving, he scratched his shoulder absent-mindedly – and to his horror a huge fat tick fell into the basin. He must have picked it up from a bush or a tree and it had burrowed into his flesh, so much so that when I had looked all I had seen was a tiny part of its black back under the skin. An angry red circle developed around the place where it had been, and then the red circle expanded all over AW's shoulder and over his back, and we became alarmed. AW showed it to Elena, the doctor at the office. Elena was baffled but did some research and eventually diagnosed Lyme disease – a tick-borne illness, which, left untreated, can lead to madness and death. Thanks to Elena, AW survived, sanity intact (I think), but to me it was another black mark against Kazakhstan.

I can't remember exactly what we were doing when Hester telephoned from England to tell us that she was engaged (major happy events don't seem to leave that indelible stamp on your memory in the same way that tragedies do), but I do remember that AW and I were thrilled as we liked her fiancé George, an architect, a lot. They set a date for their wedding in the autumn that year.

The mother-of-the-bride responsibilities seemed to me so weighty that I was secretly hoping that they might run away and get married in Las Vegas, or on a beach in Thailand, or opt for a handful of friends at a hotel in London – or at least go for the sort of wedding that couples in my generation had, i.e., champagne, speeches and snacks after the service, and then everyone off home a couple of hours later, as soon as the bride and groom had left. But Hester wanted to be married in our village in Somerset and do this whole new wedding thing of an afternoon service followed by drinks, followed by dinner, followed by dancing into the early hours of the morning. Then she disappeared off to Paris to do some sort of legal pupillage and I went home on a visit to start organising the marquee, tables, chairs, champagne, wine, tablecloths, glass, cutlery, plates, portaloos, disc jockey, florist, printer, organist, singer, priest, and caterer (speaking of which, I have not recovered from the canapés yet).

Hester did find her own dress – a spectacular one in white, printed with big red roses. She looked amazing: everyone gasped as she came into the church (and again, I like to think, when they saw the tent which Claudia and I had decorated with 200 red hydrogen balloons). All went remarkably well until the party ended and AW and I and the bridesmaids tried to get back into our house in the early hours and found that Hester and George had locked the door and gone off on honeymoon with the key. AW and a guest had to break in like burglars.

That December – our last in Kazakhstan – the family came out for a final visit before Christmas on our air miles. They very nearly didn't use the return tickets. One afternoon, driving back from a little ski resort in the mountains, AW skidded on some black ice and our car drifted unstoppably towards the edge of the precipice. I said, incredibly calmly, 'We are going to go over the edge.'

And AW said, equally calmly, 'Yes we are.'

In the back no one said a word. I prayed, though there didn't seem much point. Suddenly there was a telegraph pole in front of us, which just caught the corner of the bumper of our car – enough to stop it going over – but it was such a close shave that I couldn't get out on my side as it was already over the abyss. I have always viewed the sudden appearance of the telegraph pole as a real miracle, but AW says he had already seen it and was trying to steer the car towards it. I have my doubts. (Perhaps I should explain that AW is a Buddhist and I am a superstitious Catholic of Irish origin.)

Bella, the enthusiastic press attaché at AW's office, went into overdrive when the family arrived. Hester and Claudia and I were asked to record a message to the nation, to be broadcast on television, like the Queen. Cameras and crew turned up and filmed us artfully decorating our tree, and then we each had to say something. I spoke first: 'I would like to wish all Kazakhstanis a happy, healthy and prosperous New Year,' I said unoriginally.

Claudia followed. 'IwouldliketowishallKazakhstanisahappy healthyandprosperousNewYear,' she rattled off, terrified.

Then Hester, the lawyer-in-training, was given the microphone. 'I would like to wish all Kazakhstanis human rights and press freedom and democracy and right of assembly and—'

'Could we record that again,' interrupted the cool TV person who had an American accent, 'with you saying the same as your mom and sister?'

The annual office Christmas party was always a bit of a worry to AW: it was a huge family outing for the staff (who contributed to it) and it had to include amusements for children of all ages, as well as their parents, and of course, masses of food and drink and music. That last year AW found a fantastic venue which had bowling, go-karts, a great restaurant, dance floor, and disco. We had a very successful party in it, and AW highly recommended the place to his successor, but after the next Christmas we heard that a terrifying mafia gunfight had broken out during the EU Christmas festivities, and AW's old colleagues had to spend most of the evening crouched under tables, while bullets whistled to and fro.

Before the office closed for the holidays, I flew home to get things ready for our real family Christmas in Somerset, where AW's parents had lived. AW would follow on Christmas Eve.

The stewards on my flight home were so outrageously camp that I almost forgot my fear of flying in irritation. One of them put on a passenger's fur hat and did a little hip-wiggling dance for his colleague behind the door of the coat cupboard where the other passengers couldn't see, and then, after the routine safety speech, he added that the whistle on the lifejacket was for attracting sailors and rolled his eyes saucily. During the flight I asked him how he would manage if he had to overpower a terrorist, and he said, 'Oooh, I don't know, dear, I've only got a blackbelt in flower arranging.' I couldn't help smiling.

On the subject of air crew, the weirdest thing once happened on a flight back to London. At the start of it I told the air hostess that I was terrified of flying, which is why, shortly before the plane began its descent a few hours later, she came and asked if I would like to sit in the cockpit for the landing in London. 'The pilot thinks it might help you to get over your fear,' she said. (This was before 9/11.) I was strapped in and given headphones and told not to speak unless spoken to. After a while the pilot asked me where I lived.

'In London,' I piped up. (Perhaps I should explain here that ever since Hester was at school in London, and Claudia not far away, we have had a base in town; Claudia still lives there and that's where I stay when I come home because I am too scared to be in Somerset on my own.)

Some minutes went by, and then, 'Whereabouts in London?' he asked.

'Pimlico,' I squeaked.

More time passed and then he said, 'Which street in Pimlico?'

'Gloucester Street,' I replied, thinking this was slightly odd.

'Which number?' he persisted.

'Number sixty-eight,' I said, now believing he must be a bit mad.

'I live at number sixty-six,' he told me.

It turned out that his bedroom and my bedroom were on different sides of the *same wall* – only a foot or so of brick-work separated our sleeping heads at night. He was the annoying man I could hear flushing his loo in the early hours of the morning, because he was a pilot of course. I couldn't believe this was just a coincidence, and waited for some deep meaning to reveal itself: Captain Morgan and I would fall in love (he was about half my age) or he would save my life when I was run over or mugged in the street outside our flats, but all that happened is that he gave me a lift home from the airport.

The week after Christmas I had to make a grovelling mental apology to Olga, the fortune-teller, because Claudia announced that she was going to marry Aled, her nice new Welsh boyfriend. Aled had only just been staying with us in Somerset; apparently he'd come to ask AW for permission to marry Claude, but after a conversation in which Aled thought that AW had looked straight at him while saying how awful it would be if a father disliked his son-in-law, he lost his nerve and went back to London, and proposed without it. AW has no recollection of this discussion.

The wedding was pencilled in for 3 June the following year and, with this happy event to look forward to, AW returned to work in Kazakhstan and I went to London to prepare for the publication of my book.

The most exciting news about the launch of *Diplomatic Baggage* was that the *Daily Mail* wanted to serialise it over three days, starting on a Saturday. I was over the moon. The Wednesday before the first instalment was due out, I went to the hairdresser's, and there I met Annabel Elliot, who is Camilla Parker Bowles' sister. I knew her slightly because she used to have a nice antique shop in Somerset, not far from our home, so I greeted her enthusiastically and told her how excited I was that my book was coming out in the *Daily Mail* on Saturday. She made all the right noises, but inside she must have been thinking, 'Oh no it's not, because my sister's engagement to Prince Charles is going to be announced tomorrow . . .'

And so it was: every single page of the *Daily Mail* was taken up with stories about Camilla or Prince Charles or royal weddings for weeks.

In *Dip Bag* I told a tale that I was slightly uneasy about because it seemed too outlandish to be true – it was about friends of my parents who were called Rose. When they had a daughter, my mother told me, they whimsically christened her Wilde – but then she grew up and married a man called Boar. Now out of the blue I got a letter from a woman in Canada saying she had known Wilde herself, and she didn't marry a man called Boar but one called Bull. I was thrilled.

Another nice letter came from Paul Richings, one of the kids on the school run in Barbados, now grown up. In my book I mentioned that, as a seven-year-old, he used to ask the most irritating questions, e.g. 'Bri-gid, how long would it take for a snail to get to the mo-oon?' (We call these sorts of questions Richings Questions in our family to this day.) He wrote now: 'I've worked it out! The average snail travels at approximately 58.42 cm per hour; the distance from earth to moon is 38,240,000,000 cm so it would take a snail 654,570,352.6 hours which is 27,273,764.7 days.'

When I showed a copy of *Dip Bag* to Shirley, my Filipino cleaning lady, she studied the photograph on the inside flap and said, 'Who is this?'

'It's *me*!' I cried cheerily, thinking she was joking.

'No, that is never you,' she said firmly. 'It is much too young to be you.'

This made me depressed because I genuinely thought I still looked like the picture, though I have to admit it had been taken about ten years before.

It is so hard to believe you are getting old – apart from pains in your back, hips, knees, you name it – you feel just as you did when you were thirty. It is easy to flatter us oldies because we want so badly to believe that nothing has changed. I tried on a scooped-neck T-shirt in a shop in London not long ago, and when the assistant said, 'That's nice, you could wear it to go clubbin' or whatever,' I was so thrilled that she thought I could possibly be young enough to go clubbing, that I nearly kissed her. And of course, I bought it.

Then there's that phrase, 'I know it like the back of my hand.' I looked at the backs of my hands the other day and realised I don't know them at all: where had all those bulging blue veins and brown spots and wrinkles come from all of a sudden? How had my 'real' hands disappeared without me noticing?

When Claudia was a little girl she once caught a glimpse of my eighty-year-old mother with no clothes on. 'Why is Granny wearing a wrinkly body suit?' she asked. Now I notice that my own skin is getting that deflated-balloon look about it and my body looks as if it needs a spot of ironing – I suspect it won't be long before I have my very own wrinkly suit.

What to do? I once went to see a wonderfully practical Irish beautician in London. 'Is there any way I can get rid of these little wrinkles that seem to be appearing round my mouth?' I asked.

'Yes,' she said. 'Smile.'

That's probably the best advice for all of us oldies.

Film fun and last days

Eventually, book promotion over, I went back to poor neglected AW in Kazakhstan. I flew KLM even though there were hours to wait at Amsterdam's Schipol airport for the connection to Almaty – this was because there is a really good Japanese sushi bar there, and I had bought a sushi-making set (mat, ginger, seaweed, sticky rice) for Nina, who was keen to learn anything Oriental for the day in the not-too-distant future when (she predicted) the Chinese take over the empty lands of Kazakhstan. (I wasn't going to tell her that sushi is Japanese.)

I hung around the bar watching the chef's every move and asking him questions about the different fillings, but communication was not his strong suit and all I got was grunts, so I just had to keep looking and taking notes. I was there so long I thought they would call the police – what would the charge be? sushi stalking? – but I learned enough to show Nina when I got home, and at our farewell party we had plates of perfect sushi rolls, the first I'd ever seen served at a party in Kazakhstan. (The last new recipe Nina and I had tried together before I went to England was for pitta breads which came out exactly like cardboard beer mats.)

I had been nearly four months away, breaking AW and my rule of never being separated for more than three: that's the time limit which, in our experience, husbands and wives can be apart from each other without consequences. In fact, in Russia, as well as any ex-Soviet Union country such as Ukraine or Kazakhstan, those three months should probably be pared down to about ten days, as these places are full of beautiful girls honed in the arts of seduction and keen to get to the West.

Happily, AW was still at home, and even seemed pleased to see me, and I had missed the whole horrible Kazakhstan winter. But Almaty had changed even in the few months I'd been away.

One of my favourite places, the lovely old one-storey Soviet Hall of Receptions, with plaster decoration like over-the-top wedding cake icing, had been pulled down. I couldn't believe it. (And how I wished I had been there so that I could have collected up the demolished plasterwork and taken it home.) More and more of these old Russian and Soviet buildings were – and still are – being demolished to make way for high-rise apartment blocks. And in the old apple orchards around Almaty, where AW and I liked to walk in the evenings, bulldozers were encroaching further and further, clearing land for development. Almaty was a very pretty city when we were first posted there, but it probably isn't now.

Somehow or other – I think it was hauling my heavy suitcase down three flights of narrow stairs from my flat – I had hurt my back before arriving in Kaz, and could hardly move. Someone recommended acupuncture with Dr K (I'll call him) at the Korean hospital. (Kazakhstan is a country full of minorities: as well as the third of the population who are Russian, and the Germans, Chechens, Greeks, Georgians, Turks and Armenians exiled there by Stalin, there are a quarter of a million Koreans living there, descended from those who came to the Russian Far East as refugees from famine and disaster in their own country in the nineteenth and early twentieth centuries.)

No one at the hospital spoke a word of English but I went in clutching my back and Dr K seemed to understand what was wrong and put in the needles. Some were so painful that I had to use the technique we were taught in childbirth classes of getting on an imaginary surfboard and riding over the pain. After a couple of treatments I wasn't sure if anything was improving, and one day as I lay on my tummy, my lower back bristling like a hedgehog, I suddenly wondered if the needles had been sterilised or had they just come out of someone else's flesh before being put into mine. The thought became obsessive – I was going to get AIDS or Hepatitis C. I carefully manoeuvred myself around so that I could see the doctor's tray with the needles in it, and the good news was they were mostly in paper packages, but the bad news was that they were about ten times longer and sturdier than I had thought they were, like enormous darning needles.

After that it felt even more painful, and then I became concerned about the rather primitive electric massage machine they put on my back each time the needles were removed. I noticed it was made in China and began wondering if I could be electrocuted by it – I could see the headlines: DIPLOMAT'S WIFE DIES FROM MASSAGE, which sounded so spoiled. I decided to stop doing acupuncture. I looked for Dr K to say goodbye after my last appointment, and saw him reflected in the mirror in his office – he seemed to be picking his nose, so I gave it a miss.

Elena, the doctor heroine in AW's office who had diagnosed his Lyme disease, recommended Tamara for massage instead. She came to the house and did her treatment on the kitchen table, which I covered with a duvet for comfort. Not that comfort came into Tamara's treatment, she was brutal – the squeezing and kneading were bad enough but then she would suddenly pick up an arm or a leg and, with enormous strength, move it into positions that if God had meant it to be in he would have given you ball bearings in your joints. Then she would hold my head in her two hands and twist it so far round that I felt like that girl in *The Exorcist*. But her treatment really did seem to improve my back and it only cost ten US dollars.

AW's bosses at the EU have never paid the slightest attention to me (or any other of us wives as far as I know) apart from the time they refused my request to change the hideous, patterned, shiny brown floor tiles in the reception room of our house in the Gambia for matt white ones. They wrote a rather rude letter in French saying, 'It seems Madame wishes to turn the Residence into a bordello.' AW wrote a brilliant one back saying that he had never visited a brothel and so, unlike the writer of the letter, he 'was not an expert in their interior decoration . . .' We later heard it had been pinned up in the office in Brussels. Now I got another rap on the knuckles, this time for using the EU office address on a letter protesting about an injustice done to the Palestinians, that had recently appeared in the *Herald Tribune*. I realised at the time that this was probably against the rules, but we didn't seem to have a credible home address, and I never thought they would publish my letter anyway, so I took the chance. (I am always writing letters to papers because I support the Palestinian cause and believe that the wisest words ever written are Edmund Burke's: 'All that is necessary for the triumph of evil is for good men to do nothing.')

One day AW got a phone call from the Dutchman who was to replace him in Kazakhstan. He was serving in Cyprus, and, because he had a dog and a cat, he said it would be easier for him to bring them straight here when his posting ended in July, rather than taking them back to Brussels with him for the summer. AW said he'd be damned if he was going to leave Kazakhstan before the scheduled date at the end of September because of a dog and a cat.

This call brought everything into very sharp focus: we suddenly really truly knew that our four years were up and we were leaving. I felt so bad for AW: he loved Kaz and he didn't want to go back to Brussels – the 'home' base for EU diplomats – especially as at his age he might not get another overseas posting, so this could be the end of his years as a nomad. I suggested that perhaps we should go and live in France and he could do botanical drawings because he is so good at them. AW flew into a rage. 'I don't bloody want to do botanical drawings,' he shouted, 'I want to ride across the Pamirs and gallop on the steppe and explore the Wakhan Corridor.'

Our mood was not helped by the weather – it was early summer and pouring with rain. Kazakhstan is supposed to be arid and barren – the parched steppe equivalent to the desert – but the climate is definitely changing: that summer it felt more like Singapore.

We held our final Europe Day party in Kazakhstan at the Opera House. We wondered if it would be the last Europe Day party we would ever give, in which case I couldn't say I'd be sorry because every year the stress is awful: will any Ministers come? Will the important Ambassadors come? Will *anyone* come? No one ever seems to answer their invitations, and every year AW panics at the last moment and threatens to go out into the street and ask a few dozen total strangers just to be sure the opera/ballroom/museum, or wherever it is we are holding the party, will not be empty.

That year, having been away so long, my main stress was remembering people's names: AW's number two, John, said it was fascinating to watch me pretending I knew who people were. What I did know is that lots of good friends were missing: Nira from the Canadian embassy, Joan, the Greek Ambassador's wife, Catherine, the Dutch Ambassador's wife – they had all moved on. The most tragic departure had been that of the charming German Ambassador who lived next door to us. Out in the steppe on a picnic with his wife, he choked on some food and became unconscious. He was medevac-ed back to Germany, but the last I heard he was still in a coma. Of course, nice replacements for these friends were arriving but we would be gone before we could get to know them properly.

The new Dutch Ambassador seemed particularly friendly; he was keen on telling me that they, the Dutch, would have ruled the world, linguistically speaking, instead of the English, had they not swapped New York for Surinam. I told him that my ancestor, who was a sea captain, captured Curaçao in the Caribbean from the Dutch on a New Year's Day long ago, because all the Dutch were drunk – but then I had to admit that they got it back again when the British got plastered celebrating their victory. I admired his wife: she had been his maid or housekeeper in West Africa and knew even less about being an Ambassador's wife than I had done – talk about being thrown in at the deep end . . . But she was beautiful and elegant and learning very fast.

Because of it being Europe Day, AW was interviewed on TV, and next day when we went to the Green Market all the Tajik nut sellers gave him a terrific welcome – and loads of free nuts – because they had seen him on the telly. I think AW has become a bit of a celeb in the market. Four days later he had to open an exhibition celebrating 'European Culture' at the main museum in Almaty. There were all sorts of exhibits supplied by the various EU member states' embassies, especially the Eastern European ones like Lithuania and Slovakia (no one in cynical, spoiled old Britain can imagine just how glad these countries are to be joining free Europe after years of Soviet domination). I was guided round an exhibition of photographs of Hungarian rural life by an enthusiastic man from their embassy. The problem was that he kept calling the cows in the pictures *cats* (I think he'd got muddled with cattle). 'Here you see a typical Hungarian shepherd looking after his cats in the hills,' etc. When he said,

'This is a big cat with long horns,' I had to use every ounce of willpower not to burst out laughing.

Then AW had to go to Bishkek in Kyrgyzstan to investigate their recent revolution (this had actually happened, as these things always seem to, when we were on holiday in France, which meant AW spent the whole time on the telephone). The press called it the Tulip Revolution, but basically it was a struggle for power between two political rivals, one from the south and one from the north, with a drugs warlord called Erkinbayev in the middle. AW had an appointment to meet this warlord, but a few days before it, someone tried to assassinate him (the warlord, not AW). The bullet just missed its target and AW was transfixed to see that there was a hole at the end of Mr Erkinbayev's nose. It had a plaster over it, but AW said it was still quite apparent.

(This warlord came in quite handy later. AW left his sponge bag with his gold cufflinks in it in a hotel in Osh, the warlord's territory, but when he phoned to ask about it, they said they hadn't found it. 'Perhaps I will ask my friend Mr Erkinbayev to send someone who can look for it,' bluffed AW, before hanging up. About a nanosecond later there was a call to say they'd got it. We felt quite sad when, a couple of months later, the assassins tried again and succeeded.)

Then – huge excitement – a film crew came out to Kazakhstan to shoot a picture called *Nomad*. The film, which was basically the story of how Kazakhstan became the greatest country in the world, was lavishly funded by the Kazakhstan government. People said it was a publicity ploy intended to counterbalance recent scandalous stories involving US oil companies and the President of Kaz having USD$23 million in his Swiss bank account. Whatever the reason, it was fun for us because Marit Allen, one of the costume designers, was a friend of mine from my fashion-editor days. Impressively lifelike sets were built on the empty steppe: an enormous castle here, a huge nomad encampment there, a Chinese-style medieval village in a shallow valley near a river, and everywhere you looked there were suddenly hundreds of horses and spectacular riders from Kyrgyzstan (who lay dozing on their mounts when not required for filming) and camels. It all looked exactly how you imagine the steppe to be, but isn't. (The real steppe can be seen perfectly in the photographs AW took on a five-day car journey he made across Kaz. In these, there seems to be a line across the middle of each picture – above the line is blue sky, and below the line is yellowish steppe, and that's it; though to be absolutely fair, some pix had eagles sitting on mile posts in the yellow part – there is nothing for eagles to sit on in the steppe except mile posts.)

The film director was Ivan Passer, who made the picture *Cutter's Way* (described by the *Guardian* as a masterpiece). Sometime during his stay in Kazakhstan he was given a wolf skin, which he asked us to look after when he returned to the States for a break, because he knew the US customs would definitely not let him take it into the country. We put it in our basement and then promptly forgot about it. Months later the film crew departed, and it was only when we were packing up to leave Kazakhstan ourselves that I found it – leading to the most peculiar question I have ever asked: 'What shall we do with the film director's wolf skin?' It sounds as if it is code for something. (Until then, my oddest question – also asked in Kazakhstan when we got lost one day – was: 'Please could you tell me where is the Dutch Ambassador's yurt?')

We had such fun with them all that summer, but it ended so sadly: *Nomad* was the most beautiful film but it had a hopeless script and was a monumental flop, and poor Marit died suddenly not long afterwards, working on a film in Australia.

There were lots of places we'd never been to in Kazakhstan. One of them was Semipalatinsk, where the Soviets exploded 800 nuclear bombs; another was Karaganda, the town of Solzhenitsyn's gulag. (Apparently, when they opened the gates of this terrible prison camp after the collapse of the Soviet Union, many of the inmates stayed put because they had nowhere to go. I wanted to write something about this, but the authorities wouldn't allow it and being a diplomat's wife, I had to obey.)

There was no time to catch up on these famously grim places now, but we did make an excursion to Jarkent on the Chinese border, where there is an extraordinary old mosque shaped like a pagoda, and where we visited the elderly Catholic priest, a bit of a hero of mine – though I can't say I saw eye to eye with most of his views – because every Sunday he drove four or five hours to Almaty to say Mass for his few parishioners there, and then all the way back again. (We might have needed him for the last rites in Jarkent had AW not noticed, just before we used it, that there was a naked electric wire hanging in the shower cubicle in our hotel bathroom.)

A month before departure day, our satellite radio suddenly started broadcasting the BBC news in Swahili; AW said this was the clearest hint that we should be moving on. Now we embarked on the inevitable farewell parties – including our own (with sushi rolls) – ending up with a wonderful goodbye treat arranged for us by great friends: two Brits, Ray and Jane (she was my exploring/shopping partner), Barry and Laurette from South Africa, and a German couple, Richard and

Ricarda. He was head of the Goethe Institute in Almaty, and so passionate about trains that when he was at university he used to get jobs as a sleeping-car attendant in his holidays.

Between them, they arranged for us all to stay a night in the old *cosmostantzia*, or observatory, on top of a mountain near Almaty. The observatory had been abandoned when the Soviet Union ceased to exist, and become derelict, but some enterprising person had organised a bar and some basic rooms up there. We took a picnic and were sitting around eating it when Jane gave Richard a present (it was his birthday). She had found a marvellous old photograph of a mighty Soviet steam train with Second World War Russian soldiers on their way to fight, posing in front of it. As she handed it over, Jane asked Richard, who speaks Russian, to translate the words written in man-sized letters along the sides of the carriages. There was a brief pause and then Richard spoke softly, 'It says something like "Kill the fucking German pigs".' After a moment's shocked silence we all burst out laughing because the embarrassment was so great there was nothing else to do. We are all still friends.

The packers arrived, and I vowed that this time I would go through my wardrobe and chuck out everything that I hadn't worn in the last few years, instead of lugging it all back to Brussels. The trouble was, though, that, as always, my cupboard was full of things waiting for the day when I have lost a stone and am slim enough to wear them again. If I got rid of them now, I reasoned, that would be admitting that I will never be slim enough to wear them, and then that would become a self-fulfilling prophecy and I would be fat for ever. On the other hand, if I kept the thin person's clothes, that would encourage me to try a bit harder to lose weight. Packing up and moving involves so many decisions – you'd think I would be good at this by now having done it so often

– but I am hopeless at making up my mind about anything. I kept all the clothes.

The packers had taken the last boxes, the heart-rending parting from my beloved Nina and Ira was over, and AW's official driver Leonid came to take us to the airport at four o'clock in the morning. There, to our surprise, and huge delight, in addition to the official man from Government Protocol, were lots of AW's staff who'd got up in the middle of the night to come and say goodbye (though not his number two who *should* have been there but had obviously elected to stay in bed, hmm).

AW and I don't usually travel together – since our daughters grew up this is no longer a deliberate policy, it just seems to work out that way – and normally I can never sleep on planes because just as I'm dozing off I remember with a heart-thudding jolt that right under my feet is 33,000 feet of *nothing*. But this time, with my AW by my side, I slept like a baby, until he tried to step delicately over my legs to get to the loo, missed his footing, and fell on top of me with his full body weight. I woke with such a fright I really didn't know if I was alive or dead.

I

Commuting to the Continent

Brussels, 2 October

Coming back from an overseas posting to your 'home' base is what the Victorians would have called a sad falling off. Apart from feeling slightly surreal and like a lost sock in the laundromat of life (as we once saw printed on a greeting card), there is no more free living in a nice embassy-provided house or Residence; now you have to look for your own accommodation, and pay for it yourself like everyone else. AW has found a service flat not far from the European Commission and has moved in, while until this weekend, I have been in London trying to unpack, re-enter life in Britain and catch up with our girls.

The Brussels flat has a bedroom, a *living* (as they say here), small kitchen and bathroom, and is furnished in exactly the opposite way to how I would have done it, i.e., wipeable beige wallpaper, big telly, black fake-leather sofas and chairs, and worn brown carpet. Depressing. I never went to university, but I think from the cooking point of view this must be a bit like living in student digs: the extractor-pad thing over the hob is in greasy shreds, there is a tiny fridge, two saucepans, five lids, three old brown plastic coffee-filter paper holders (but no filters) and the sink is stained stainless steel. You wouldn't really want to cook anything much more than toast here. I keep forgetting to buy a bowl so I have to make our salads in a saucepan.

The good part is that there are hundreds of cheap places to eat in Brussels and the sofa is a sofabed so AW and I can sleep separately, which is great for me because of his snoring. He says I snore too, but he seems to be able to sleep through mine – I definitely can't through his, even with state-of-the-art earplugs. I mean, you can hear him halfway down the road. My father snored in the same way and none of us children could ever understand how our mother got a wink, but she seemed immune to the noise. I haven't ever got used to it – at one point I was so desperate that I took out a subscription to a magazine called *Snorers' Monthly* (I think it was) which was full of tips and ads for anti-snoring gadgets, plus snorers' and victims' stories and the latest research. I've just googled it and it doesn't seem to exist any more, maybe because Google itself has this kind of info now.

AW has always been very good-natured about trying out snoring remedies – apart from one, which is a large plaster with a hole for the mouth. You are supposed to stick this to your chin and then pull it up and stick it to your cheeks – the object being to stop your mouth falling open, but as AW says, your mouth might still fall open – and drag your cheeks and bottom eyelids down like a bloodhound and they might never go back to normal.

We once bought a weird contraption called a Noz-o-Vent, which involved springs to keep the nostrils open (*Snorers' Monthly* recommended it highly). We ordered it because we were going on holiday in France and had to share a room in the hotels we would be staying in. As it happened, we left the gadget behind in the very first place we visited and, as we drove on next day, AW and I became quite hysterical imagining the hotel staff trying to puzzle out what it was. We decided that being French they would think it was a sex toy. Right now in Brussels with our two separate rooms we don't have to worry, but AW has found a new gadget for emergencies, it's a sort of plate that holds your jaw in a certain way and seems very effective – AW says that is because it is so uncomfortable that it keeps him awake all night.

AW is now on the Azerbaijan desk at the European Commission while we wait to hear what his next job will be. In the meantime, we have to find a proper flat for us and all our furniture that has been in storage here since we left for Kazakhstan four years ago. The plan is that AW will go to England on alternate weekends, and I will come to Brussels for others. I am really looking forward to that: people scoff at Belgium, but I love Brussels with its wonderful food, auction houses, antique and flea markets (someone we know knew a person who bought a Manet, or maybe it was a Monet, in the Place du Jeu de Balle flea market in the seventies), not to mention all the new films that open here before they do in London. And we have a small handful of long-suffering friends in Brussels who are used to us turning up every four years. Plus our best diplomatic colleagues from Syria – the Canadian Ambassador and his wife Sue – are posted here now.

London, 16 October

AW and I were driving up to London this afternoon for him to catch his train back to Brussels after a weekend in Somerset, when my mobile rang. It was Hester.

'Mum, I've got something really exciting but a bit scary to tell you,' she said.

'You're pregnant!' I guessed immediately.

'How on earth do you know?' she asked, not yet understanding about mothers' instincts. She told me the due date

– and her and our future lives flashed before me: she has been trying to get a job in the Sierra Leone War Crimes Court – that will have to be abandoned – and, I did a rapid calculation, the baby was due on Claudia's wedding day, 3 June. Oh God. I sense trouble ahead.

As AW kissed me goodbye at the station he said: 'Bear up under the burden of all this happiness,' smiling ironically.

Actually, I know I ought to be thrilled – and of course I am – but to be honest, I am also in a bit of a panic. I don't want to be a grandmother yet; I adore my family but I feel I have only just escaped from my own children. I suddenly yearn to be half-child, half-woman, young and free, wild and irresponsible – and I'm only semi-joking. I can feel a trap closing.

2 November

Something really embarrassing happened today. I was in the queue for the checkout in Tesco's in Pimlico with Claudia, when I heard the rather shrunken old lady in front of me (who wasn't wearing any stockings and it was cold) say to the cashier that she only had £5, so everything in her basket that came to more than that should be left behind. I felt so fortunate compared with her that I whispered to the cashier that she should put all her things on my bill (which of us wouldn't have done the same?).

It took the old lady a while to realise what was happening, and then she shouted out at the top of her voice, 'This woman is a saint, everyone. A total saint, I am telling you, she is a saint!' and then she started having some kind of seizure.

Claudia darted round to the other side of the checkout and caught the old lady, and the manager, who was brilliant, rushed up with a chair and called an ambulance, and we calmed her down. By the time it arrived she said she was okay, shrugged off all help and plodded off home. Since then I have been racked with guilt that I didn't go with her to carry the parcels and see that she was all right.

9 November

They say no good deed goes unpunished and this seems to be true. On my way to catch the train to Brussels, I passed a tramp outside McDonald's in the King's Road. I offered him a quick hamburger, but he said he was vegetarian and so he'd like a Filet o'Fish. I rushed in to get one and found they had to be made to order. I was running late and only just caught my train and almost had a nervous collapse in the process.

Brussels, 10 November

I love coming to Brussels, it's like dropping off the edge of the world. We try not to tell anyone I am here so that we can just be quiet and go to the movies or eat *moules et frites* together. And we don't seem to be having quite so many rows as usual. Also, when I am here I can forget all about weddings and pregnancies (though I did dream that Claudia wore black knickers under her wedding dress and they showed through). And I love the journeys on the train: Eurostar are always trying to make them shorter, but I rather wish they'd make them longer instead.

On the other hand, there are some really annoying people on the train. In the past weeks, next to me, there have been a couple snogging noisily, a girl filing and painting her toenails, a man who took his shoes off and put his feet on the table, and parties of sports fans who have had a few drinks, shouting and yelling down the carriage at each other. And of course there is *always* someone on a mobile phone. The other day there was a chap who talked on his mobile for the entire journey except in the tunnel. I found myself getting off the train next to him in Brussels and, still burning with rage, I said, 'Have you ever considered going for therapy? You have been on your mobile phone for two solid hours, perhaps you need help?' I thought he might punch me but he just looked astonished. (People can be extraordinarily passive: AW and I were in the station restaurant in Amsterdam once when a man came in and sauntered from table to table picking up people's glasses and drinking their beer or wine, and eating chips and bread from their plates. No one tried to stop him; no one said a word. AW was just longing for him to arrive at our table, but he never did – I think he could probably feel the waves of testosterone emanating from it.)

London, 13 November

On my way home on the train today there was a good-looking young couple sitting round a table for four, with five or six big knitted bears wearing T-shirts and shorts. The girl had two of them on her knees and the man had one. I thought they must have bought them as Christmas presents and were playing with them for fun, so as I passed to go to the loo, I said, 'I like your friends,' and smiled.

The man looked at me earnestly and said, '*Family*, not friends.'

I thought he was joking but when I passed them again on the way back I saw the girl kissing her two and then leaning over and stroking the head of one that was in the seat next to her. When the train got to Waterloo they tenderly placed them into three backpacks, talking to them all the while. I couldn't believe that they were both involved in the fantasy. You would think that one of them would say, hang on, these are stuffed toys . . .

19 November

We have decided to bring the date of Claudia and Aled's wedding forward to 20 May. This is on the basis that first babies are usually late and so there will be less chance of Hester going into labour as Claudia is walking down the aisle. Claudia and I started looking at wedding dresses today. We have decided that Claudia's bouquet will be spring flowers and we'll have fresh spring flowers on the tables and swags of artificial ones wound around the poles of the marquee. I googled artificial flowers and found they were much cheaper in the US, so I have begun to order them. I had to open a Paypal account, which took me about four hours and nearly cost my sanity. Have also booked the marquee, caterers, portaloos, etc.

Brussels, 2 December

At the Gare du Nord in Brussels this evening there was a huge long line of people waiting for taxis, so I asked a friendly-looking man much further up than me if I could share his taxi and jump the queue. Once in the cab he told me he was Dutch, and we introduced ourselves, and then he laughed and said, 'But you can call me Cheesehead.' I hadn't a clue what he was talking about, and I must have looked bewildered because he reassured me, 'It's okay, I know everyone calls us Dutch people Cheeseheads – like the French call you English *Rosbifs*, ho, ho, ho.'

I laughed along, but I have never actually heard a French person call a Brit a *Rosbif* in real life, and I had no idea that Dutch people are called Cheeseheads – AW is half Dutch, but he has never revealed this to me.

3 December

I am stocking up with food for Christmas. The meat here is so perfect – no fat, no horrible bits, no blood. Sometimes I think my local butcher's looks more like an art gallery (in a Damien Hirst kind of way) and I don't think a Belgian butcher would even recognise a British pork chop, it is so crude in comparison. When AW eventually retires I think we'll have to do a meat run to Brussels in the way that other people do booze cruises to Calais.

My nights are getting weirder and weirder: last night I dreamed that I was a prawn's head and even though I had no body – it was just a gungy mess where that should have been – I felt quite perky and energetic. Must be all the food shopping I'm doing.

5 December

Oh dear, I spoke too soon about AW and me not having rows – we had a corker in the flea market yesterday morning. It was all over a plaster cake – the most wonderful object, obviously made for some patisserie shop window, with piped 'icing' and 'cream' and flaked 'chocolate' on it. I wanted it to give my artist friend Candace for her birthday, which is coming up soon. AW thought it was a piece of rubbish and wouldn't give me any euros to pay for it with, so I had to do a deal with my English pounds. We *always* end up having a row in flea or antique markets because there is inevitably something I want to buy and AW doesn't – though he often comes round to whatever it is later, and sometimes even claims that it was he who spotted it.

14 December

Hester had her second scan today and she is having a boy! In the very first pictures that were done a few weeks ago he looked just like a tiny crocodile curled up so we called him Crocky. In this scan he is beginning to look like a proper person.

The other news is that AW has been appointed Special Envoy to Azerbaijan starting in January and that he has found a lovely flat in Brussels, in Square Marie Louise, a really pretty park, which has a lake in the middle and is within walking distance of his office. I am going over to sort out the furniture and everything in January. He will have to spend part of every month in Brussels, and part in the Azerbaijan capital, Baku. Is this why I dreamed last night that AW was sitting in the bath wearing a curly black wig?

Brussels, 7 January

Today I dropped and broke a mirror, which is supposed to be seven years' bad luck, but it was a magnifying mirror, so I am wondering if you have to multiply the seven by the degree of magnification.

In the meantime I have walked so often from AW's service flat to our nice new flat and back, that I know where every mound of dog poo is on the pavements in between and could probably do the journey with my eyes shut and not step in any.

12 January

AW has been in touch with the people who have our furniture in storage, and they seem to have lost most of it, including the beds. We are moving into our new flat in a couple of days so tomorrow we have to go to IKEA, on the outskirts of Brussels, to buy new stuff.

13 January

Unlikely as this may sound, AW and I had never been to IKEA before because we are always abroad and we hadn't a clue how you shop there; we probably wouldn't have gone if we'd known it was all self-service. I'll never be rid of the YouTube-type movie clip I now have in my mind of poor AW loaded with two flat-packed wardrobes and a ten-foot-high kitchen dresser in long boxes on his shoulders, creating a Mexican wave of ducking customers as he staggered to the exit.

We are not allowed to transport furniture in the lift to our new flat, so we have had to arrange a special delivery by outside elevator. Most moves in Brussels are done this way actually, it's much simpler than it sounds; none seem to be in Britain – I wonder why not.

16 January

This weekend I dashed home to collect the car so we could use it for our move in Brussels and this afternoon we loaded it to the brim with all our clothes and bed linen and bits and pieces from the service flat and drove it over to the new place, leaving it parked outside while we finished cleaning the apartment. A couple of hours later we went down to collect all the stuff and found the car had been broken into – the thieves had managed to open one of the front windows with an iron bar (which we found, lying in the gutter) without the alarm going off, and from there they had succeeded in searching the car, turning all the linen and clothes over, and found AW's briefcase and my bag, which were really well hidden underneath. My purse had no money in it but a lottery ticket (which of course is the winning number), and AW's had money and both our passports, so then we had to spend half the night reporting all this in the central Brussels police station where there was a big sign saying 'No Smoking', with all the cops puffing away underneath. Then we got lost going home and found ourselves on the autoroute to the airport with no turn-off till we got there. What an utter nightmare – and now we have to get new passports.

17 January

Oh God, the storage people found our furniture this morning – luckily they telephoned just as the delivery people were about to put the IKEA things on the elevator; now most of the IKEA stuff has gone back to the shop (who have been incredibly nice about it). We decided to keep the new beds though, so we gave the crappy old ones to the storage people when they delivered *their* load this afternoon. This is all so nerve-racking.

18 January

The flat looks lovely; it has big windows and would be full of sun if there was any in Brussels. The only worrying thing is the fire escape. We are on the seventh floor and the fire escape is the flimsiest, most vertiginous, metal circular stair-case down the back of the building. I feel sick with fear just looking at it, and had begun waking up in the night worrying about how we would find the courage to get on it in an emergency – until yesterday evening when, just before going to bed, I stubbed my toe on the sofa leg which was so painful that I didn't sleep a wink anyway. I think I have broken it.

Aren't bad things supposed to go in threes? So many seem to have happened lately that I don't know which set of three we are on any more.

20 January

It's sad to be leaving Brussels, just as we have sorted every-thing out and the flat is looking so nice, but AW is off to Baku for his first stint as Special Envoy this week, and I am going to London to start planning Claudia's wedding in earnest.

London, 23 January

Went to Peter Jones and bought two new magnifying mirrors, one for London and one for Brussels. I need them because a) I can't see to put on my make-up without reading glasses – but with glasses on you can't do your eyes, and b) I live in dread of getting one of those long hairs on my face that you sometimes see on other people and long to tell them about but don't dare. (There's a terrible story about a man saying to a woman at a party, 'Excuse me, there is hair on your cheek, do you mind if I take it away?' Then he gently tries to remove it, but finds it's attached.)

The doctor sent me to have my toe X-rayed and I *have* broken it but there doesn't seem to be anything to do except tape it to the toe beside it.

Brussels, 8 February

AW and I were reunited in Brussels today. He likes Azerbaijan and thinks he will enjoy this job for a year or two. And he says that I can visit Baku if I want to – or come to Brussels, or stay in London, depending on my whim. In fact, AW summed up: I am in a whim-whim situation.

London, 28 February

Claudia has found a dressmaker who is the mother of a friend of a friend to do the bridesmaids' dresses, which are going to be very simple and white. We went to see her today, and discussed the whole thing; it was only at the end that I asked what it would cost. When she told us, I thought the price was for all three dresses – but it was only for one. I nearly passed out, but we were so far down the line by then that I didn't have the nerve to back out. I can't tell AW. He will have a fit, especially as he has just organised a trip to Morocco for a few days. We have never been to Marrakech and this is a present to ourselves to celebrate AW's new job and our move.

27 March

We returned from our trip yesterday, and AW is already back in Brussels and off to Azerbaijan again for three weeks, which is sad, but Marrakech was all we'd hoped for. The sun shone and we were gawping tourists in the Djemaa el-Fna, staring at the weird mix of people and eating at the food stalls every evening. I couldn't believe that we'd never before heard of Morocco's unique argan nuts which have to go through a goat's digestive system (the goats actually climb up trees to eat them) before they can be crushed for oil. AW wondered if, long ago, there'd been some sort of mis-hearing and the Golden Fleece story was really about Jason and the Argan Nuts.

One slightly worrying thing cropped up: our hotel bathroom in Marrakech was brightly lit, and when AW came in while I was cleaning my teeth with no top on one evening, he noticed, in my reflection in the big mirror above the basin, that there is a sort of dimple in my breast exactly where the underwired part of my bra ends, in front on the left side. I spotted it ages ago and have just assumed it is a dent made by the wire, but AW doesn't think it is, and has made me promise to show it to the doctor.

Later. Just after I wrote that, I went out and the day collapsed. I couldn't find the car anywhere, so I rang the police, praying it had been stolen, and they said: no, it hadn't – phone the car pound, so I rang them and, sure enough, the car had been towed away while we were abroad because the parking permit had run out. (There are several Rules of Life: one is your car has *never* been stolen, it has always been towed away. Another is you always weigh more than you think you do – but on the other hand you always have less in the bank than you thought you had.)

Normally you get a reminder about renewing the permit but I didn't get one this year, so I forgot about it. I had to go and get the car from the Marble Arch pound where I was charged not only the parking and the towing-away fees, but also £25 a day for each day it had been there while I was away. I am too ashamed to write down the total. I felt sick with self-hatred, guilt and the sheer bloody waste of money. You can't ever relax having a car in London, there is always something you've forgotten or overlooked that you get absolutely clobbered for, and there is no mercy, not even if you are getting older and more forgetful. Once I'd got the car, I sat in it and cried.

30 March

I've been suffering from shock and misery about the car, but today I finally got round to ringing the doctor about the dimple in my breast. I thought I'd have to wait a week or so to see her, but she gave me an appointment this afternoon and now she has referred me to the Royal Marsden Hospital, which deals with cancer. My appointment is on 19 April, so I have to try and put it out of my mind and get through Easter with the family.

6 April

I thought I was doing a really good job of being normal and jolly, but my cousin Frances (who is the family illness counsellor since she has had a double mastectomy) rang today to say that she'd had a phone call from our daughter Claudia saying, 'What's up with Mum?'

'You've got to tell her what's going on,' said Frances, so I did, and of course she was very upset – you only have to say the word 'cancer' and people are already mentally at your funeral (I am as well, actually). This is especially true in our family, because my beloved older sister, Moira, died of breast cancer in her thirties and my aunt (Frances's mother) in her forties.

17 April

I am wondering if perhaps I have a dimple in my boob because I do bust exercises every day? Perhaps I have developed an extraordinary muscle in a place where most people don't even have places, as they say. Actually, I secretly *know* I have cancer because a) I threw away the Marie Curie Breast Cancer appeal which came in the post just before we went to Morocco, and b) this would be the worst time in everyone's life for me to be seriously ill, with the wedding and the baby only a few weeks away, so obviously that's what's going to happen.

18 April

Over Easter I suddenly developed a dreadful pain in my back: cancer of liver or kidneys is what I am thinking. I always have problems with my back, but this is different. Perhaps they can check it out at the hospital tomorrow? My appointment is at 9.30 and Frances is going to come with me.

I walked round and round the streets near my flat this evening, praying that I will get a clean bill of health tomorrow. I have become incredibly superstitious and see everything as an omen or portent. For instance, if I come round the corner from my flat in time to catch a bus arriving at the stop – that means everything is going to be all right, but if the bus is pulling away and I've missed it, that means it's not. I have two front door keys that look very similar but they are for two different locks – now, if I put the right key in the right lock first time, I am going to be okay, if not, I've had it, and so on.

The suspense reminds me of a famous film that came out in 1961 called *The Day the Earth Caught Fire*. In it, a nuclear explosion has knocked the world off its axis, and it is drifting nearer and nearer the sun and is going to be burned up unless someone can think of a solution. The world's scientists decide to explode another bomb in order to push it back on its proper course. The film ends with everyone waiting to hear whether the experiment has succeeded: the *Daily Express* prepares two headlines for their next-day edition: one says EARTH SAVED and the other EARTH DOOMED – and then the film ends and you never know which one is used.

I have always remembered this film rather fondly because I worked at the *Daily Express* at the time it came out, but right now I feel those headlines relate directly to me.

19 April

I took a taxi to the hospital to meet Frances this morning and had one of those drivers who chats while you have to kneel on the floor at the back, craning to hear what he is saying. I wished I hadn't, because at one point he said, 'You know, luv, we just have to live each day as if it is our last,' and I thought 'Oh my god. Is this a warning? Is he giving me a message to say my last days are now?'

Frances had brought a big plastic file for me because, she says, from her own experience, you get so much paperwork and it all gets lost unless you have something to keep it in. Very thoughtful.

There was a big handsome man with his elderly mother in the waiting room at the Royal Marsden – of course we all thought he was the moral support for his mother with cancer, but then it turned out that *he* was the cancer patient (I never knew men could get breast cancer) and she was the moral support. Somehow this was infinitely sadder than his mother being the ill one.

Frances waited while I was sent off for a mammogram and then for an ultrasound. I knew almost immediately that things were not going well when the ultrasound doctor put the machine on my dimple – and then never moved it again.

'Have you found something there?' I asked, and she nodded and said she had found a lump. 'Would you say it's a bad lump?' I asked, somehow very calm.

'I would say it could be,' she answered. She showed it to me on the screen and pointed out the sort-of tentacles coming out of it, whereas an ordinary cyst, she said, was round and smooth. I thought it looked evil, and I cried, and she passed me a box of Kleenex tissues. As I threw my used one in the bin I noticed it was full and thought what a lot of women must have had bad news today.

(I forgot to mention the pains in my back but they seem to have disappeared.)

Then I went back to the waiting room to tell Frances, and she rang AW who was in Azerbaijan waiting for news (I couldn't speak to him because I knew I would cry again and possibly never be able to stop), while I went off to the dreaded mammogram again for a biopsy. This time they put my breast in the clamp and then stuck seven long needles through it and into the lump. If anyone had told me in advance that this was going to happen I'd have bunked off the hospital appointment this morning and gone into hiding, but somehow you get this my-life-in-your-hands acceptance of things they do to you in hospital, and, surprisingly, it didn't hurt nearly as much as it sounds. The doctor who was doing this horrible thing to me turned out to have heard me on Libby Purves's *Midweek* programme last year promoting *Dip Bag*, so we chatted about that. Surreal.

Then I was sent to see the surgeon, Miss O'Neil. Just the other day my nephew, who lives in Dublin, told me that long ago in Ireland the Keenan family were humble bards to the grand O'Neil family, but when I told her all this (that's the other thing that happens in hospital, you get verbal diarrhoea) she gave me a funny look as if to say it's your brain we ought to be looking at, not your breast. It was only when I left the hospital that I realised that I was in there under AW's name so she wouldn't have had a clue that I was called Keenan.

Miss O'Neil went through it all in a very kind way – the various types of cancer, forms of treatment, etc. They will inform me the day after tomorrow whether my lump is malignant, and next week I will see the main surgeon, Mr Gui, who will tell me what they plan to do. She cheered me up slightly by saying that once in a million there are rogue cells that imitate cancer but are not dangerous. That, basically, is the only chance their diagnosis might be wrong.

Later, at home with Frances, I smoked fifty cigarettes and then I drank a few glasses of wine. I think alcohol might be the way forward. Then I asked Frances whether the operation was called a masectomy or a mastectomy and she said, 'Don't ask me, I've had two but I am dyslexic.'

I went to bed thinking how strange it is that I woke up in one world this morning and now I am in a completely different one. For one thing, I can't imagine what I ever worried about before. And I don't know how to tell people. I don't know what to say when people ask how I am: 'Oh fine, just a tiny touch of cancer but otherwise all's well.'

20 April

I met a very dear old friend, Cynthia, for lunch yesterday (she was in the Gambia with us), which might not have been the cleverest thing as she has had a very aggressive form of breast cancer and her doctors are not holding out much hope for her, so I got home full of panic and depression.

I thought I would cheer myself up by taking Claudia and heavily pregnant Hester to the movies for a nice relaxing evening. I chose *Junebug*, a new film that all the reviewers say is highly entertaining. *Not one single one* of them mentioned that it is about a woman whose baby boy is born dead. (I am quite surprised that the ushers didn't stop us entering – or at least warn us – when they saw Hester's enormous bump.)

The first thing that happened in the cinema was that Hester, who was sitting next to me, stomped off to another seat, groaning, because I told her she was too noisy with her popcorn, but then we innocently settled down to watch the film, until it gradually dawned on us that something terrible was going to happen to the pregnant heroine. 'We've got to get Hester out of here *now*,' I whispered to Claudia. 'Fetch her, quick.' Claudia went and grabbed her – Hester was already in floods of tears – and we rushed out. Now I am racked with guilt for choosing such an incredibly inappropriate film.

I haven't told Hester there is anything wrong with me yet; she is so full of hormones and emotions at the moment. I am going to tell her when I know exactly what is going to happen.

21 April

Back to the hospital today, and yes my lump is malignant – which I really knew anyway so it wasn't a big deal. The wonderful news is that I don't have to have a mastectomy (I finally learned the word) unless I would feel safer having one (which I wouldn't). But I can't have my operation on the National Health because there are no free slots in time for me to recover for Claudia's wedding. On the other hand, it can't be left until afterwards, so it's been arranged that I will go privately, next Saturday. AW says, do I want him to come home? But I said, no, it's only a lumpectomy, I can manage.

Isn't it curious how relative everything is: you wouldn't think anyone could be over the moon to be told that they have to go into hospital and have a lump removed from their breast and lymph nodes from their armpit and then have radiotherapy for five weeks – but when the alternative is a mastectomy and chemotherapy, you are dancing on air.

All my women friends are so impressed that AW spotted the dimple in my bosom that they want him to hold a clinic in which they all come and show him their chests. I haven't told AW about this yet, in case he thinks it's a good idea.

Everyone who rings up tells me about their aunt, mother, sister, best friend, cousin who has had breast cancer and is still alive. I realise that this is exactly what I have always done too – whatever the problem, you somehow think it will console people if you tell them all the success stories you know. But now I find I don't really want to talk about it, I just want people to say, 'Hi, Bridge. So sorry. Ring if you need me. Love you. Bye.' I don't want to sound ungrateful; I am truly truly thankful for the calls, but I find I am suddenly exhausted.

2

Operations and Preparations

London, 22 April

My main trouble is that all this is happening at exactly the same time as organising Claudia's wedding. I have to think about the questions I have for my surgeon next week – e.g., will he be removing my nipple – as well as talk to the mortgage company about the fifteen-grand loan we are asking for, and confirm our massive order with the wine merchants. I live in dread of asking Majestic for breasts instead of bottles or Cheltenham & Gloucester for 15,000 nipples.

Today is Saturday and I decided I must break the news to Hester before she hears from someone else, so I rang George, her husband, and told him so that he is prepared, and I asked Claudia if she could come round, and then I popped over – Hester lives almost next door. Of course she was upset but then we ended up having a lovely day getting Claudia a trial wedding make-up at Peter Jones, and buying a pram for the new baby. I felt a bit sorry for George who started the morning with breast cancer and then moved on through cosmetics to baby buggies.

He was stoic, but actually I am the star of the day because I managed to get a refund on an expensive coffee-making machine that Hester and George have had for months – and used – but hate because it uses little aluminium tins of coffee

and is (they say, but then again they are obsessed) environ-
mentally unfriendly. They had no receipt and no packaging
but the shop assistant agreed to give back half the money –
sixty-five pounds. He was called Mana – Mana from heaven
I say because, for once, someone wanted to help, rather than
ruin your life like they do in Lupus Street Post Office in
Pimlico or in the Marble Arch car pound or at the ticket
barrier at Paddington where the woman attendant wouldn't
let Hester and Claudia through to buy their tickets to
Somerset on the train, even though it was obvious Hester
was eight months pregnant, and most of the ticket machines
at the station were out of order and there were queues at all
the others, and the train was about to go. They missed it, and
Claudia had to restrain Hester from physically attacking the
woman – I am not surprised. The other day, a friend of ours,
Camilla, was issued with the wrong return ticket at her station
in Somerset, but they wouldn't allow her past the barrier at
Paddington either. She said, 'If you don't let me through to
catch my train home I am going to scream.' They didn't, so
she stood there and screamed as loudly as she could and they
opened the barrier in a nanosecond – but by that time the
train was almost leaving so she had to run to catch it and
sprained her ankle. I hope Mana the shop assistant becomes
chairman of the John Lewis Partnership.

And now another good thing has happened: ages ago I
emailed someone at Westminster Council to tell them the
tree in the road outside my flat had died, and now (I admit it
is seven emails later) they have come and planted another
one.

I love my son-in-law George, but he is such an architect.
He is going to paint the baby's nursery dark grey.

25 April

I found the weirdest message on my voicemail last night: it said something about a fitting, and how the bad news was that it couldn't be done until next month and did this suit my plans? I couldn't think of anything that needed 'fitting' in my life, and then I wondered if this was some sort of euphemism for my operation, so I rang Anne, my 'breast nurse' (I hate that, it sounds like a wet nurse), and asked her and she said no, a lumpectomy is *never* called a fitting, and then this morning I found an email from a joinery firm in Somerset who are making us a new window. I'd forgotten all about it. Basically I am just a zombie these days.

26 April

Off to see the main surgeon, Mr Gui (he is of Chinese origin) today with Hester and Claudia who want to hear, officially, what is happening. We had to wait for nearly three hours, and he looks about fourteen, but it was worth it because he made it all sound very simple and very curable and we left with me wondering what on earth I have been making such a drama about. I asked him if I should give up smoking and he said, 'Certainly not.' On the other hand he is stopping my HRT and giving me anti-oestrogen tablets so I will end up looking like a withered old man I expect.

Then Claudia and I, and Gwen, her lovely future mother-in-law, went up to the Welsh Club to hear the choir who are going to sing at her wedding, and discuss the music. There are twenty of them – all rather jolly middle-aged men – and looking at them you would never know what a fabulous sound they make. We wanted them to sing 'Oh Happy Day!' as the last hymn, but they really want to sing the Welsh national anthem or 'Day-O'. Claudia and I couldn't quite imagine her and Aled coming out of the church with the choir singing, 'I see deadly black tarantula; Daylight come and me wan' go home', so they are going to sing the one about 'There's a Welcome in the Valleys', which they performed for us then and there. By the end I was sobbing just as hard as Gwen, who is Welsh.

27 April

Have just come back from loading up a really nice chest of drawers that I found dumped on the pavement near my flat. I saw it on the way to pray in church, and reckon that painted white and with new knobs it will be really nice. Hester and George helped me to heave it into the car.

The girls are being wonderful; they ring every two minutes to see how I am. It makes me cry. My worry is: am I forgetting something vital for the wedding or the baby? When I am not composing letters to newspapers about the injustice of not letting Hamas rule Palestine even though it won a free and fair election, I am neurotically going through my lists.

I have just heard that my cousin Jenny has had a lumpectomy – how strange. That makes seven out of ten women in our family who have now had breast cancer.

28 April

Every day I seem to learn about some new procedure I have previously never heard of (and Frances was right, my file is filling up with paperwork). This morning I had to go to the Royal Brompton Hospital for a nuclear injection into my nipple so they can track whether the cancer cells have gone into the lymph glands, and if so how far. (This is apparently a good new thing in cancer treatment, meaning they don't automatically have to remove all the lymph nodes.) Such a nice nurse from New Zealand did it; for some reason I thought her name was Stephanie so I called her that all the way through – Stephanie this and Stephanie that – until, at the end, she said, 'I don't mind at all, but actually my name is Angela.' Still, she gave me a kiss and a little arm rub when I said goodbye. What is this new rubbing thing that people do now? To start with I thought it was soppy, but now I like it, and do it myself.

Just after I got home my cleaning lady Shirley arrived. I haven't seen her for ages as she has been having her gallstones removed. She brought them with her in a plastic tube and rattled them for me; they looked just like small pieces of gravel, I felt quite ill. Then she told me about her operation and how agonising it was, and how she had to have five morphine injections. As I was putting on my jacket to go out, she wished me luck and said, 'You will feel pain, maybe terrible pain.' Oh thanks a bunch, Shirley, I wanted to say, I love you dearly but please go and rattle your gallstones somewhere else.

I had lunch with my best man friend, Chris, who cheered me up and we did lots of hugging and arm rubbing, and then we walked down the road together and I nearly got killed by a little boy on a fairy cycle whizzing along the pavement, which would have saved a lot of trouble.

I have to be at the hospital at 6.30 tomorrow morning as I am first on the list. Is it better to be first on the list? Aren't doctors supposed to drink a lot? The surgeon might be suffering from a hangover and have trembling hands, but then again, if you are last on the list his hands might be shaking even more, from exhaustion. Claudia was going to come with me to pray the Hail Mary as my stretcher is wheeled down to the operating theatre, but we decided no one will be wheeling stretchers at 6.30, so she's coming a bit later.

Hester came round tonight to have a supportive chat, which ended in an argument because the doctor has told her the baby might be early, and she says we were silly to have brought Claudia's wedding date forward.

Oh dear, I wish AW was here, I miss him so much. He is longing for me to go to Azerbaijan, or at least see more of him in Brussels, but I am trapped by my health, the wedding and the baby. I feel like a maypole with my ribbons being tugged by my family in all different directions.

Later. I thought I lay awake all night worrying about everything, but I must have slept at some stage because I dreamed I was in charge of making blackcurrant yoghurt for a school in France. It was a nice dream actually because all the children eating my yoghurt were slim and healthy, while the ones who refused it were fat and spotty.

29 April

I woke up on Operation Day feeling exactly as though I was about to go on a long flight. I had ordered a cab the night before, so I arrived at the hospital on the dot of 6.30 a.m. Claudia turned up at seven, and then we sat around for nearly five hours, until they took me for the op at midday (we did say the Hail Mary then). I wonder why they do this. We were so bored. AW texted me a medical joke: Have you heard about the man who goes to the doctor with a strawberry growing out of his head? 'I've got some cream for that,' says the doctor. Ha ha ha.

Then it was all so easy, I walked down to the basement, climbed on to my trolley, and the anaesthetist put a needle in my hand. 'Are you going to send me to sleep now?' I asked.

'In a moment,' she replied.

And the next thing I knew I was trying to say, 'I mush get to the lavatory before the operashun,' and they said the operation is over.

Hester and Claudia came with huge baguette ham sandwiches and biscuits, and we had tea and rang AW and I fell asleep talking to him. Claudia got me to lend her my credit card and give her my pin number on the flimsy excuse that she could go and buy me a bra with no underwiring in it (and, as I discovered later, some treats for herself). There was a clock in my room that ticked very loudly and I became obsessed about how stupid it was to put a noisy clock in a hospital patient's room, but mostly I slept all afternoon. As a matter of fact, I have felt so tired recently that I think they could have done the op without anaesthetics, I'd have fallen asleep on that trolley no matter what.

30 April

AW rang me this morning to say that I had sent him masses of text messages in the night, but I can't remember writing any of them, and Chris rang to give me the verbal equivalent of an arm rub. Then Mr Gui came to see me with his twins, two adorable little boys. I asked if they were going to be doctors but Mr G said, no way, they are going to be footballers or pop stars. He checked my dressings and said he'd see me next week at his practice and tell me if any further surgery is on the cards. What I can see of my nipple at the edge of the dressings is bright blue, as blue as a Bombay Sapphire gin bottle, but at least it is still there, and my pee is bright blue too. Claudia came in with the bra she bought from M&S yesterday: it has no underwires, but is so huge it looks like the kind of thing you hold up in the store to make your friends laugh. Didn't she know my size? I will have to return it.

Mr Gui told me I could go home this afternoon. I didn't really want to. I think one could become addicted to being in hospital, it is so cosy having people knowing what is wrong with you and looking after you, whereas the outside world just rushes on regardless. Hester and George brought me back in their car – and they had stocked up my fridge with lots of nice things to eat. And I found lots of loving emails, which was a great morale-booster. How lucky I am. Chris told me on the phone that his headmaster's wife used to say, 'A friend in need is a bloody nuisance.' This has got to be true but nonetheless friends have been marvellous.

In the post was a flyer for a Meet the Local Authors event in Somerset just before Claudia's wedding. I am a Local Author, but needless to say I am not on the list. I think I must be recovering because I feel quite annoyed about this.

1 May

I flopped about in the flat today feeling tearful and depressed, and then I started feeling resentful about AW. It is all very well for him to say that he is with me in spirit, but I need him here physically. I howled at him down the phone, which was really unfair because it is my fault he is not here – I told him not to come back. But I feel we should be bonding over the blue nipple and pee and he hasn't been involved with any of it. Incidentally, I no longer see a bosom as a sexual thing, and I have the urge to show my blue one to everyone because it is so peculiar, but so far I have managed to restrain myself.

2 May

Had my first outing today, to Price's Candles in Battersea to buy some for Claudia's wedding dinner, as well as flares for the car park. Then Ahdaf, my dear Egyptian writer friend, came round and told me that even in the generous, hospitable Arab world there is a phrase that says, 'A friend in need is no friend of mine.'

3 May

I spent today shopping. I only meant to change the female giant's bra that Claudia bought me, but I decided to look and see if I could find something to wear at Claudia's wedding, and then get some saucy bits and bobs from the Ann Summers shop in the King's Road as a contribution to her hen party on Friday. The trouble with shopping for clothes (apart from having what looks like two cleavages nowadays) was that I still have all the dressings and dried blood and bruising on my chest, and though I was wearing a pretty camisole top you could still see some of it and I thought the salesgirl was going to come into my cubicle and go 'Oh, yuk!' and confiscate all the clothes, so I gave up on garment shopping and went to buy the hen-party presents.

I was so nervous going into the sex shop that I tried not to look to left or right, but even so I couldn't help seeing the vibrators – they were about two foot long and black and shiny with extraordinary bits sticking out of them and I was so shocked I got quite dizzy. After that I more or less *felt* my way to the hen-night section (though feeling could be worse than looking in Ann Summers). I didn't understand what half the things were for.

'What are Teasing Tassels?' I asked the assistant, looking at yards and yards of black thong with mauve feathers on the ends.

'Oh that is, like, to tie up your partner,' she said.

I had a brief vision of tying up AW and nearly became hysterical. The girl was completely unembarrassed, which made it slightly easier; whatever you asked, she told you straight: 'Oh that is, like, for clitoris stimulation.'

In the end I bought some drinking straws with willies on the ends, Willies, Boobs and Bums chocolates, some saucy thong knickers and fishnet stockings, and at the last minute threw in a little book that looked a bit like the Ant and Bee books that Hester and Claudia had when they were little. (I managed to resist the 'glow-in-the-dark' willie earrings, and the egg cosy shaped like a huge penis.) From Ann Summers I moved on to Petit Bateau children's shop to buy something for Crocky, and then, worn out, I went home. As I unpacked the hen-party presents I glanced into the little Ant and Bee book and there was a picture of someone licking someone else's bum; it was the rudest thing I have ever seen.

There is a message in my inbox from a company called Spend-a-Penny. They are doing the loos for the wedding and want a site visit. I have decided that AW can deal with them: it is his punishment for not being here for my op. I told him this on the phone and he said he expected it was only the first of many.

4 May

Phew. Lots of things I've been dreading are over today. First and foremost I saw Mr Gui for The Verdict. It was brilliant: no more surgery required, just radiotherapy and Tamoxifen, starting in July, and then three-monthly checks at the Royal Marsden. And they are going to do genetic testing to try and find out how much Hester and Claudia are at risk.

To me the Royal Marsden Hospital is the most wonderful caring and efficient place in the world, and when I think of Mr Gui and the staff who work non-stop and seem completely dedicated and selfless, in comparison with our greedy bankers, corporate CEOs and politicians, I feel quite sick at heart.

Popped into Claudia's hen party – I was only dreading this in case no one turned up, but I needn't have worried, there were all her beautiful friends and Gwen, and my pal Sandy, whose daughter is one of the bridesmaids, and it was fun. I handed over the gifts, stayed for about an hour and then us oldies left. Later in the evening I got a text saying, 'Your little book has been officially voted as the rudest present of the evening – but a great conversation maker.' Oh dear.

Today I managed to get through a *whole day* without telling anyone that I have breast cancer – normally I am compelled to bring it into every conversation: with the postman, with random people on the bus, in Tesco's, etc. But I suddenly realised today that I can't talk about it any more because *I don't have breast cancer*. It has been taken away. I don't have anything wrong with me.

By the way, George has painted the nursery pale grey, not dark grey as he'd threatened, and it looks wonderful.

Tomorrow, after the last fitting of the bridesmaids' dresses (Sandy is coming to cast an eye over them too), I am catching the train for a few days with AW in Brussels. I can hardly wait.

5 May

Today turned out to be a total nightmare. I got into the car to go to the dressmaker's and it wouldn't start. I couldn't believe it – this car has *never* not started. (The last time something was wrong it was overheating, but then the needle fell off the temperature gauge and that seemed to cure it until I could get to the garage.)

I rang Claudia at the dressmaker's, and she passed me to Sandy, and I found myself sobbing down the phone about how I couldn't go to Brussels leaving the car where it was because it would be towed away again, and the AA rescue people would never get to me before the train to Brussels left. She said to keep calm and try the engine again in a minute, so I sat and prayed – if you can call muttering furiously to God, 'How could you *do* this to me at a moment like this?' a prayer. Then I tried to start the car again and it worked.

At the dressmaker's, I was really disappointed by the frocks; they looked quite amateurish, rather as if I had made them myself on the kitchen table. I was about to point out a bad bit of sewing when the dressmaker said, 'You know, these are hand-made couture garments,' and I suddenly heard myself saying, 'I know about couture; I knew Christian Dior . . .' (This is a complete lie, but I did write a book about him.) Anyway, Claudia's bridesmaids are so pretty that it doesn't really matter about the stitching, they'll still look gorgeous.

Brussels, 8 May

Was just trying to chill out with AW in Brussels for the first time in weeks when the phone went and it was George to say that Hester has been taken into hospital with possible pre-eclampsia, whatever that is. (Sounds to me like something to do with parking, but then again I am extra-sensitive on that point.)

I was going to have my hair cut tomorrow and I have to buy delicious Belgian cocktail sausages for Claudia's wedding. Oh dear, what a shallow person I am, torn between being a good mother and having my hair done. Reluctantly, we decided I'd better go back to London.

London, 9 May

Arrived back in London at midday and went to Chelsea and Westminster Hospital to see Hester. She wanted to go home but her midwife said she must stay for more tests. I managed to persuade her not to leave, and settled her into a bed, but it seems that after I'd gone, the woman next to her went into labour and was groaning loudly, and Hester decided to leave. She is now at home with George, crying.

I have just finished ironing Hester's wedding veil for Claudia. The way my luck is going I thought I would probably make a huge iron-shaped burn hole in it, but all went well: it's perfect.

I was asking myself while I was doing this, why all these things keep going wrong – it can't really be because I broke a magnifying mirror in Brussels, and I was idly wondering if it could be that Ceesay, our old steward in the Gambia, has been to a *marabou* (witch doctor) and had the Evil Eye put on us. Ceesay lost his job soon after we left, and, since he has a family and there are no safety nets in Africa, we decided to give him the money to buy some land and build a simple house. But then he lost some of the money (buying a plot from someone who didn't own it) so we had to send more, and then he asked for a well, so we paid for that, and now it's a generator and we have said *no*, not yet anyway, and so maybe he is getting his revenge. Ceesay was the living image of the comedian Eddie Murphy – I don't think he ever realised that the only thing that stood between him and AW giving him the sack was me, because when he writes to AW now (using a scribe in the market) he always signs off his letters 'in expectation of the usual consideration, your old pal Ceesay'. I loved him and at the end of our four-year posting, when we said goodbye I couldn't resist giving him a kiss. As I leaned forward Ceesay realised what was going to happen and held up his hands to protect himself with the result that, as I closed in, my bosoms fitted neatly into his palms. We both screamed.

My only wish at this stage is that Hester will start feeling better and that her baby will be born safely, and not on the wedding day or the eve of the wedding, and that Claudia's big occasion will go brilliantly well. If I only knew all that was guaranteed, I could relax. Did I say relax? I can't even remember what that means any more.

Somerset, 11 May

Under the direction of Candace, my artist friend who lives near us in Somerset, Frances (the family illness counsellor) and I have started making three thirty-foot-long swags of spring flowers to wrap around the tent poles for the wedding reception. There are boxes and boxes of sprigs of artificial blooms and greenery that have been arriving over the weeks from the US, and it is not as difficult as I thought it would be to tie them on to long ropes. Our village Flower Arrangement Club is going to do fresh spring flowers on all the tables; it will look lovely.

12 May

Things are looking up. AW is back from Azerbaijan (in time to meet the Spend-a-Penny people in three days' time) and I have been invited to take part in the Meet the Local Authors event after all.

15 May

Something so awful happened today that I can hardly bring myself to write it down. The phone rang and it was Claudia,

hysterical. 'Mum,' she shrieked, 'there's a catastrophe ...'
Oh no, I thought, please God, not more trouble. What on
earth has gone wrong? Is bridegroom Aled dead? Or his
beloved Grandma – who is only hanging on by a thread
– gone?

No, it was almost worse. The registrar had just informed
Aled that something was wrong with the reading of his banns
in London and that the wedding will have to be cancelled as
there is *no licence*.

I only got through the morning by deciding that whatever
the registrar says we'll just go ahead and have the wedding
service and the reception anyway, and they can do a proper
civil marriage later. Then I spoke to our vicar, who said he
would not do a service if there was no licence. I pleaded: 'But
people get married on beaches in Thailand, and on the
bottom of the sea, and sky-diving, surely they can be married
in their village church?' He said, no, not on his watch. I hate
him – he'd already said we couldn't have our own Catholic
priest helping with the service. Unless a miracle happens we
are going to have to cancel the church wedding – 180 people,
Spend-a-Penny, flowers, food, fireworks, Welsh choir – all
of it. I am numb.

Claudia is one step ahead of me; by lunch she'd planned
the email to friends: 'Slight change of plan for Saturday. We
are giving a party in a tent in a field and I will be wearing a
wedding dress.' Why not? Perhaps we could all just go and
sing hymns in the church with the Welsh Choir. Would the
vicar actually bar the door? In the meantime, Aled is contact-
ing his old RE teacher, who knows someone in the
Archbishop of Canterbury's office. He is working on it, he
tells me.

16 May

They came to put up the marquee today. It is in a field on the top of a hill. AW and I went to look and were slightly taken aback that the farmer has only mowed the bit of the field where the tent is. Visiting the site, AW and I could see clearly that the whole success – or failure – of this wedding reception, or party, or whatever it turns out to be, entirely depends on the weather. It is drizzling rain now, but we have four days to go.

Aled says the archbishop's office is doing their best and it looks hopeful. Claudia rang to say that her future father-in-law has slipped and cracked three ribs. When this is over I am going to go and live on a desert island with no computer or phone.

17 May

I had a sleepless night imagining people trapped in the marquee by unmown grass six foot high all round like a jungle. No one will be able to saunter outside with a drink in their hand without being swallowed up by vegetation and feeling like Humphrey Bogart in *The African Queen*. And where will the firework people set up their launch pad – they have to be a safe distance from the tent in a clear space.

Thank heaven there was a distraction this evening: the Locals Authors' party. I had no idea that there are so many Local Authors, or that they are so distinguished. I am feeling humble.

18 May

All of us now spend the whole time watching the weather forecast on the telly; it's definitely not good. This evening there was a special warning that no one should put up tents or temporary structures outside in the next few days as they could be blown down – and there's our marquee on top of the hill being buffeted by the elements. This is May; isn't that supposed to be the most glorious month of the year? I am now thinking in terms of making a human sacrifice to placate the gods and stop the rain. My chosen victim would be the vicar, but then of course he wouldn't be able to do the wedding service (if we have one) and that would be cutting off my nose to spite my face, so I will opt for the man in Lupus Street Post Office who made me cry once in front of the whole queue.

On top of all this is the continuing baby saga. I have rung Yeovil hospital to find out if Hester can go there if need be, and asked if they do epidurals on demand. The midwife was really nice and assured me that all will be taken care of if the baby arrives. Hester is in a complete panic about her pregnancy and delivery. I tried to tell her on the phone what I was taught in childbirth classes: '*You are in control.*' She thought I said, 'urine control', and didn't know what I was talking about.

Another misunderstanding: Claudia spoke to AW this morning and told him she was having a full body wax today and will come down here afterwards. AW thought she said full botty wax and asked me anxiously if there was anything wrong: was this a euphemism for something bad? Everyone is too stressed. Only a short time ago – it seems like yesterday – I wondered what on earth I worried about before I got cancer; now I know.

Later. Aled is in touch with the vicar and it seems that it's all sorted. The wedding is *on*!

19 May

On the TV weather forecast this afternoon there was '24' written over Somerset. AW said, 'Look! That's not bad; that's *warm*.'

'Unfortunately,' said Malcolm, my brother-in-law, 'that's the wind speed, not the temperature.'

21 May

It's all over! The baby didn't arrive. Claudia looked fabulous (the sight of my little girl going down the aisle with AW had me sobbing almost uncontrollably – just as it had at Hester's wedding). The rain held off until after midnight – but then it really pelted down and the last departing guests' cars, including a taxi, were getting stuck in the mud. (Apparently, when the taxi came to a halt the passengers asked the driver what was the matter, and he replied, 'Some effing idiots decided to get married in a field in the middle of nowhere. That's what's the matter.')

There is so much to do. AW and I spent today cleaning up the hideous mess in the tent and sorting out glasses, plates, linen, chair covers and so on. The field is so muddy that they can't get any big vehicles in and so they are leaving the marquee up until later.

AW and I crawled home, knackered, and when a friend came round this evening and all innocently said, 'God, I am absolutely exhausted,' I wanted to pick up the kitchen knife and stab her.

22 May

Last night I looked forward to eight hours of tranquillity and peace without my stomach churning with worry about the wedding or the baby, but instead I lay awake all night torturing myself imagining how appalling it *would* have been if the wedding had been yesterday in the pouring rain, with all the women guests teetering across fields of long grass in their stilettos because no cars could get into the field. Why can't I just revel in the fact that it all turned out so well?

23 May

AW and I drove back to London via Fleet today so that I could put Claudia's bouquet on Mum's and Dad's grave, as I did with Hester's. Both times I found myself in floods of tears, wishing that my parents could have been at the weddings.

3 June

AW has gone to Azerbaijan and I still can't sleep because ages ago I agreed to take part in the Paris Literary Festival, which means going away for two days in the middle of next month. What if the baby is three weeks late and arrives while I am there? Why did I ever say I'd go?

It has suddenly turned really hot and I am trying hard not to remember that today is the day Claudia's wedding *should* have taken place and that, as it turns out, it would have been perfectly okay.

All my neighbours are having barbecues on their balconies and Pimlico suddenly smells like Samarkand where the restaurants all serve sizzling kebabs cooked outside.

3

Baby Business

Fantastic news – we are grandparents!

Hester had to go to hospital for a regular check-up yesterday, and I drove her there to make up for having to go to
Paris later. We expected to be about forty-five minutes, but
they told her that her blood pressure was too high and they
wanted to keep her in while they did some tests. (I decided
to stay with her so I nipped out to move the car.) The tests
showed that she was getting pre-eclampsia and that she must
remain at the hospital, and they would induce the baby
tomorrow. I waited with Hess until, ages later, she was taken
to her ward. At lunch she had said she was getting funny
tightening feelings in her tummy, and it seemed that these
were still going on so they put a foetal monitor on her, which
revealed that she was having *real contractions*. (I went and
moved the car again.)

After an hour or so, the contractions were becoming really
painful. Remembering my own childbirth classes I said
encouragingly, 'Come on, Hester! Do the breathing, ride the
pain.'

'Oh Mum, do shut up,' said Hester. 'You aren't feeling the
pain, I am.' Then she said, 'I can't believe that *you* are going
to be my birthing partner. Get George!' (I had been trying to

75

get George for ages, but he wasn't answering his mobile.) A friend of mine was at her daughter's confinement and I felt a bit jealous now: she was allowed to massage her daughter's shoulders.

'Do you want me to massage your shoulders?' I asked Hester.

'No!' she said, but I did manage to massage her feet without her really noticing. Suddenly George arrived with all Hester's things. She was overjoyed to see him – and so was I.

I went home and spent the rest of the evening biting my nails with worry. No squeak from George about what was happening (turned out later he had sent hourly texts to someone else whose name begins with a B). At 11 p.m. Hester rang saying she had moved from hell to heaven because they had put in an epidural. I lay on my bed with my clothes on in case there was an emergency. At 5 a.m. got a text saying 'We have a beautiful baby boy.' *Pheeew!* I rang AW in Azerbaijan to tell him the great news (I'd been giving him regular updates all evening) but could hardly speak for the lump in my throat.

For the first time this year I feel there is truly nothing to be anxious about.

Later. Went to meet our first grandchild. I walked into Hester's cubicle and my heart turned over when I saw her lying back in her bed with Crocky on her chest. He is going to be called Malachy. (This is good in almost any language except French in which it means 'wrongly acquired', i.e., stolen.) He is adorable – a little pink shrimp with long fingers and toes and bright red soles to his feet. Hester is besotted, but also a dragon: no one is allowed to pick him up if they have smoked in the last five years.

11 June

Hester is back home and has washed all the new baby clothes and now they look second-hand. Apparently one of the midwives told her this was a good thing to do to make sure there were no germs on them. I took the clothes home and ironed them and folded them to try and make them look nice again.

I am discovering that I don't know anything about looking after babies now. 'You could put the baby on his side with a rolled-up towel behind him,' I suggested.

'*On his side?* Definitely not. The midwives say he must be on his back.'

I gave Hester what I thought would be some useful items, including soap, and zinc-and-castor-oil cream. *Soap?* The midwives say *never* let soap anywhere near him, and as for zinc and castor oil – apparently they laughed at the quaintness of it. The midwives are the Oracle. I see them as a witches' coven in pointy hats stirring a big pot.

But the midwives didn't show Hester how to bathe him, and nor did they teach her how to swaddle the baby. I did, and it works. Neh neh ne ne neh.

12–15 June

Malachy is asleep most of the time; he is so sweet, I adore him. I can't bear to go to Paris.

17 June

Back from the literary festival (my very first), which was beautifully organised, i.e., I was met at the Gare du Nord by a young man with a bunch of flowers and a taxi. It was all very small scale and cosy: the events were held in a little tent pitched in the park next to the Shakespeare and Co. book-shop (they were the organisers). My own 'gig' was a conversation with Celia Brayfield, once a colleague on *Nova* magazine, now a bestselling author. I was scared stiff, but she was friendly and nice and so was everyone else.

There was much hilarity when William Dalrymple lost one of his front teeth – and in that instant ceased to look like the charismatic, dynamic man-of-the-world he is, and turned into a derelict tramp. He was due onstage so there wasn't much hilarity from him. I loved it all.

18–19 June

Poor Hester, she rings every night at about midnight in floods of tears. We had been worrying that Malachy sleeps all the time, but now he throws up and screams after every feed and doesn't sleep at all. Tonight she came over here to try and get some herself. She has asked the midwives what the matter is but they don't seem to have any idea.

20 June

Last time AW was in England he talked about retiring when his job as Special Envoy to Azerbaijan ends. This has put me in a bit of a panic because now that Hester and Claudia have left home, I know he will make me sell the flat in Pimlico, which has been our base for ages – and still is mine. I have decided to get a jump ahead of him and downsize, so I can pay off some of the mortgage.

I was walking home this afternoon, saying to myself, I really need someone to advise me what to do, when there was a touch on my shoulder and there was Guy, the estate agent who found me my present flat. I hadn't seen him for years. 'Hello,' he said, 'long time no see. I don't suppose you are looking for a smaller flat because I've just this minute been given a really nice one to sell.'

I looked at him as if he was an angel sent by God. We went to look at the flat and it was just what I wanted so I made an offer for it straight away – provided he can sell mine, of course. I have now prepared my flat for viewing by stuffing all the mess behind the sofa.

21 June

Hester sent me a text this evening saying that she had fed the baby for four hours and he showed no sign of being satisfied and what should she do? As if I knew. I remember it all horribly clearly. When I had Hester, the schedule they told me to aim at was to feed the baby every four hours for forty minutes but I seemed to be feeding her every forty minutes for four hours, and was in despair. I think the year she was born was the most difficult of my whole life.

It's a good thing you don't know all this in advance because you'd probably never have children if you did. Once you've been through it though, you forget and think you might as well have another. That's how nature cons you into having a family. I would do anything to help Hester but I don't know how.

Somerset, 23 June

I drove Hester and the baby down here on Thursday. I think I got a speeding ticket because Hester was in such a panic about feeding the baby on time I was going at about ninety-five miles an hour. Stress stress stress.

Today George and AW joined us (AW from Brussels) for the weekend. AW is not good at babies; he tends to spend most of the time at his desk. I find this quite annoying. Why is he exempt from helping?

24 June

Today I feel like the most hopeless and incompetent mother and grandmother in the world. Every time I try to help I seem to do something wrong – spill the milk, get poo on the baby clothes while changing the nappy, etc., etc. But this afternoon I really surpassed myself. I thought I would lend a hand by sterilising the bottles and the breast pump, so I put everything into a big saucepan and then went to watch the World Cup on telly with the others . . .

About three-quarters of an hour later I smelt burning rubber. I hurled myself into the kitchen, but it was too late – everything in the pan had melted together into a large, grey-pink, modern sculpture with nipples sticking out in every direction. Hester is distraught, all the shops are shut and I don't know what to do. I am in disgrace.

Later. Hester and George are upstairs now and I know they must be talking about what an idiot I am, so I have hidden the baby monitor in the kitchen cupboard so I don't accidentally overhear what they are saying. (It's easy to forget about baby monitors – apparently there are all kinds of horror stories about parents and in-laws overhearing things they were never meant to.)

I decided to go to church this evening so that I could ask everyone after Mass if they had a breast pump. 'Breast pump?' they all repeated in disgusted tones as if I had asked for something obscene. I hardly dared go home but then I had an inspiration: my friend Sandy who lives in our village has her daughter-in-law staying and she had a baby a couple of months ago – maybe she has a breast pump. Why didn't I think of this before?

Later. She did have one. I was saved. Claudia is going to John Lewis on Monday to buy another one and AW and I will pick it up when we get to London in the evening.

I don't know why I have lost all my confidence and find myself terrified of what mistake I might make next. Recently I do things like crossing the road without looking, or forgetting the last two steps on the stairs. Just getting through each day without doing some major damage seems the best I can hope for. And then there are the mad things I find myself doing, i.e., the other day, as I approached a pedestrian crossing, I took out my car keys to 'open' it.

London, 26 June

I am pretty sure we got another speeding ticket driving back to London today. The baby was crying and so was Hester, and all we could think of was getting them home.

Then AW and I went to collect the breast pump from Claudia – and managed to leave AW's jacket in her flat with his new passport in the pocket. He has a 7 a.m. departure tomorrow to catch the Eurostar back to Brussels so we have just driven all the way back to Claudia's to get the jacket. What is the matter with us?

28 June

Mr Gui, my surgeon, told me I should try and rest before my radiotherapy treatments, which start in three weeks, so AW and I are going on holiday now. In four days' time I am off on the train to meet him in Brussels, and then we will continue the journey to France. (We have a little house there, which I bought in 1968 with the proceeds of a TV washing powder commercial I appeared in.) I am quite scared about travelling without him in my new confused mode – I'll lose the train tickets, forget my passport, leave the stove and/or the iron on in my flat and burn the house down, forget to close the front door, or abandon my suitcase on the pavement (as I have done before). I just don't trust myself any more.

I feel so bad about leaving Hester that I have organised (with her mother-in-law) that we will pay for a doula to go in and help for a few days. I had never heard of a doula before, but apparently it is someone who supports you when you have had a baby – not a nurse or a midwife, more of a kindly assistant.

Later. Hester has just rung to say that maybe she will come to France with the baby. I have to admit my heart sank, I really want to be able to do *nothing* – I told her this in what I thought was a kindly way, but she was upset and I realised that one must never tell an unpleasant truth to anyone – least of all your daughters – unless you really have to. Now we've agreed that if she truly needs to come, she can.

16 July

Back from France. Hester didn't come after all and AW and I have just seen Malachy for the first time in two and a half weeks. He has totally changed from a newborn baby into a perfect, plump little cherub. He is also focusing and smiling and Hester says he is incredibly advanced for five weeks because he can roll over and yesterday he punched his teddy bear.

I needn't have worried about the journey: all went well, apart from the fact that as I got on the train for Brussels I realised I had left my swimsuit behind. I couldn't bear the idea of having to expose my body trying on swimsuits in a shop in France, so I rang Guy, the estate agent who has the keys of my flat, and asked him to find it and send it to me. It arrived three days later.

AW was ill on holiday: he has had a kind of flu for weeks so we went to a doctor – his name was Dr Tricky which didn't inspire confidence – but he gave AW antibiotics and at long last he is better.

18 July

Was in the deepest sleep this morning when the doorbell woke me up. I looked at the clock and it was 10.30 – I'd forgotten to set the alarm. Dashed down to answer the bell and it was someone from the estate agent's with a client to see the flat. I had to go and hide in the bathroom.

Quite a few people have seen the flat but no one seems to want it. It doesn't actually matter because the people whose place I want to buy haven't found anything they like yet, so it is all on hold. A charming Iranian woman came to have a look at my flat the other day and I had high hopes of her, but I don't think she wants the flat, I think she wants *me*. She keeps telephoning and inviting me to things.

As I hid in the bathroom I despaired. My routine is hope-less: it's not just now, it always has been. Every single night since I was a teenager I mean to go to bed at a reasonable time, and every single night I don't put my light out until 1 a.m. (or later if AW is not around to nag me) and then (when I can) I don't get up till nine as I need my eight hours. Hester has a book by Gina Ford that gives you the routine to follow with your new baby right down to the last minute every day. I am seriously wondering if it would be possible for me to hire Gina Ford to come round and draw up a routine for me. I think I need her almost as much as Hester does.

For some unknown reason, this evening AW and I were invited to the opening of the new Jameel Gallery of Islamic Art at the V&A, and in AW's absence I took Claudia. We had to leave early as I had promised my friend, Ahdaf Soueif, to join her on a protest outside Parliament against the horrendous bombing of Lebanon. At one point the word went round the huge crowd of demonstrators that we should all go and lie down in the middle of the road alongside the House of Commons. I am such a coward, I really didn't want the police to pick me up by my arms and legs and throw me into a van, plus I get claustrophobia hemmed in by lots of people, plus I was in my high heels and my smart black suit which I'd worn for the gallery opening, but I had to do it or Ahdaf would have thought I was a wimp. Claudia was deeply embarrassed by the whole thing and edged away into the crowd muttering, 'Oh God, Mum, do you really have to do this?' as Ahdaf and I stretched out flat on the tarmac. The police let us protestors stay there for quite a long time, maybe eight minutes, and then their vans came – I was first back on my feet and ready to run.

19 July

Had to see Mr Gui today to make sure all okay for the radiotherapy. He was very pleased with me and sent me on to the radiology department to be marked up for my treatment. It's very hot at the moment but the room where they keep the huge radiotherapy machine was freezing cold and I had to control my shivers and lie still while the radiologists took measurements and then tattooed blue dots on my chest to guide the angle at which they will aim the rays, or whatever they are, on to the right spot. From now on I will watch out for women with little blue tattoo marks on their chests; it is like a secret code meaning we have had the same treatment.

21 July

Today I paid a call on the Syrian Ambassador who is a friend because Damascus was AW's last posting before Kazakhstan and we lived there for nearly six years. I asked him if there was any chance of getting an interview with the President of Syria's young British-born wife, Asma, and he said he would ask. He told me that the President was proposing to hire a PR and what did I think? I said I thought that the President didn't need a PR, he needed to make serious, basic reforms in his country, and that would make him popular and admired around the world without him having to spend a single penny. Of course the Ambassador couldn't make a comment on this, but I had the feeling he agreed.

25 July

Day 1 of Radiotherapy. (My nephew William says his idea of radiotherapy is lying in bed listening to *The Archers*.)

I took lots of newspapers as I thought I'd have to hang about for ages, but no sooner had I arrived at the Royal Marsden than I was whisked off into the freezing room and given the treatment – two lots of thirty seconds of radiation – and then I was out again. My main worry is what would happen if there was an earthquake and the machine fell on me – it would burn a hole all the way through me and I'd end up like a huge polo mint.

26 July

Day 2. Same as yesterday and have now discovered the cafeteria in the hospital. It's brilliant: today I had couscous with little chunks of melted Camembert cheese in it and a tomato sauce. I wonder if I could use it as an ordinary restaurant and meet friends there. It even has a little terrace where you can sit outside.

27 July

Day 3. I am walking to the hospital and back every day. It takes about forty-five minutes each way, but I am hoping that exercise might conquer my aches and pains: right now I feel as if I need a back replacement, hip replacements, knee replacements, and a neck replacement. One good thing is that Mr Gui says that he is not putting me on Tamoxifen, the wonder cancer drug, because it will make all my aches and pains worse. 'We have to think of your quality of life,' he says.

En route to the hospital, I met a woman I know slightly. We chatted, and I told her I was on my way to the Marsden for my radiotherapy course. 'Oh that's wonderful!' she said. 'Retraining in mid-life, that's what I like to hear.' I couldn't be bothered to correct her and so she has gone off believing I am learning to be a radiologist.

28 July

Day 4. As I walked through Pimlico today I saw a *Westminster and Pimlico News* hoarding saying GRANNY IMPALED. Perhaps she was an incompetent granny like me and was impaled by her daughter. On the other hand I might impale Hester, she is driving me mad about my carbon footprint. Every time she comes to my flat, which is almost daily, she switches off the TV and the computer (she says everyone leaving their computers and TVs on is the equivalent of four power stations a year of electricity). And then she tells me to relax.

Hester's old nanny, Sue, came to visit us today. She works for the NHS now, and among other things, she teaches people how to massage their babies. Years ago, when she first started this, she named the life-size doll she demonstrates on, Hester, and then later, when she bought another, boy, doll she called it George — little knowing that the real Hester would marry a real George one day.

29 July

Day 5. I've never been able to resist scavenging recipes from old magazines. Now, since I am always in hospital waiting rooms these days, I have become really skilled at coughing sharply as I tear them out, or doing it millimetre by millimetre so no one hears.

It's all ridiculous because I never get round to cooking any of the recipes and they just clutter up the kitchen in untidy files making me feel guilty.

30 July

Day 6. AW is in Azerbaijan, and the rest of the family, including Malachy in his pram, are off to a rally in Trafalgar Square to protest against the continuing attacks on Lebanon.

Later. There were about a thousand people at the rally, though there should have been a million. There are too many good men out there doing nothing.

1 August

Day 8. My chest is a bit sore and itchy from the radiation. Am smothering it with aqueous cream. Also trying hard to get a proper routine going but have still not yet managed to put my light out before 1 a.m.

I took Malachy for the evening. I've babysat him in Hester and George's flat, but this is the first time I have had him here for several hours. I had imagined an idyllic, quiet evening writing my diary while he slept peacefully nearby, but of course he had to be played with, fed and winded, which took hours, and then, after I'd put him to sleep on my bed upstairs and crept down to the kitchen to have a cigarette (with my head out of the wide-open window of course), I had to keep dashing up again every two minutes to make sure he wasn't a cot death. I had forgotten that if you have babies or children around you can't do anything else.

I must stop quoting Malachy to my friends. 'He's amazing,' I hear myself saying: 'Yesterday he said *owa* and then he went *aah boo gah*!' The friends look stunned with boredom but I think they are putting it down to the radiotherapy. I have only just realised how idiotic I must sound.

2 August

Day 9. Waiting next to me in the hospital today was a little girl who told me eagerly that she loved skipping. I suddenly remembered the utter thrill of skipping when two others were turning the rope, and how you had to wait, swaying forward and back with the rhythm of the rope, your heart in your mouth, waiting for the exact right moment to run in and start jumping. I wonder if I could take it up again instead of starting Pilates, which everyone tells me I must do.

I had supper with my friend Lesley this evening. She was telling me about a place to buy pot-pourri but I thought she said 'buying Popery' and was discussing corruption in the Catholic Church. It's funny how mishearing something can set you off on the wrong track. I think I might be going a bit deaf because this is not the first time this has happened. AW keeps telling me I am deaf, but I maintain it is him mumbling.

7 August

Day 14. AW came home three days ago. I was thrilled to see him but he brought havoc in his trail. First, he threw out all the magazines I've been saving for their recipes. (Mind you – and I am not admitting this to him – this was probably a blessing, as I explained earlier.) Next he decided to clean my computer by wiping it with a damp cloth. He must have pressed some fatal combination of keys because the whole thing was disabled and we had to have the computer man round for five hours to save all the stuff on it, and then we had to go to Currys and buy another computer for £590.

Then, in the evening, AW took me to the movies in the West End and we were clamped. I don't think we can afford AW. So far his trip home to 'look after me in my hour of need' has cost about £300 a day.

12 August

I have lost more than a stone. I don't know whether it's the walk to the hospital every day or what, but suddenly I am the size I've wanted to be since I had babies. I took out all the clothes that I have been too fat to wear for years and tried them on today. Shock, horror! I fit into them perfectly, but they are all too young. They have cut-away armholes or low necklines, or the skirts are too short; I can't wear any of them. Sadly, I took them all to the local charity shop – it was like disposing of the last links to my youth, especially as I am very conscious that the comfy shoes I am wearing for my walk to the hospital are just the sort of thing that I swore I would never wear when I was old. They are trainers and there is something about an older woman (you might even say an elderly woman, though I wouldn't) wearing trainers that is definitely not cool, especially if, like me, she is carrying a plastic bag. My long-ago fashion-editor self would have been appalled.

14 August

Day 21. My last treatment! I felt really sad saying goodbye to Sam and Aliya, my lady radiologists. I will miss them – I mean how many people do you spend time with, undressed, every single day for three weeks? Sam had bought a copy of *Diplomatic Baggage* and asked me to sign it; I was so touched.

It's Claudia's birthday today and I am going home to Somerset for a celebration supper with her and Aled, who are there on holiday.

Later. My train pulled out of Waterloo station, stopped, and then reversed back to where it had been before, at which point there was a lemming rush of passengers off it and into another train on the adjoining platform. I have no idea how everyone else knew the secret that this second train was going to our destination, Gillingham, Dorset; I certainly didn't, and was slow on the uptake, which meant that when I finally climbed into it there were no seats and nowhere to stand either. I went into a lavatory and told everyone outside that I would be sitting in there and, if anyone wanted to use it, please just tell me and I would go out (only two people did).

In the end, quite a few people came in as well; a nice boy, Dale, sat in the basin – he wore astonishing clothes: long black fishnet sleeves looped over his fingers, T-shirt underneath with the crucifixion and skulls on it, and a fantastic black floor-length magician's coat. He told me he bought them all in Salisbury.

Somerset, 15 August

Hester had a terrible day yesterday – and was revealed to us all as a total hypocrite. Ha ha ha. Ever since Malachy was born she has been a complete tyrant about people smoking i.e., if you have had a cigarette in the past twenty-four hours you have to change your clothes before you are allowed to hold the baby. But now it turns out that she is back smoking herself (to be fair she did give up for nearly a year when she was pregnant and after). This is how we know.

She went on to the rickety fire escape of her flat on the third floor to have a quick fag, and somehow the door, which has no knob on the outside, slammed shut behind her and she was trapped and – worst of all – she could hear Malachy crying inside. She yelled down to passers-by that she was stuck and to fetch Mark from the Halifax Building Society office opposite her flat (she knows him from when she and George were house-hunting). People looked up and saw her waving and shouting and walked on by, but then at last some Good Samaritan went and fetched Mark. He shinned up three floors of the fire escape like the Cadbury's Milk Tray man, but he couldn't get the door open either. Luckily, though, he had his mobile phone with him, so they rang George and asked him to come back from his office and open the door from inside. It was too dangerous for Mark to get down the fire escape again, so he and Hester had to wait together on the fragile iron platform making polite conversation. Hester said it was surreal.

The whole thing reminded me of when my cousin Simon came to stay in London long ago, before mobile phones existed. After I'd gone to work one day, he was in the bath when the doorbell rang. He wrapped a skimpy towel around his waist and went to answer it and somehow the door slammed shut behind him and he was left almost naked on the landing. He had to knock at my elderly neighbours', Mr and Mrs Baum, who got a horrible fright seeing him there and were not convinced he wasn't some kind of pervert. They let him in eventually but didn't offer him any clothes, and he had to spend the day waiting for me to come home, clutching his bath towel, miserably embarrassed and sure that the loose budgerigar that was flying round their flat would do a poo on him.

20 August

Hester phoned this evening in her dead voice. Seems she and George left the key of their flat down here when they set off for London today, and they can't get in. They do have the key to *my* flat so are going there for the night, and luckily they have the baby things they used at the weekend.

Why does this sort of thing happen to our family all the time? And it is not as if it's always our fault – sometimes we are the victims of random, weird events. For instance, almost exactly ten years ago, AW and Hester and I met up in Marseilles to look for student accommodation in Aix-en-Provence, where Hester was to spend a year of her uni course. On the way back, our high-speed train was stopped in its tracks just outside Marseilles station, surrounded by hundreds of members of the SNCF workers' union, and *taken hostage*.

The doors were locked but we climbed up on the seats and, putting our mouths to the narrow window openings at the top, begged and pleaded with the workers – telling them it was Hester's twenty-first birthday and she had to get back for her party (all true); but it made no difference. We sat there for hours while negotiations went on around our train, and it was only in the afternoon that it was allowed to shunt back to Marseilles station and we could get off and catch a taxi to the airport where we found places on some obscure airline flying to Luton (was it Guernsey Airlines?) and Hester got to her party in time.

London, 22 August

Saw AW off to Brussels on the train this morning with a sigh of relief. Yesterday the car broke down on the motorway on our drive up to London and we had to call the AA to fix it. Then the wheels came off our shopping trolley in Sainsbury's and AW had to carry it home, full of stuff, in his arms as if it was a person. Then he lost his Brussels wallet with all his euros in it, and just after he'd gone this morning I found his mobile phone, which he'd left behind. I am not sure I can take much more of this.

My chest suddenly looks as if someone had left an iron on it, but Sam did say it would get worse before it gets better.

23 August

Oh dear, in spite of everything I was much happier with AW here – without him my routine goes to pieces. It is midday and I have only just had a bath – not that I haven't been up for hours doing things, it just seems to take me so long to get around to getting dressed. I really do need Gina Ford. The trouble is that I haven't planned my life properly, I haven't thought about the future – everything stopped for me with my radiotherapy. Now it's over and I am just drifting along and have no energy to do anything.

Forgot to mention that we *did* get speeding tickets for those journeys we made with Hester and the baby to and from Somerset. I appealed them, explaining about baby crying etc., etc., but was refused and had to pay up. Right now the car is away at the garage being repaired and I must say it is a relief not to have it here.

Brussels, 26 August

I went to say goodbye to Malachy yesterday because Hester and George are off on holiday to our house in France and I have come to Brussels to spend a long weekend with AW. Malachy was supposed to be having a nap when I went in to kiss him goodbye, but he had escaped from his swaddling and was lying on his back beaming at his baby mobile. I just wanted to hug him for ever. He has such a lovely smell, which I know is from washing powder, but will always be Malachy to me.

There is some talk of George getting a job in Kabul. I can't bear to think of them going away – it gives me a pain in my heart and makes me realise how awful it must have been for my mum when we took Hester and Claudia away from them for months at a time.

London, 28 August

When I kissed AW goodbye this morning in Brussels, he smelt terrible. 'Oh sorry,' he said, 'I've just sweetened my breath with a slice of Camembert.' He has to entertain six ministers from Azerbaijan tomorrow.

On the Eurostar home I fell so fast asleep that my snoring must have entered my subconscious and made me think I was being attacked by a lion – or perhaps that I was a lion myself – because the next thing I knew was that I woke up snarling, my lips drawn back and my teeth bared. When I opened my eyes my fellow travellers round the table were looking at me anxiously, but they quickly looked away. Not just embarrassing but positively disturbing.

Hester telephoned from France to say that someone has broken a flower-painted bowl (the pieces were left there), and she was telling me now so that I wouldn't think it was her. I realise that this is my favourite bowl that I had stuffed into the very back of a cupboard so that no one would use it. There is an odd thing about possessions – why is it *always* your most favourite objects that get broken or damaged, or disappear?

At the moment I have lost a green jade pendant my mother gave me (it fell off its chain), a stick-man picture by Sir Edmund Hillary of himself and Sherpa Tenzing climbing Mount Everest that he drew for me when we were posted to Delhi (for a donation to charity), as well as an old letter to my engineer grandfather from workers on the railway line in India that he was constructing, explaining why they had had to kill a tiger. All of these are pretty well valueless but priceless to me, and have vanished.

My other theory is that objects are able in some way to attract the right buyers. There are lots of examples of extraordinary treasures being found in junk shops by the *only* people able to recognise them for what they are. I remember the story of the portrait of Mary Seacole, a black nurse in the Crimean War: it came up for sale, unidentified, at an obscure auction in the country where it just so happened that among all the punters viewing things was the one person able to recognise the woman in the picture. Now it is in the National Portrait Gallery.

I told someone this theory – that objects call out to be bought by the right people – and, knowing my shopping habits, he said, 'God, Bridge, when you go into a junk shop the noise must be deafening.'

I found AW's wallet with the euros in it under the fruit bowl in the kitchen. It's a pity it didn't call to me before, and save a lot of angst.

31 August

Today I went to see a hormone specialist about my aches and pains. I sobbed over his desk telling him about these, plus my tiredness and lack of joie de vivre, etc., etc. He said my symptoms were all to do with not taking HRT. He suggested that I should try out some plant oestrogens such as Red Clover, and if that makes no difference, Mr Gui might put me back on HRT, but I have to give it a few months.

My dreams are getting weirder and weirder – and they all seem to have something to do with babies. Last night I dreamed that Hester was a baby who could discuss things with me like an adult, and that she had a handle on her back for easy carrying.

4

Humdrum

George is off to Kabul on Friday for his job interview. We have been spending all our time discussing whether he and Hester should go to live out there. Hester is longing to move abroad. It's curious: she wants to recreate her nomadic childhood in foreign parts for her own family, whereas Claudia definitely wants to stay put.

Someone has finally made an offer for my flat in Pimlico but the trouble is that the people I am buying from haven't found anything they want yet. Everything is on hold until they do.

7 September

Hester rang: the end of their holiday was like a good news/bad news story. First bad news: they ran out of fuel on their way to the airport, but then good news: they pulled into a lay-by where somehow they found a man with a jerry can of petrol; next, bad news: they arrived at the airport knowing they'd missed their plane, but, good news: take-off had been delayed for two hours and they were allowed to check in. (A year ago they went to France forgetting their credit cards, and they had to pawn their passports at a hotel to get some money to fill up their car.)

8 September

Oh God! A huge suicide bomb went off in Kabul today – for the first time right in the centre – and George is due to catch his plane in a couple of hours. I wonder if he will cancel the trip.

Later. He didn't, he is on his way.

10 September

Today I arranged to take Malachy with me to Peter Jones to meet up with my dear pal Julia and her friend Mimi for lunch. It took me all morning to pack nappies, shawls and blankets, rain cover for pram, changing mat, wipes, toys, clean outfit, muslins, bottles, milk powder, water – I kept wondering if I'd forgotten something vital and re-packing all over again.

I struggled up to the top-floor restaurant with the baby in a pram almost hidden by the plastic bags balanced on it and dangling from its handles – not to mention my own handbag slung across my body. Julia hooted with laughter and said I looked like a whole Bedouin encampment on my own, but she did help me change the nappy in the Ladies' room for which I was deeply grateful because it was a particularly frightening shade of green.

It's odd but quite a few of my friends have just become grandmothers: Julia, Jossy, Sandy, Didi, Mary. It turns out I am not the only one finding it difficult: we are all having the same problems with car seat/pram/pushchair fastenings and buckles (in our day we just used to put the baby in a carry cot on the back seat) – let alone the supposedly 'easy' travelling cot which requires the brilliance of Einstein and the strength of Hercules to put up. And all this comes just as our eyesight is getting worse so we can't do anything without our glasses, and our grip is getting weaker so sometimes we just can't press hard enough on a clip to undo it. Mary knows someone who actually put a whole pushchair on a swing because she couldn't undo the safety straps to get her grand-daughter out. We are all finding it exhausting, and it's a relief to be able to confide in each other about our tiredness and the mistakes we make as we are far too scared of our daughters or daughters-in-law to tell them. And none of us can remember our mothers being so hands-on with *our* babies.

12 September

This morning at 8.45 a.m., I got one of those irritating tele-phone calls from a call centre in India or the Philippines. I said, quite nicely, 'I'm sorry, I don't want an unsolicited call right now.'

The man at the other end said, 'How you know this is an unsolicited call?'

I replied, 'Because I didn't solicit it; I didn't ask you to ring me.'

He said, 'Why don't you cut your line?' And then yelled, '*Go get some scissors and cut your line!*' and slammed down the phone.

What a world when someone you don't know rings you from halfway round the globe and shouts at you. You can't just be rude at the outset or you might find yourself in an embarrassing situation, as I did not long ago when our phone rang in Somerset and it was a man with an Indian accent asking for AW. I said firmly, 'I am so sorry but we do not want to buy anything,' and was about to hang up when the Indian voice replied, 'And I most certainly do not wish to sell you anything. I would merely like to speak to my old friend from university.' It was a distinguished Pakistani buddy of AW's from his time as a student.

13 September

AW is back for a few days' leave. The first thing he did was knock over the flower arrangement in the sitting room of our flat, so there was water all over the place, but I am so happy to see him.

14 September

Poor AW: his few days R&R have turned into nothing but stress because George is in Kabul and Hester is at the end of her tether with Malachy crying and being sick all the time, so this morning we took her to Chelsea and Westminster Hospital children's section and saw a nice doc who says the baby has probably got acid reflux and *at long last* gave her the medicines that will help. Thank goodness George is back tomorrow and we are escaping from London to go to my niece's wedding in Dorset.

Somerset, 15 September

My aches and pains are no better in spite of taking Red Clover herbal oestrogen, and nor is my miserable mood. I cried all the way down to Somerset and all the way round Sainsbury's in Frome because I thought if I feel like this now, what am I going to be like in ten years' time? AW got really fed up.

Incidentally, the mother of Richard Reid, the Shoe Bomber, comes from Frome. The local paper said, 'Spare a thought for his poor old mum who has to cope with having a terrorist for a son *and* living in Frome.'

Years ago, in the summer holidays, while I was shopping in Frome one day, Hester went to Woolworth's to try and get a job. She was gone for hours so I went to look for her but couldn't see her anywhere in the store. I asked a salesperson, 'Where would you go if you were looking for a job here?' and she said, 'You'd see the Personnel Manager upstairs, but don't bother, luv, there's no vacancies at the moment.' I didn't realise for a second that she thought *I*, the one-time fashion and beauty editor of the *Sunday Times*, was looking for a job at Woolies in Frome. I resolved that from then on, I would force myself to put on my lipstick and eye make-up every morning, instead of being lazy. And maybe I should have my hair cut instead of scraping it into a ponytail.

17 September

Today was bittersweet. On the way to my niece's wedding we went through Whitelackington, a village we used to live in after my parents returned from India. It was sad: our old house looked a bit derelict and the pretty flower garden Mum created at the back had vanished. My sister Tessa and I were about seven and ten when we lived there; I was given a camera one birthday and took what I thought were very arty photographs of a tree in the village that was being cut down. I looked at them in an old album the other day, pages and pages of very small, bad, black-and-white photos captioned: the Wych elm (about six of these); the Wych elm cut; the Wych elm falling; the Wych elm fallen (another six assorted views); the corner without the Wych elm, and so on. I remember my kind parents being full of praise at the time.

London, 19 September

Had the most terrible nightmare last night – one of those ones that you have to put the light on and wake yourself up so you don't fall back into it again. It was all about AW and I discovering secret catacombs under our house – they were lined with fresh wet skulls. Why should I dream something so horrible?

Brussels, 26 September

I went for a walk in the pretty park outside our flat today and passed a group of late-teenage boys hanging about; two of them ran ahead of me and then looked back and shouted to their friends in French, 'Forget it. She's an old bag when you see her from the front.' I don't know if they actually said 'old bag', but that was definitely the gist of it, I was mortified. I believe this is called the '1776 syndrome' – meaning you look seventeen from the back and seventy-six from the front. So embarrassing.

Some of the Flemish words in Brussels sound comic to British ears: there is a pub down the road called *Wopper* and on a nearby building site there's an advertisement for new flats which have exciting-sounding things called *slaapkamers*. I asked AW what these could be – turns out they are bedrooms.

Somerset, 1 October

My artist friend Candace had her birthday today and I gave her the wonderful plaster cake from the Brussels flea market that nearly caused AW and I to divorce. The only problem was that another woman had made a beautiful, surprise real birthday cake and she nearly cried when she saw mine, thinking it was a rival. Once she realised it was a fake, she was happy again.

Later. Holy Moses! AW has just emailed to say that Malaysia is coming up among the postings next autumn and he is going to apply for it. This means he would not retire next spring but we would go to the East for two years. Malaysia! Sun! It would be worth it.

7 October

Malachy came to stay last night, and my dear friend Meriel came to supper. It got off to a bad start because Malachy wouldn't feed properly and then it turned out that I had left the lid on the bottle under the teat so no milk was going through. Once we'd sorted that out everything went hunky dory and he slept till eight the next morning. I didn't sleep at all because of worrying about cot death, or intruders stabbing us both, or me dying of a heart attack and no one being able to get in to look after the baby.

9 October

George is not going to work in Kabul as the situation is getting worse there and he would not be able to take Hester and Malachy. The decision is out of their hands. Thank goodness.

19 October

In the last twenty-four hours I have been to Basel in Switzerland and back. I was asked to talk in a bookshop there. Why do I agree to do these things? I get so worked up and panic-stricken – though once I am actually doing it, it's fine.

Got up at crack of dawn to catch the 8.30 plane but it was cancelled, and so instead of arriving early to be briefed and have a good look round, I arrived only just in time for the talk. As I went slowly through security I saw tables covered with assorted bottles and I thought, 'What a fantastic idea! They've set up a bar so that you can have a drink while you wait in the queue.' Then I realised that far from it – these were the bottles they'd taken off passengers. I quickly swigged back the miniature bottle of brandy that I keep in my bag to numb my fear of flying.

To my amazement when the plane finally left hours later, they upgraded me *without my asking* because of the delay. I am always trying and failing to get promoted to business class. The worst time was on a Lufthansa flight to Syria when I asked at the check-in for an upgrade. They said they'd look into it, but nothing happened, so I went and sat in my economy seat, which happened to be next to a Syrian woman I knew. Suddenly an air hostess appeared at the front of the aircraft and asked loudly, 'Vill ze voman who asked for an upgrade, please identify herzelf.'

Before she noticed my hand shooting up, the Syrian woman sighed and said, 'There's always someone who wants more, isn't there?'

That was bad enough, but then the air hostess walked slowly down the aisle to me and said, 'It eez not possible,' with a look of triumph in her eyes, and then walked back again.

London, 20 October

We have just heard that a great friend of ours, Maya, has been arrested and imprisoned in Damascus. It seems that someone she knows in the United States sent her a rude cartoon of the

President of Syria having it off with the President of Lebanon and she forwarded it to a friend who panicked and reported her to the secret police. (The cartoon is not really explicit and has been going around on the Internet for a while with different faces on the two figures, e.g., George Bush and Saddam Hussein.) She must have been insane to send it on, but no one deserves to go to prison for a joke. I feel desperately sorry for her.

The actor Simon Russell Beale lives in the flat below Hester and George, so tonight we went to see him in *Galileo* at the National Theatre and afterwards he invited us for a drink backstage (thrilling) and then we all shared a taxi home. He showed us his books – there was a wall of them – and told us that when he first became an actor and made some money he bought a pair of diamond cufflinks. He hid them in the bookcase but, knowing he would forget where, he decided to put them behind the most boring title he had: *The Anglican Church in New Zealand*. Not long later his brother came over to play on his piano and, glancing at the books, noticed *The Anglican Church in New Zealand*. Just *because* it sounded so excruciatingly boring, he took it out to look at it and found the cufflinks. Obviously not such a good hiding place after all.

Simon Russell Beale comes from a military family (like ours), and has a theory that children from those kinds of nomadic backgrounds are often good at acting because they have learned to project themselves and get on with strangers very quickly.

22 October

Malachy came to spend the night again. I had instructions to get seven ounces of milk into him before midnight but I couldn't (I'll say that I did). To distract him I put on the telly but it was a programme about a giraffe having a Caesarean – will he be traumatised?

There was a piece in the paper today saying that a survey of parents aged over fifty revealed that they didn't feel extra stress. Well, all I can say is who were they talking to? I know from my own survey of grandmother friends over sixty that we are all worn to a frazzle.

Brussels, 11 November

AW and I are in Brussels and Claudia has come for the weekend with her friend Jemima. Before she left London yesterday morning she rang me and spoke in a funny voice (she's had this weird voice for about a week now and I've been wondering what's up) and then announced that she is pregnant! Yay! Now we are all having a great weekend together, mostly eating.

Later. Decided to get the ironing out of the way but AW has a new iron that is so complicated I can't understand how to work it. (Incidentally, am I the only person who still does ironing? – neither of my daughters seems to press anything.) I am completely dyslexic about gadgets and machinery – I barely know how to put on a DVD. I just want an iron with HOT, WARM and COLD written on it and a mobile phone that only does calls and texts (it upsets me that apparently I am using only about a hundredth of its capacity), and a TV with just an ON/OFF switch like they were in India when we were posted there.

And while I'm about it, the other thing that drives me mad is that instructions are always printed so small – especially on shampoo and conditioner. So there you are with water in your eyes, trying to see if you have to leave the product on for five minutes or if you can rinse it off straight away, and you need a magnifying glass to read what it says. And another thing, I used to enjoy buying clothes in the old days when stores didn't have dozens of different shop franchises in them, but put all red dresses or all black coats together on a rack so you could see the whole spectrum. And I feel sad for the days when you could go to a hardware shop and buy one screw or an individual cup hook, rather than having to get a packet of twenty that you will never use.

13 November

We walked round the lake in our square today and noticed that someone had dropped a packet of chocolate fingers – they looked exactly like the turds of some cute little dog and AW had the urge to pick one up and eat it to shock the passers-by into thinking about the dog-poo situation in their parks.

I found AW sitting staring into space this evening. I asked if anything was wrong and he said no, he was just thinking that once we were two and now we are going to be eight, and he is trying to take it in.

London, 15 November

Got a message from the Syrian Ambassador to say the President's wife says she doesn't want to do an interview but she'll think about it next spring.

Tonight was the launch of Barnaby Rogerson's new book *Meetings with Remarkable Muslims*, which I have contributed to. It was held at the Moroccan Embassy Residence, which was interesting for me as AW and I are not involved in the diplomatic world in London at all – the only embassy I have set foot inside is the Syrian one. Across a crowded room I saw a new friend, Eleanor O'Keefe, who helped organise the Paris Literary Festival. I rushed up to say hello but when I opened my mouth the words that came out were, 'Do you think we could organise a literature festival in Palestine?' As I have written earlier, the Palestinian cause is dear to my heart, and there has been talk of a literary festival in Petra, Jordan, lately, so I suppose the two came together in my mind all of a sudden. Eleanor thought it was a bold and brilliant idea and we are going to ring our friend Ahdaf Soueif who, being an Arab writer, is the perfect person to head it up.

Later. Ahdaf is really excited about the idea, and if AW doesn't get the job in Malaysia he can help organise it all. (It may not sound like it from this diary, but AW is an excellent organiser.)

18 November

I had to do a talk at the Richmond Literature Festival today. I was even more scared than usual as Simon Hoggart was in the audience and he is a *really* funny writer, but I was being interviewed by an old journalist friend Valerie Grove, so it wasn't just me up there, which made it easier. The audience were nice – apart from the three people in the front row who were asleep. I like to think that is because the room was very hot.

22 November

What has happened to my brain? A good friend, Anthony Sattin, rang today, and at the end of our conversation he said, 'So . . . we'll see you later for dinner.'

There was a pause while I realised I had forgotten all about going to dinner with the Sattins, and then I explained that I was babysitting Malachy and couldn't get out of it. 'Oh God, I am so sorry,' I said. 'Have you already bought the food?'

There was another silence and then Anthony said, 'No, not actually, because we were coming to dinner with you.'

Then I went to the photocopy shop to get a duplicate of my insurance certificate for the sale of my flat, and I pressed sixty-five copies instead of one; I didn't know how to stop the machine so I got thirty copies (at 20p each) before the man came to help me.

Some years ago I was asked to write a book on the models who had appeared in *Vogue*, and they gave me a temporary desk at the magazine to do some research. I pretended that I was well used to working in an office and knew my way around, even though I hadn't actually been in one for about twenty-five years and was terrified. The first thing that happened was that I pressed one hundred on the photo-copying machine instead of one, just like today – but I didn't dare ask for help because then I would have had to admit that I didn't know how to work the machine, so I just stood there coolly while the machine churned out the copies, and I then hid them in my bag and took them home for scrap paper.

Next thing was that I tried to get hold of the Eileen Ford Model Agency in New York, but though I rang and rang I couldn't get any reply. 'Can you think of a reason why the Eileen Ford Agency in New York is not answering their phone?' I asked my glamorous neighbour at the next desk.

'Could be because New York is five hours behind us so it's six in the morning there and they won't have opened yet,' she said coldly.

28 November

Julia came to have lunch today and checked my babysitting schedule (we grannies are all given schedules so we know what we should be doing next). It's quite ridiculous really: she and I have both brought up families, we are both professional women, but we find ourselves giggling guiltily about our little misdeeds. I confessed that I pour milk out of Malachy's bottles so that Hester will think he has drunk more than he has, and Julia revealed that she once made up her baby granddaughter's meal with unboiled tap water.

Julia has written a book called *Approaching Death* and, because I helped her slightly, she sent me a copy. I left it on the kitchen table to read, which has caused a family drama as everyone who's been in here since has thought that I am preparing for my own.

5

Moving Events

London, 29 November

Have been feeling fed up as AW went off to Baku, and then on to Kazakhstan for a meeting, a few days ago and I have hardly heard from him.

Today I went to lobby my MP at the House of Commons about the Palestinians, but the queue in security was so long that I missed my appointment. I was hanging about waiting to see if he could fit me in somehow, and got chatting to a handsome man whose views on the Iraq War and Middle East seemed to match mine. Then, *he asked me out for a drink* and, though I couldn't go (babysitting again), I was over the moon to be invited – ME with my aches and pains, and back/hip/neck that need replacing.

Walking home I had a sudden urge to go back and find him and pour my soul into his deep dark eyes, but I knew that way madness lay – for a start he'd probably gone home by now – and plodded on to my flat.

30 November

AW rang today to say it is minus twenty-five degrees in Kazakhstan and he has left his fur hat in Brussels.

It makes me nervous when he is in the ex-Soviet Union: as I have said before, you cannot overestimate the danger to husbands there. Even our colleague, the Swiss Ambassador in Damascus – happily married, Catholic, children – left his wife for a secretary when he was posted to Ukraine. Last time I saw AW he showed me a picture of his new Azerbaijani assistant on his mobile – she is the most beautiful woman I have ever seen. Thank God she's engaged to be married.

6 December

This has been my medical week: appointments with the chiropractor, the acupuncturist, and a cancer check-up. The check-up was fine, but the other treatments don't seem to have made any difference, which is depressing. A neighbour in Somerset who used to be a nun (she is writing a book called *Kicking the Habit*) says that from her own experience, the Last Rites do wonders for bad backs.

There are so many extraordinary characters in our village; you could make a soap opera without having to move more than 500 yards. We have a rather dour farmer, Caroline the ex-nun, the war photographer Don McCullin, as well as a famous theatre director, a well-known furniture-maker and bridge-builder, a railway signalman who is an expert on the queens of England, a respected newspaper columnist, a former editor of *Brides* mag, a country and western musician, a stonemason who is exactly like the leading character in the play *Jerusalem*, and someone who really knows Dominic West from *The Wire*.

2 December

Malachy is coming to stay with me for eight days in January as Hester and George have to go to a wedding in India. Will I be able to cope?

I have been longing to have my teeth whitened with laser treatment, but Charlie Brooker has just written a piece in the *Guardian* saying that he tried it and he would rather have had his smashed out with a hammer and replaced with false ones, it was so excruciatingly painful. The alternative is to have trays of bleach that you put on your teeth at night, but doesn't that keep you awake?

Brussels, 8 December

AW and I met up in Brussels today for the first time in three weeks. He was supposed to get to the flat before me but his plane was two hours late leaving London. He arrived fuming about British Airways – the World's Most Hated Airline, he calls it. The stewardess on the long Baku–London leg of the journey (he was travelling BMed for that part) gave him a nice bottle of wine, but it was taken off him as he went through London airport to catch the BA flight to Brussels – a bit silly since it had been on the previous plane with him for six hours. I wonder what they do with all the confiscated bottles.

AW brought me a second-hand mobile from Baku: it's the old flip-top design by Nokia, which I love but you can't buy new any more, so I was thrilled. Then he put my SIM card into the new phone, and I was thinking what a kind man he was when he announced that he had deleted all my messages 'to help me'. I was furious. I had been saving the one from Hester telling me the baby was born, and another from Candace when I was having my cancer op. AW is a complete control freak. I dread to think what would happen if I deleted his messages – or even read them for that matter. Men go on about being henpecked but why isn't the word *cock-pecking* in use? I feel I am being cock-pecked right now.

We had some friends for supper tonight. I think one of them must have been high on something because he kept calling AW darling. I am not sure any woman friend of ours has ever called AW darling, let alone a man – he isn't really that kind of person.

12 December

Went to the wonderful Belgian butcher today to buy meat to take to London. There was a pool of yellowish liquid on the floor and I thought one of the cabinets must be leaking melted ice or something. It turned out to be dog pee ... gross. Too Brueghel-esque for me; things in Belgium are often a bit on the dark side.

London, 15 December

Malachy's christening at Westminster Cathedral today. We have a family christening robe which goes round the relatives like pass the parcel; I retrieved it from my cousin Simon. Malachy is five months old now and a real boy; he looked rather as though he was in drag in the long lacy robe. He played peekaboo with his White Garment, which made the priest laugh.

I am not sure any of the godparents are religious. When the priest asked, 'Do you believe in God the Father Almighty?' there seemed (to my Catholic ears) to be a deafening silence, so I sidled over and stood near them so that I could boom out, 'I do'. Luckily (no one else thought of it – I don't know what would happen to this family without me) I remembered to bring the second tier of the wedding cake from Somerset where it was being kept for the christening.

17 December

AW strikes again. He has lost his set of keys to our flat. Don't ask me how: he only went out to get milk and next thing he can't find them anywhere.

As the rain pours down I am getting more and more enthusiastic about Malaysia, but AW noticed in the small print of the application form that it says you must have been in Brussels for two years before applying to go abroad again, so he is not optimistic.

20 December

Malachy has got bronchiolitis. His breathing sounded so scary this afternoon that AW and I decided to take him, with Hester, to A&E.

We set off, me driving and AW holding some of the baby paraphernalia. Outside the Conran Shop in Sloane Avenue we stopped for the traffic lights and AW noticed that the bottle of baby milk he was carrying had leaked into its lid so he opened his door to tip it out – and knocked a cyclist off his bike. There was an almighty crash and the poor chap landed on the pavement. (To be fair to AW, the cyclist was creeping up the gutter and was impossible to see.) Within a nanosecond the security chap from Conran was out of the store phoning for an ambulance and the police, and telling Marco (the cyclist) not to move a muscle. He lay there looking dramatic for about ten minutes and then said he was fine and sat up.

We had to wait for ages until the authorities arrived, and then for the police to take statements and meanwhile, in the back of the car, Hester was muttering, 'Oh God . . . parents,' in exasperation and I can't say I blamed her. At long last we were allowed to continue on our way without any further action and got to A&E where they checked Malachy out and said he was okay.

Somerset, 1 January

New Year and AW, who is home for the holidays, and I feel full of gloom about the state of the world: the so-called War on Terror, the threats to Iran, the long-suffering Palestinians – not to mention double standards, hypocrisy and lies from our leaders, etc., etc. Then I realised that we go through this every New Year and I felt better.

8 January

My back is so painful I can hardly breathe. Could I have broken a rib in my sleep? I am knocking back Nurofen non-stop. The chemist suggested a thermal-wrap thing that you swaddle yourself in – hmmm, glam. It does seem to help though. Perhaps it's all psychosomatic because Malachy is coming to stay in a few days' time.

13 January

Malachy was delivered to me today by his other grandparents, who have had him for a week. I have an empty diary for eight days, apart from having to interview the designer Kaffe Fassett for a magazine in Brussels.

My friends Chris and Wendy dropped by to meet Malachy this evening and to check out my grandparenting skills. They told me he hadn't eaten enough supper and that I was trying to do it all too fast, which is probably true.

Hester rang from India to say she was missing him so much she was going to come home.

14 January

Hester phoned again to say she is okay now, it was just jetlag.

I am not okay. According to the schedule, Malachy has to drink eighteen ounces of milk every day, but he is hardly taking any, and spits out most of his food.

I cried today. Is he going to starve to death here? *The Good Granny Guide* makes it all sound so easy. I wonder at what point you must start really worrying about a child not eating.

I made some delicious baby meals and tried to tidy my flat, which already seems to be ankle deep in dirty muslin cloths and toys – and all my clothes seem to have baby food or vomit on them, and he's only been here a day.

London, 15 January

It would all be much easier if he would go to sleep when I put him down in the evenings at 7 p.m., but he doesn't, so I am still sitting by the cot with my head against the railings singing to him tunelessly at 9.30 p.m. (Poor child, I am probably ruining his musical ear; Hester and Claudia are only able to identify the songs I sang to them by the words, not the melody.)

I went to the Indian chemist to try to get teats with bigger holes in them as I thought that might help with the feeding. The shop assistant didn't understand what I wanted so I said again very slowly, 'Teats with big holes for a baby's bottle.'

'I see,' he said. 'Big tits' – and went off to look for them.

Ahdaf came for supper to discuss 'Palfest', the Palestine Festival of Literature, but I had to keep going up to Malachy who wouldn't sleep so we couldn't really have a conversation. We have already formed the board, and decided to ask Harold Pinter, Seamus Heaney, John Berger and Chinua Achebe to be patrons.

16 January

Today I went off to interview Kaffe Fassett and do the shopping (Malachy went to the babyminder for a couple of hours). He (Malachy, not Kaffe) still isn't eating or sleeping properly.

London, no idea of the date

Malachy woke before five and it took more than half an hour to get him to go back to sleep, and then it was for only twenty-five minutes. The gap between 6 a.m. and his first rest seems an eternity that I don't really know how to fill.

This afternoon I gave him the wrong bottle of milk by mistake: an old one I had prepared earlier, instead of the nice warm one I had just got ready. But how old was the bottle? From this morning? Yesterday? Feeds are only supposed to hang around for an hour. How do babies survive their grandmothers?

Later. No ill effects as far as I could see, so I took Malachy to tea with Meriel this afternoon. I had to meet up with her urgently to discuss what to do: there is to be a Sixties Fashion Study Day at the V&A shortly, and, though we were both really important fashion editors in the sixties (I was once described as a 'Young Meteor' but when I married AW I became a fallen star), we have not been invited. We felt upset enough to complain, which is a bit humiliating, but we don't care: we can't just be written out of fashion history.

London, 20 January

Having made such a fuss about not being invited to the Sixties Study Day, Meriel and I *had* to go today, so Claudia and Aled came to babysit.

There were lots of friends and faces from the old Swinging London days at the V&A, all forty years older now (perhaps it was right to hold the event in a museum). It was a jolly trip down memory lane, but when I got home there was a phone call to tell me my darling brother had died at lunchtime that day. I am dazed and miserable. AW is going to come over from Brussels tomorrow.

22 January

AW has been wonderful; thank goodness he came home. I feel desolate about my brother. I had counted on seeing more of him when AW retired, but now I never will.

Hester and George are back tonight and Malachy is going home. I will miss him, he is the most companionable and entertaining little chap and I adore him.

14 February

AW sent a sweet email: 'Will you be my Valentine for the thirty-sixth year running?'

I spent the evening babysitting. Hmm, romantic. I am longing for the day when AW and I can be together.

Have lost my social skills: my publishers gave a party the other night and I found I could barely communicate with other grown-ups, I can only talk to babies. Luckily I met my old friend Irma Kurtz there, who also has a grandson of nine months, so we could chat about nappies and feeds and the amazingly clever things our grandsons can say and do.

Somerset, 22 February

Today was my brother's memorial service at Downside in Somerset (he was at school there). The abbey was packed and the service incredibly moving. I felt so proud of him. He had been Adjutant-General of the British Army, plus ADC to the Queen (who sent a representative), but I will always think of him with his handsome head thrown back, laughing mightily, and making life more fun.

London, 23 February

I rang my friend Chris today, but he was at the doctor's. His son said he would ring back in an hour, but I said, 'No, *I* will be at the doctor's then.' That's how it is these days.

I have a trigger thumb all of a sudden, as well as my permanent back ache. My doctor has started talking about 'pain management', but I don't want to manage it, I want it to go away – can't we have 'pain elimination'? Or perhaps even 'cure'? She has suggested having a steroid injection in my spine and referred me to a specialist. In my referral letter she has described me as 'This charming lady author'. I told this to Chris later, and he said that in a similar letter his doctor called him 'This right-handed gentleman . . .' We agreed he must have been pretty desperate.

6 March

Went to the Thai unisex beauty salon, which is round the corner from our flat, to have a pedicure. There was a notice on the wall saying PLEASE DO NOT ASK FOR SEX.

15 March

The couple who own the flat I want to buy have found something they like, and so the whole deal is now being activated, and I should be able to move in about four weeks, but I am going to have to go to Brussels as well as find friends to stay with here because I am having some changes made by a builder. He is a bit of a gamble – I just found his card on the doormat – but he has given me a really reasonable estimate.

The last time I had to move out of my home for builders was years ago and a friend from Brussels days, Pauline, who had a very important government job, said I could stay in her house as she was going away to the US for two weeks. I went round so she could show me the ropes, and noticed that there were about seven locks on the front door. 'Gosh, Pauline,' I laughed. 'You certainly go in for security!'

'Yes,' she said seriously, 'that's because I am on the IRA hit list.' HIT LIST? OhGodOhGod, I thought, this is the last place I want to stay, but I didn't know how to get out of it. Every morning I'd come out of the front door talking to myself very loudly: 'I wonder how *Pauline* is getting on *in California*,' I'd say. 'It's so kind of her to *lend* me, an *Irish person*, her house.' Apart from the fear, her place was lovely and I am still grateful.

9 May

It's *weeks* since I last wrote my diary: my computer has been packed away, and I have spent most of the past two months in Brussels with AW, or staying with various friends in London.

The move into the flat last week was catastrophic – not because the builders hadn't done a good job, but because I discovered they had thrown out all my most treasured possessions (the ones I hadn't already lost) by mistake.

When I first came here I put all my precious things into a big cupboard on the landing to keep them safe. For some unknown reason the builders thought that everything in the cupboard had to be thrown away, so just before I came back from Brussels to move in, they emptied it all out on to our skip. It was only when Shirley (the cleaning lady) and I started unpacking that we discovered things were missing: a wooden rocking horse (bought for Malachy), a little Persian rug, pictures, a small nursing chair, my Victorian saucepan rack – but, most heart-breaking, my boxes of antique French Les Islettes plates painted with roses, which I have been collect- ing all my life. My first instinct was that the builders had stolen the stuff, but the old Italian lady who lives below me asked why I had put a lovely rocking horse on the skip so I know their story is true.

I offered a huge reward to the skip people but no one has found anything. The insurance company is not going to pay (I was on the 'wrong level' whatever that means), and I can't be too harsh on the builder because he told me he had a nervous breakdown last year and I don't want to bring on another one. There was a story in the papers recently about an electrician who found discarded pictures by Francis Bacon on a skip and sold them for £96,500. I hope someone found all my stuff and got some pleasure out of it, I'd rather that than it all got dumped in a landfill site.

My first night in the new flat the lights fused and I was so scared that I had to drag the bedroom chest of drawers in front of the door, then I lay awake all night listening to the people in the flat next door bonking non-stop and decided I must be next to a brothel (I discovered next day that there isn't a flat next door, only a roof, so the noise must have been a TV aerial, or pigeons, or something).

Finally, when I came home from shopping yesterday afternoon, there was a huge crow flapping round the sitting room. (Actually I don't know what it was, only that it was black and felt the size of an albatross.) There is a definite voodoo feeling about this — I mean how often do you find a bird in your flat — but I opened all the windows and managed to shoo it out.

12 May

Last night I dreamed that all my veins were on the outside of my body and kept catching on door handles.

Claudia's baby is due in only three weeks; she is having a girl and has decided to call her Maisie, after my mother, which I am very touched about.

My parents died more than a decade ago but I miss them all the time; Mum was known in our family as Doomwatch because she always expected the worst to happen — I realise that I am turning into her now. She used to stand in the bay window of their sitting room, puffing on a cigarette, watching the cars on the road and worrying that one of them would park across the entrance to the garage — no one ever did. I worry that the man who comes to read the electric meter is a serial killer who will turn on me when the front door is closed behind him, that if I sit under one of the huge chandeliers at Mass in Westminster Cathedral it will fall on top of me, and that a neighbour might play music too loudly or keep a barking dog. None have so far.

One good piece of news is that our friend Maya has been released from prison in Syria. What a brave woman she is. She is going to stay on in Damascus and open the hotel in the Old City she was working on before she was arrested.

Somerset, 30 July

Claudia and little newborn Maisie are down here with me now so that I can help. I have been conquering my fear of the underground and going to her flat in London every day on the tube, but it is easier in Somerset.

Maisie's birth was horrendous: Claudia was in labour for thirty-six hours and ended up having a Caesarean. After the first twenty-four hours I couldn't stand the worry and went up to the hospital at 2 a.m. There was a pool of dried bright red nail varnish in the centre of the waiting-room floor that looked like blood – I wondered if it was an omen.

The worst part about it was that Claudia's midwives were really surly and unhelpful and I watched my poor daughter, in the middle of her own ordeal, trying to win their support by asking them about their families and so on but they were unsmiling and cold. I wanted to kill them all. Luckily in the last stages she had a gentle Frenchwoman to help, and then a kind lady surgeon.

Afterwards Claudia was in a ward where there was a young girl of thirteen or fourteen who'd had a baby and whose birthing partner was her even-younger sister. It was so sad.

London, 8 August

Malachy is now at nursery school; I fetch him most after-noons as Hester is back at work as a lawyer. Another baby at the nursery bit him last week and I felt so sad because I realised that this was only the first of the many hurts he will get in life. Grandchildren seem to grow on you: at first I saw it all as a terrific interruption to normal life, but now I can't imagine the world without Malachy and Maisie. I am not sure there is life after grandparenthood though – every time I go to Brussels I feel guilty that I am not helping one of my daughters. Have got to conquer this or I will never see AW again. I told him the other day what a wonderful mother I am being right now and he said, 'It's a pity I'm not your son.'

London, 15 August

The Evil Eye seems to be growing dimmer, its powers have definitely lessened, though I have locked myself out of my flat twice in the last few months. And I am still desperately trying to be disciplined enough to turn my light out before 1 a.m. and get dressed (with full make-up) before midday. My resolution has been slightly dented by the fact that I have had a really terrible cold and cough – in fact I stayed in bed until 10.30 this morning; then my friend Lesley phoned, and I told her I felt so guilty because I was only just getting out of bed. She said, 'Don't be silly, at our age people should be astonished that we are *ever* out of bed – my grandmother sat all day, knitting, but look at all the things we have to do. Anyway,' she went on, 'you might get pneumonia, so go back under your duvet.'

Perhaps as a result of all this bed rest my back was much better – until I made the fatal mistake of telling AW, after which it started hurting again.

29 August

Today on my computer I suddenly got an email from William Dalrymple asking if I would be his friend on Facebook and it seemed rather rude to do nothing, so next thing I joined. (William has been a friend in real life since he came to stay with us in Syria for a night and stayed six weeks.) Now I am getting messages from people saying they're happy to be my friend, which makes me feel pathetically grateful. One good thing is that my birth date came out as fifteen years later than it really is: don't ask me how, I don't think I filled anything in, it just appeared there.

I have hardly any Facebook friends. I must get Hester or Claudia to teach me how to do this or it will be such a loss of face. I read some of our children's friends' messages: they mostly seem to say they are hanging out of their arses with hangovers (whatever that means); I'm not going to read them any more for fear of what I might find out. People keep telling me how brilliant Facebook is because it puts you in touch with all the people you used to know – but my feeling is that if you haven't seen someone for forty years there is probably a good reason for it.

2 September

Something so embarrassing. Claudia has been feeling a bit down in the dumps so I sent her an email saying, 'My darling little fat baby, it will all be okay in the end so don't worry and just remember your mum loves you and you can climb back into her tummy any time' etc., etc., etc.

Not long afterwards I got an email from the famous cookery writer Claudia Roden to say she had received my message and could only imagine that I had sent it to her by mistake. 'It sounds as if it's meant for a daughter,' she said kindly.

I don't know the famous Claudia at all, but her name was in my computer addresses because she once asked me about good restaurants in Syria. I am mortified, but she has been so sweet and has invited me to supper.

10 September

We are still waiting to hear whether AW got the job in Malaysia – he had an interview which he said didn't go badly. I keep seeing signs and portents everywhere, i.e.: Claudia bought a stuffed snake for Malachy and it says MADE IN MALAYSIA, and on the bus the other day there was a teacher with some children on an outing and she turned out to be from Malaysia. The truth is that whether we go to Malaysia or not I will be disappointed. If we don't go, AW will retire and we will be sitting in Somerset in the pouring rain wondering what to do for the rest of our lives, but if we do go I will miss the family desperately.

Going back to MADE IN MALAYSIA, I have a friend, Valerie, who has a wonderful shop on the Fulham Road. She ordered some ceramic pots from a firm in Korea some time ago and asked them *not* to write MADE IN KOREA on them. The pots arrived with NOT MADE IN KOREA stamped on them. This is true.

20 September

Yay! Have just heard that Russia have bought the rights for my last book. What a random list of countries have bought it: Thailand, Latvia, Holland, France and now Russia. *Dip Bag* must be the only thing they have in common.

23 September

I went to Mass at Westminster Cathedral and lit a candle and prayed we'd be sent to Malaysia. The candle went out – another omen?

25 September

AW has just rung to say that the rumour is that he won't get Malaysia, he'll be offered Azerbaijan. At the moment he is Special Envoy there, visiting every couple of months or so, but a posting would mean him going to live in Baku and setting up an embassy. Oh dear, I really and truly don't want to leave the family to go to Azerbaijan. Perhaps AW should stop work after all, but I think he will miss it too much. Maybe we should retire to Brussels – we both love it there, and there is a beautiful house up the road with a granny flat and stables and a garden. But there is no *reason* for us to live in Brussels. Do you need a reason to live somewhere? Plus it rains even more than in Somerset.

The writer Philip Hensher has ignored my Facebook request to be my friend. It's pathetic how rejected you feel when people don't respond. I have met him once, and I only wanted to tell him how much AW enjoyed his book *The Mulberry Empire*.

6

Fresh Horizons

I have a new thing now, I open my mouth to say a word and the wrong one comes out, but with the same first letter e.g., Salisbury or Singapore, instead of Sainsbury's; hotel instead of hospital. The other day AW and I were in a church and I said, 'I like the stainless-steel windows,' meaning of course stained-glass windows.

My sister Tessa has put her finger on it. 'I talk in predictive text these days,' she said when we were chatting on the phone the other day. 'Once I've started a word my brain comes up with any random ending to it.' Exactly.

Last week I tried to tell Hester that I'd killed a spider of enormous size, but it came out that I'd killed a spizer. Then there are the conversations AW and I have now: 'Do you remember that time, I think we were in the Gambia, when we met that man, you know, what was his name, he had a bald head and a moustache, and we went to that extraordinary restaurant, what was it called? And he told us that weird story about, what was it? A dog that swam down a river to find his owner, or was it his owner who swam down to find the dog.' And so on. Luckily AW and I can usually mind-read what the other is trying to say, but it occurred to me that if either of us had to take the Good

News from Aix to Ghent, we would have forgotten it by the time we got there.

29 September

I am full of anxiety about what AW will do if he retires and I've come to the conclusion that if they offer him the job as Ambassador in Azerbaijan he should take it and go there and I should go with him. It's another ex-Soviet country: oil and gas and corruption and cold winters like Kazakhstan, and I was getting so excited at the thought of going to the tropics, but I could probably stand it if it was just for a year.

9 October

I am going to Syria in a few days' time with the photographer Tim Beddow to do a story for the *Telegraph* magazine on the women who have saved the Old City of Damascus. (All the house restorations, hotel openings and efforts to improve the tumbledown old town have, so far, been initiated by Syrian women, not men.)

I needed a picture for my Syrian visa so I went round the corner to Snappy Snaps and had one taken, but the photographer said it was too unflattering to show me, and that I must go down to the studio so he could do it again in better light. Imagine a *passport photo* being too hideous to show the client. It must have been appalling: I wish I could have looked at it.

23 October

I love going back to Damascus, it feels as if I had never left, and the shopkeepers in the Old City remember me and give me a big welcome. Tim and I stayed with a Frenchman whom we didn't know, but who invited us because he loves our book on Damascus and didn't like the idea of us staying in a hotel.

An exciting thing happened: I was suddenly summoned to the palace for a meeting with the President's wife. I was sure it must be about the interview I'd requested ages ago, but no, it seems she wants me to do a book, with Tim, about her office. She has been given a very charming historic building for her NGO projects (it is where poor King Faisal of Syria spent the few months of his reign before the French kicked him out), and she wants a glamorous-looking publication about it that she can give to VIP visitors. She is young and pretty and bright, with three children. She told me how much she loved her husband and lots of quite intimate things, but absolutely refused to let me open my notebooks and write anything down for an interview. (If I were ruthless I'd write it anyway, but I'm not.)

The official Palace photographer did a photo of us sitting on the sofa together. At the end of the interview I was given a copy: the President's wife, sitting elegantly with slanting legs, looked like a model and I looked a bit like an old potato in a wig.

25 October

We have been trying to raise money for Palfest and I got my first financial contribution of £15,000 from a friend who has worked a lot in the Middle East yesterday. It looks as if we really might be able to stage the first festival next spring.

5 November

AW and I are back from France, where we were closing up our house for the winter. We had a lovely time, apart from the fact that we had to dash out of a restaurant just as we were settling down to a nice meal because I suddenly remembered I had left artichokes boiling on the stove at home (except that when we got there, I discovered I had turned them off – which was a double memory loss). The waiter put our food on paper plates for us to take with us.

Then, worse, AW filled up the hire car with diesel instead of petrol on our way to catch the train back, and so it came to a halt in the middle of Montpellier and we had no alternative but to leave it there and take a cab to the station. God knows what Avis will charge us.

What is the matter with us? Is this the beginning of dementia? They say that if you are going dotty you don't realise it, but after our mum died we found her notebook and on one page she had scrawled '*I am not going mad I am not going mad . . .*' and the awful thing is that she was; she had Alzheimer's. Remembering this makes me want to lie on the floor and cry.

The poor old lady who lives opposite our flat went out the other day with no skirt or trousers on, just a jacket over her knickers – I ran down to help but by the time I got there she must have realised and had gone back indoors again. It was such a shocking sight. Each of us thinks we are inviolate, but it will probably happen to us all.

This evening I had to give a talk to the Women's Institute in Fulham – it was in a pub and the audience were nice but no one offered me a drink, or supper, or my taxi fare there and back, and I thought: why am I doing this?

7 November

Lesley telephoned to say she is just back from a meditation course; she was in a wonderful calm, peaceful state of mind, she said, and then she made the hideous mistake of buying *Vogue* and suddenly she was miserable about her face, her figure, her income and the fact that she didn't know anyone in the pictures on the social pages.

Speaking of which, in a brief moment of glory a couple of years ago, I was photographed with Suzy Menkes of the *International Herald Tribune* and Shirley Conran at a *Harpers & Queen* party, but when the picture appeared in the magazine some time later, I had been cut off and it was just famous Suzy and Shirley left. Note: if you are photographed with celebrities, make sure you are in the middle.

10 November

I left my make-up bag on the bus coming back from Claudia's place yesterday, so I rang London Transport Lost Property and got talking to a very nice woman there. Once we'd finished the business about my loss I asked her what kind of things people left on buses and she said, 'Oh you'd be *very* surprised,' in a mysterious voice.

'Oh, go on, do tell me,' I insisted.

'Well,' she said conspiratorially, 'we get lots and lots of sex toys – and artificial limbs . . .'

'*Sex toys on the bus?*' I cried.

'I suppose people buy them to take home and forget them on the way,' she said, but she couldn't explain the artificial limbs.

I went to get replacement make-up this morning and found that most of the things I like have been discontinued.

I wish the cosmetics people wouldn't change their ranges; just when you've found the perfect eyeshadow/mascara/lipstick it goes out of production. Hester has put me on to a Maybelline lipstick that is wonderful for people my age because it has no grease in it so the colour can't run into the lines round our mouths – it's a bit like using Dulux paint. Sometimes at the end of a day after I've put on several layers it starts peeling and my mouth looks like something out of *World of Interiors*. (The writer Diana Athill once suggested that women whose lipstick has leaked look like werewolves caught in the act of eating their victims. Not a nice image.) I'm wondering if I should buy enough of this wonderful product to last for the rest of my life, in case they decide to discontinue it.

I understand now what that phrase about one's days being numbered means: at my age you can look ahead to the end; you can almost count the days. But hang on, I am panicking too soon. My mum died at eighty-five which is so far ahead of me now that it would mean buying seventy-two lipsticks (and that's counting only four a year). I think I'll put it off.

11 November

Norman Mailer died yesterday. I remember going to a talk he gave at the Roundhouse in London years ago. He had just made a film called *Maidstone* and it must have been known that he had received some sort of corporate funding for it, because during the Q&A session afterwards, a young man stood up and said in a whiny voice, 'The point I want to make, Mr Mailer, is that it's all very well for you, compromising your integrity to get funding, but what have you got to say to someone like me who is trying to raise the money to make a film *without* betraying their principles? What do you say to me?'

And Norman Mailer replied, 'I say *hard snot.*'

12 November

Had my first ever flu injection today and the nurse recommended the pneumonia one as well and gave me a leaflet with a picture of an old couple smiling bravely. I can't identify with them, and I don't really believe I am this age, so I am going into denial and not having the pneumonia jab.

I spent ages googling the sculptor Anthony Caro today because we were going to meet him at a dinner party this evening; there were more than a million entries for him so this wasn't as simple as it sounds. Then we arrived at the dinner and he wasn't there as he had flu. I used to look people up in the cuttings library at the *Sunday Times* when I worked there, but Google is a hundred times easier. You have to be careful with your questions though, it's a bit obvious you've done research if you say, 'I believe you have 431 cattle on your farm.'

AW wonders if Google in Russia is called Gogol.

14 November

Went round to babysit Malachy and noticed that outside his bedroom window there was a big red balloon with streamers, which seemed to be stuck in the angle of the roof – just like something from the film *Le Ballon Rouge.* I thought it was so thrilling that a random balloon had somehow floated to the flat and I was determined to get it for Malachy, so I fetched a broom to try and pull it down, but I couldn't seem to budge it.

Then Hester came home and I told her about it all excitedly and she went, 'Oh no! What have you done? That's the anti-pigeon device which George and I spent *ages* putting up there . . .'

Thank God I hadn't succeeded in dislodging it. I crept away quietly.

23 November

Listened to the last episode of Katharine Whitehorn's memoirs being read on *Book of the Week*. She says that at one point in her life she had felt sorry for herself having to buy her shoes in Marks and Spencer. This annoyed me as I always buy my shoes there and think they are wonderful.

24 November

We all (daughters, sons-in-law, grandchildren) went to the second-hand clothes market in Portobello today. Hester tried on a fur jacket and Malachy looked at her and said, 'Dog!'

I bought an old black, rabbit fur coat (the label says 'Made in Croydon', *Croydon?*) because the man on the stall told me I looked like a Russian countess in it.

27 November

Have had a letter from the NHS asking if I would like a bowel cancer testing kit. I said yes. Told Chris about it and he said, 'They'll be sending us our own home colonoscopy kits next.'

Actually I wish they'd send me my own face-lifting kit: I can pull up the sides of my face to look about twenty years younger and just need the equipment to keep it there.

30 November

AW came home last night and it seems that Malaysia is not going to happen because he is *definitely* being sent to Azerbaijan. In fact, he heard this while he was in Baku and has already pinpointed an apartment looking out over the Caspian Sea to be the Residence. The sitting room (which is also the dining room and study) is sixty feet long. How will we sit in it? I asked AW, and he said you will sit one end and I will sit the other. I will have to furnish the Residence myself (Brussels never helps) which means getting three quotes for every single thing that goes into it – from curtains to cookers – and AW says you can't really buy anything in Baku itself. Stress. Stress.

2 December

Wonderful news! Hester is having another baby, due next July. She was telling me about it in the car and I couldn't hear her properly and suddenly found my hand on the volume switch of the radio, thinking I could *turn up her voice*.

Last night I dreamed I was in prison but I was determined not to let the warders know I cared so I ran round and round the exercise yard with my arms wide open like a child playing aeroplanes saying, 'Isn't this marvellous!'

10 December

Returned from a weekend in Brussels today – arriving on the Eurostar at St Pancras instead of Waterloo for the first time. It was horrible: the tube to Pimlico broke down and we had to change trains and then the new train was so crowded that

I suddenly got a panic attack and had to push and shove my way out of the carriage with my voice getting more and more frantic: 'Please can you let me through?' 'Let me get to the door please . . . *Let me oooout!*'

19 December

AW has just rung from Brussels to say his blood pressure is very high – in spite of the fact he is already on medication for this – and the doctor wonders whether he should go to Azerbaijan. I am not surprised his blood pressure is up because he spends all the time these days sorting out staff and signing contracts for his new embassy – and these things are a complete nightmare in the European Commission because there are so many procedures to follow (to prevent corruption). I asked my friend Barbara what can happen from high blood pressure and she said, 'A stroke of course.' A stroke! Nothing like that had ever crossed my mind. Now I am worried all the time.

While I was doing the washing-up this morning and my mind was in neutral I suddenly had the most peculiar flash of insight – in a split second I absolutely knew the whole point of life, as if a veil had been drawn aside. I thought, 'Quick! I must write this down,' but as soon as I got a pen and paper I couldn't remember a single thing about it.

I told this to Chris and he told me the story of a vicar who dreamed the secret and meaning of existence and wrote it all down in the middle of the night so that he could tell the world, but next morning when he excitedly reached for his notes he read THE SKIN IS MIGHTIER THAN THE BANANA.

Somerset, 22 December

AW came back from Brussels yesterday with quite a bit of laundry. I put it all in the washing machine – checking the pockets of his trousers carefully, all except one pair which I seem to have missed, and those, of course, were the ones with his wallet in the pocket. By the time I realised what I'd done it was too late to open the machine and we just had to watch it doing its cycle. AW was unexpectedly nice about it and joked about my money-laundering.

Made cakes for Christmas today – but some were raw in the middle, and I burnt the chocolate roulade. I cried because all I want to do is be the kind of woman who can bake a batch of brownies for the family without having a nervous breakdown. Millions of other women can do it, why can't I?

The only good thing about today is that we are past the shortest day of the year, which makes me feel that winter's end is in sight.

We managed to dry the notes in the wallet.

26 December

Was just thinking how marvellous it was that, for the first time in history, we haven't had our annual family Christmas row, when it happened.

It was all about the central heating: Claudia erupted when Hester wanted to turn it off to preserve the planet, Hester threw her plate across the kitchen into the sink and then ran off, I chased her up the stairs to kill her, George came after me, and so on. I wonder if we will ever have a Christmas without us all being in tears at some point.

1 January

Drinks with old friends, where we met lots of people who would be our new friends if AW stopped working and we lived here permanently. I could see AW thinking he was quite glad not to be retiring just yet.

5 January

Maisie's christening at Westminster Cathedral today. It all went beautifully. I wore my new rabbit-fur coat and told AW proudly that the man who sold it to me said I looked like a Russian countess in it. AW said, 'Hmm, I don't see Russian countess, I see Belgian housewife.'

Coat has been put at back of cupboard.

8 January

After church today I gave a lift to a girl with Rasta dread-locks, who told me that she looks after fourteen rabbits. People give them to her when they don't want them as pets any more (I didn't mention my coat). She was very keen to let me know that rabbits do two kinds of poo: normal rabbit poo and then a softer poo, which they eat. (I am not making this up.) If they don't have the right diet (*not* carrots and lettuce but hay, hay, hay) this softer poo gets too liquid and sticks round their bums and gets maggots in it. I didn't feel much like making lunch when I got home.

Driving up to London we passed a field that had a perfect circle of large molehills in the centre. AW said it was Molehenge.

10 January

The strangest thing: my wedding ring broke today and it is our thirty-fifth wedding anniversary. Is it a sign? When AW was in the Gambia he was given a ram (by the President), which suddenly died. Everyone in the office said that was *really good* because it meant that AW himself wouldn't die any time soon, because the ram had done it for him. Similarly, maybe the broken ring means the ring is broken instead of our marriage.

7

Countdown to Departure

Brussels, 13 January

We arrived here for the weekend two days ago, taking the ferry from Dover to Dunkirk. It was a glorious day and the journey was lovely. Going through Dover port reminded me of the time, years ago, when we were returning from Brussels and AW decided that no one had the right to ask him to show his passport, so he drove past the window where you were supposed to hand it in. Within seconds, alarms sounded, security barriers crashed down in front of us, and we were surrounded by armed men. When they asked AW for an explanation I noticed he didn't mention his theory but said his foot slipped on the accelerator.

We have acquired a beautiful, big, carved-wood Buddha. I saw it at an auction last time I was here, and though it was covered with thick black paint, there was something about it which persuaded me to leave a bid. I thought it could be a perfect wedding anniversary present for AW and me – and I got it! AW and a friend managed to struggle back to our flat with it, but this weekend is the first time I have seen it/him face to face at home. I am going to try and scrape off the paint tomorrow while AW is at work.

14 January

As soon as I got to work on the Buddha with a kitchen knife today I discovered that underneath the black paint he seemed to be gilded. I went wild with excitement and scraped away like a maniac so I could finish him before AW got back from the office, and it is true – he is covered all over with rather worn gilt. AW was thrilled – the Buddha looks beautiful now. (Unlike me who, by the time it was finished, had to be scraped and washed and wiped almost as much as the Buddha.) We will take him back to London and get an expert to tell us where he comes from.

The doctors have said that AW *can* go to Azerbaijan this spring and so we will be packing up and leaving Brussels very soon.

One of my big disappointments, these past months in Brussels, is that I haven't been able to get an appointment to visit the Hôtel Solvay in the Avenue Louise. This is a unique and fantastic art nouveau house that my friend Julia Tugendhat and I helped to save back in the 1970s, when we first came to live in Brussels, following our husbands. Old Monsieur Wittamer, who owned the house in those days and became a dear friend, died some time ago and his son inherited the property. I wanted to show the house to George as, being an architect, he would particularly appreciate it, but the son has been difficult and won't arrange a visit. Now it's reached the stage at which my pride would not let me take George to the Hôtel Solvay even if (to quote Alan Bennett) young M. Wittamer got wild horses on bended knees to beg us to come.

London, 18 January

AW drove the Buddha from Brussels to London today; I came home earlier on the train (I tried sneaking into the posh

Eurostar lounge at the Gare du Nord with AW's frequent traveller card, but was discovered and thrown out, which was deeply humiliating). AW put the Buddha in the back of the car with a seat belt across his shoulder and, with his hand up giving a blessing, he looked a bit like the Queen, waving. AW was going to cover him with a cloth but then it looked as though he was smuggling an immigrant in a rather inept way.

29 January

Window cleaner came this morning – he did the windows beautifully but made a mess on the carpet. I noticed that his card said he was a carpet cleaner as well, so perhaps this was deliberate.

Hester and Malachy popped in for a quick tea and Malachy did his usual demonstration of how he can wreck a home in ten seconds. It took me half an hour to get the TV, Digibox, DVD player and the clock on the cooker working again after they'd gone. Hester has a game with him called Running Round the Flat, which is just that – they take it in turns to chase each other. Malachy thinks it's the best thing in the world.

4 February

I took the bus to go and visit Claudia and Maisie today, and a woman (who looked more or less my age I thought) offered me her seat. I was so shocked that I wanted to say to her, 'Please, tell me what you see?' because – apart from my bad back – I don't feel old at all and I think of myself as being quite 'well preserved', as they used to say. Then again if she really told me what she saw the answer would probably demolish me, so I am glad I didn't ask.

5 February

Today was the start of my tooth-whitening adventure. (I decided to try the non-painful version which involves sleeping at night with your teeth in plastic trays full of bleach.) The hygienist did stuff with bleach and some sort of light – ultra-violet, or is it infra-red? – aimed at my teeth, and he made the moulds from which they'll cast the plastic trays, which will be ready in about two weeks.

18 February

I've got my trays and have had another treatment and the dentist seems to be pleased, but personally I can't see any difference at all – except perhaps to my mental state. I am now obsessed and have to keep flashing Hollywood smiles at myself whenever I pass a mirror.

19 February

Tonight I have to give a talk to the British Syrian Society about the houses of Damascus. I was just practising my speech for the hundredth time when there was a tremendous buzzing on my doorbell. I looked out of the window to see who was being so aggressive and there were seven policemen on the doorstep. Seems that Lina, my old neighbour downstairs, had fallen and they couldn't force the door of her flat as she was lying across it. In the end they got in through her big front window, and she was fine after I'd given her a cup of tea – but I was a gibbering wreck as there was no time left to work on my talk.

Later. All that was *as nothing* compared to what happened tonight: I was halfway through my slideshow when the projector broke down. The Syrian President's father-in-law and the Syrian Ambassador tried valiantly to get it going again but they couldn't, which left almost two hundred people sitting there, waiting to be entertained. My talk was meaningless without the pictures, and so I just had to try and tell funny stories about our time living in Damascus, e.g., how AW left his expensive Russell & Bromley loafers outside the mosque and someone stole them, leaving a pair of ancient white winkle pickers with turned-up toes in their place; and how AW loved hummus so much we decided he must be a hummusexual, ha ha. I did my best and the audience laughed, but it was traumatic, and I have now decided to have all my slides made into a PowerPoint presentation.

I sent a text to Chris saying my talk was a cock-up but apparently it came out as an 'anal-up' – quite a good description actually.

20 February

The latest news is that Hester and George are going to come and live in our flat while they renovate theirs. In theory this should have happened after I'd left for Azerbaijan, but my departure has been postponed for a week as AW has an important visit to deal with first, so now I've got to find somewhere to live as we can't all fit in. (Hester keeps saying, 'Don't worry about throwing your pregnant daughter out on to the streets, Mum, I am sure I will be okay.')

I nipped into the estate agent's to check how much it would cost to rent a furnished flat for the family in Pimlico for a week and they told me they didn't usually do short lets but they could probably find something for us for about £800. My jaw is still hanging open. When it is back in place, I am going to pluck up my courage and ask Valerie, my neighbour downstairs (who is often away in the country), if I can stay in her flat for the week before I leave. Oh dear, I thought old age would bring a slower pace, relaxation and calm, but it seems to be the opposite, life gets more hectic and complicated with every passing day.

We had a family outing to the theatre this evening to see Simon Russell Beale again in *Much Ado About Nothing*. Hester said I looked pale so she dabbed some lipstick on my cheeks and then smoothed it over and said, 'That's better,' and it was only when I got home that I saw she had left a red streak outlining the bag under my left eye, as if the bottom of my reading glasses had burnt into my skin. Still, I don't believe anyone in England looks at women over fifty – you could go out wearing a false nose or a stocking over your face here and no one would bat an eyelid.

22 February

The most exciting thing happened today. A week or so ago I sent photographs of our Buddha to the V&A and asked if they could tell where he came from, and did they have any idea of his date? This morning the head of the Asian Department rang to say that our Buddha could be twelfth or thirteenth century from north-western China in the Jin period. I googled this to discover what he is worth, and it seems Jin dynasty sculptures can go for *thousands*.

Will get someone from Sotheby's or Christie's to come and look but it is too good to be true, things like this never happen in my family, i.e., someone gave me twenty pounds' worth of Premium Bonds for my twenty-first birthday and in forty-five years I have never won so much as a quid.

27 February

We had a party for the authors and donors for Palfest last night. It was given by the Qattan family, one of our main supporters, in their house in Kensington, and Harold Pinter, our patron, came – which was a huge compliment – but how does one talk to someone so celebrated? I remember when we were posted to the Gambia I met a real American astronaut and I asked him what it was like being on the moon, and as the words came out of my mouth I realised that I was probably the three-millionth person to ask this stupid question and why didn't he howl with boredom or scream, 'Shut up!' He had a better time at the children's school where of course they all wanted to know how you go to the loo in space. The answer is something to do with suction tubes, but I've forgotten the details.

Perhaps I should explain that the reason there was an astronaut there is because, being exactly opposite Cape Canaveral across the Atlantic, the Gambia was (until 2002) the place where a space rocket would make an emergency landing if a launch failed; each time a rocket was due to be sent up, the little country was taken over by Americans in preparation for this eventuality and, in between, astronauts visited on goodwill missions.

Brussels, 29 February

Back in Brussels. The packers are coming on Monday and we have to sort out what is being shipped where, and then I have to start getting proper quotes for furnishings for our Residence in Baku.

AW will not allow me to help with the actual packing because long ago, when we left Brussels to go to Trinidad, I sent our dustbin into storage by mistake – AW likes to joke that when we came back ten years later the contents had turned into fine compost – so we spent the evening poring over AW's map of the apartment that will be the Residence, deciding what we need in the way of sofas, beds, dining table, chairs etc. I have decided that I will try Peter Jones, Oka and Heals for the quotes.

London, 3 March

Yesterday was Mother's Day. Hester was furious because George forgot (AW never sends a card because, as he says, I am not his mother). At the same time she doesn't seem to remember that I *am* her mother. I imagine there are rows going on in households all across Britain today.

Went to Peter Jones to get started on the Residence furnishing quotes and they gave me a really pleasant shopping adviser to go round the store with me, choosing things. When that was done I went to the fashion department and bought some clothes to wear in Azerbaijan.

4 March

Took the clothes back to Peter Jones as have regained the weight I lost two years ago and looked frightful in all of them. Also, I really must work on posture. I caught sight of myself in a mirror stooped over like the Hunchback of Notre Dame.

A man – actually he looked about seventeen – came from Sotheby's today to look at the Buddha. He started shaking his head as he entered the room and the gist of it seems to be that our Buddha's headdress is not carved well enough, plus he is too heavy to be really old ('the wood would have dried out over 700 years') and there is a recent crack in his head which wouldn't have happened if he was twelfth century. So he is a copy. I knew it couldn't be good news. But he is still beautiful and maybe I'll investigate more when I have time.

Later. Yesterday was AW's Big Day in Baku: the visit of the EU Commissioner in charge of external affairs who came to open AW's new embassy, announce him as the new Ambassador, and accompany him to meet the President of Azerbaijan.

AW has been in Baku this past week, preparing for all this, and when it was over he accompanied the commissioner and the Brussels group to the airport and saw them on to their plane. While he was standing at the foot of the aircraft steps he felt a strange draught on the back of his leg and when he investigated with his hand he found that his left trouser leg was ripped from the buttock to below the knee. 'Oh my God,' I said when he told me last night on the phone. 'Could they see your pants?'

'Bridge,' he said, 'not only could they see my pants, but my whole bare hairy leg.'

After this shocking discovery, AW said he went into John Cleese-mode, sidling across the tarmac, crab-like, so that only his front faced the officials, and moving through the airport building with his back to the walls, all the time trying to look cool and ambassadorial. How did the rip happen? He had no idea. Why didn't anyone mention it to him? 'Because I am the new Ambassador and I suppose they were just too embarrassed.' AW and I laughed so hard about this that my eyes are swollen from crying.

When AW first went to work for the EC in Brussels his boss gave a little party in the office so that new arrivals could meet some of the senior staff. As the guests arrived he asked AW to open a bottle of champagne. Eager to please, AW set to work – but the cork shot out unexpectedly and, as luck would have it, hit the twin neon tube ceiling lights which shattered, showering the guests with splinters of glass.

There is another ex-boss of AW's who must have him seared into his memory as well – the Head of the EC Mission in India. He kindly invited us (as junior colleagues) to a grand dinner he was hosting in Delhi. Halfway through, AW tried to be helpful by tipping some water from his glass over a clump of candles that were burning rather too fiercely – at which point they exploded and set all the table decorations on fire, and in about two seconds there was a conflagration with people running to extinguish the flames. We were never asked again.

But my favourite upsetting-your-boss story happened to AW's best friend, Adrian, when he was a painfully shy student at Oxford University. His tutor invited him to a drinks party one Sunday morning and, steeling himself, Adrian went along. Later, after a sherry or two, when he felt slightly more relaxed and was chatting to friends, he leaned his elbow on the mantelpiece in a cool, man-about-town kind of way, whereupon the whole thing came out of the wall and, together with all the glasses that had been left on it, crashed to the ground.

5 March

My saintly neighbour has agreed to let me stay in her flat for the week before I leave when Hester and her family are in my place. Thank God the accommodation problem at least is solved. There seems to be so much to worry about at the moment: the move to Azerbaijan; the furnishing of the Residence; a talk I am being *paid* to give to Shell wives in Amsterdam in a couple of months; the first Palfest coming up this spring; the project for the Syrian President's wife; and Hester's baby. I wake up every morning with my heart thumping and that Robert Frost poem, '. . . But I have promises to keep,/And miles to go before I sleep,/And miles to go before I sleep' going through my mind over and over.

The *Guardian* has done a piece about grannies, quoting one as saying that this was the most fulfilling time of her life. I would find it a lot more fulfilling if my back didn't hurt so much (the injection I had seems to have worn off) and there wasn't such a lot to do. All I want is to open my eyes in the morning and find nothing to dread, but I remember my sister Moira saying that 'maturity' was realising that this would never happen, and accepting it.

6 March

I am trying to make my flat a bit more child-proof by covering the fitted carpet with old rugs, which don't matter if things get spilled on them. My friend Lesley told me that decades ago, when she came home from Afghanistan with her first baby to stay with her parents, her father met her at the airport after the ten-hour flight and the first thing he said was, 'We've had new carpets laid at home, so I hope you'll be careful.' She burst into tears, and has never forgotten it. The awful thing is that now, at my age, I sympathise with her father.

Last night I dreamed that I went to the airport to meet a friend but he had turned into a small monkey (wearing a suit and carrying a briefcase). The big problem was that he didn't seem to realise what had happened and I had to keep talking to him as though there were nothing wrong.

12 March

Am ready to leave tomorrow. Have chosen the Residence furnishings and the quotes are coming by email (I am hoping against hope that Oka is cheapest because they have everything I need and are more stylish than the others) and I have cleaned up Valerie's flat, and packed.

It's agony going off this time because saying goodbye to little Malachy and Maisie is just too hard.

8

Beginning in Baku

Baku, 14 March

Normally it is quite unnerving waking up on the first day of a new posting because you have no idea where – or who – you are, but I had no difficulty this morning for the simple reason that I never went to sleep. My bed was so hard I might as well have been lying on the floor and all I could think was, 'Oh God, what have I done?' AW should have retired: we could be living cosily in Somerset now with a playframe in the garden and the grandchildren coming for weekends, but instead we are on the fifteenth floor of the Radisson Hotel in Baku, Azerbaijan, and it's all my fault. (I never usually venture above twelve storeys because of my fear of heights, but strangely, that seems to be the only thing I don't mind right now, because the building is very square and solid and doesn't give me the feeling that it's going to topple over.)

This morning AW went to his office quite early, and I have spent most of the time since at the tinted, sealed, rather grubby hotel windows with their eagle's-eye view over the grey city of Baku to the grey Caspian Sea, which looks like a vast, still, pool of mercury under the grey sky; geographically this is known as the Caspian Depression, I am crossing fingers it will not also become my emotional state as well . . .

I should never have persuaded AW to come here; I've condemned us to months and months of exile away from the family, and the worst part is that I am not alone in being unhappy about it: AW is under such stress having to open this embassy by himself with precious little support from Brussels – his blood pressure is up already. What if something dreadful happens to him here?

Right now though, the most depressing thing is that my watch has stopped and I don't know what the time is. I know this sounds ridiculous but I tried to text AW in the office to ask him, but our English mobiles are not working here and I don't have the office number and when I rang the non-English-speaking receptionist she didn't understand what I was asking, and I don't know how to work the pay TV. Pathetic. I thought of ringing Hester or Claudia to ask them the time in England and add on the four hours for Azzers, but I have been forbidden to use the hotel phone for long-distance calls, and anyway they will still be asleep.

Our suite (bedroom, bathroom, sitting room) in the hotel doesn't help: it has a shabby carpet, ugly brown furniture, slightly greasy upholstery on the sofa and chairs, and there is a cigarette burn on the edge of the bath. The marble and stone in the bathroom is a bit stained and cracked – which makes me feel bad about all the hotels like this one in the world and all the tons of beautiful natural stone wasted in them.

AW got top marks and gold stars from me this morning though – not only had he reminded me to bring my own pillow (the hotel's are as hard as the mattress) but he himself has bought a small cafetière and a packet of good coffee from Brussels (the hotel coffee is Nescafé). All we needed was milk so I asked room service for some and after forty minutes they brought a packet of long-life. I hadn't realised that there are degrees of quality of long-life milk – Azerbaijan's is the worst I've ever tasted, exactly like watered-down condensed milk. But the bottom line is that I don't feel the total despair that I did in Kazakhstan and I have not yet cried (a first for me in a new place) because a) I am going home in only three and a half weeks to get on with other things, and b) Baku is an old city and I know from AW that there are interesting buildings to explore down there, including the ones that feature in the great Azerbaijani romantic novel *Ali and Nino*, not to mention the one that houses our new Residence.

At lunchtime AW took me out to a Turkish restaurant in a rather pretty, French-looking part of the city near the hotel. The sun came out, the Caspian Sea changed from mercury to silver lamé, the food was delicious and I felt as if I were in Paris. Speaking of which, the French Ambassador here is an old friend from Damascus days. He is leaving shortly, but it's cosy starting off with one friend.

Later. Frightening news from Claudia: she took Maisie to a paediatrician because she has a nervous tic in her eye and he says she has to have a brain scan in case there is something wrong. AW and I are racked with worry. I emailed my friend Myrna in Damascus who has seen the Virgin Mary and asked her to pray. We will know the result in three days but in the meantime it's almost impossible to think of anything else.

Tried to take my mind off Maisie by mugging up on the history of Baku. The only thing I know is that Garry Kasparov, the chess player, and Rostropovich, the cellist, were born here. (I am quite proud of the fact that Rostropovich kissed me once – it was years ago when AW was posted to Syria. AW and I and a very pretty woman were standing, with another man, watching a concert from the side of the Roman temple in Baalbek in Lebanon during a music festival. The man turned out to be Rostropovich, and the four of us fell into a long, whispered-but-animated conversation. Then he said he had to leave as he was the next performer, and he kissed the very pretty lady – I think he'd been planning to do this for some time – and then he had to kiss me too or it would have been ageist.)

This is what I have learned now. Before the discovery of oil in the mid-nineteenth century, Baku was a small Muslim walled city on a promontory in the Caspian Sea. It belonged to Persia until the Russians conquered Azerbaijan in 1828; they allowed it to continue as an Islamic state (rather an enlightened one, with the first girls' school in the Muslim world). But when oil was discovered some decades later, the town – according to Alfred Nobel – became as frantic as the Klondike in the gold rush. People came from all over the world to try and cash in, including the Nobel and the Rothschild families, and there was a building frenzy, with the new oil millionaires (the oil barons as they were known) competing with each other to create the most flamboyant European-style houses, all built in pretty, honey-coloured stone, which is why Baku is such an attractive town now. But the oil boom lasted only sixty years – until the Soviets marched in in 1922 and seized everything. Some oil barons were killed, others killed themselves, many fled, and even more, including Zeynalabdin Taghiyev, the city's richest citizen and greatest benefactor, whose palace is now the National History Museum, ended living like beggars.

At the end of the afternoon I was called to AW's office for cake – it's someone's birthday and they have the same tradition here as in Kazakhstan, which is that the person celebrating always brings something delicious to share with the whole office. They were discussing the news that a journalist was stabbed last night. They think it's a political assassination as he had been critical of all the hideous new high-rise blocks going up in the city, and the cutting down of trees. Apparently the American Ambassador was first to rush over to the government to express her outrage – but AW says how can the US lead a protest about human rights when they have Guantanamo, and support Israel which has nearly 10,000 political prisoners.

Someone in AW's office told me a joke: A man says, 'This is my cat, Ceremony. Please don't stand on Ceremony.' Is this Azerbaijani humour?

Got back to the hotel and asked reception if they could give me a softer mattress or a topper, and they have come up with a thick sheet of foam, which will do nicely. I also asked for a plug for the basin, but they don't have one.

This evening AW took me out to Sultan, another Turkish restaurant, which has huge braziers for barbecuing kebabs and we ate the most delicious meal. How amazing to be in a place for only one day and find two restaurants that you'd be happy to eat in for the rest of your life. Plus you are *allowed to smoke in restaurants here*: you can actually enjoy a cigarette with your coffee after a meal. It's astonishing how liberating this feels, like stepping back into a better age. The irony is that I have such a terrible sore throat right now that I couldn't bear a cigarette.

Towards the end of supper, a man AW knows slightly came up to him and, in a low voice, told him something about possible changes in the government. I thought: Wow! Night-before-last I was bathing Malachy, and now I am hearing secrets being passed to AW . . . Apparently there are more spies in Baku than anywhere else in the world – it's because of oil/gas/Great Game/East-meets-West/ex-Soviet Union, and so on.

15 March

We went to see our future apartment this morning. It is stunning – on the top floor of a lovely old oil baron's building full of silvery light thrown up by the Caspian Sea, which is only a couple of hundred yards away across the Boulevard (as it's called) round the bay. The only downsides are the fact that the ceilings are so high we will have to put up scaffolding to change a light bulb, and there is an ancient, absolutely terrifying, lift. I am not sure if I am more scared of the lift crashing six flights because the rusting hawsers have snapped, or of AW and me falling through its flimsy-looking, patched-up old floor.

In the street below our flat is a whole line-up of very posh shops – Cartier, Tom Ford, Dior, Bulgari, Hermès, etc., etc. I was wondering who on earth buys anything in them, but now I've heard that they all belong to the President's wife.

Ingrid, the most senior person at the office, invited us to supper tonight where we met up with our old friend Jean-Yves, the French Ambassador, and a nice Irish girl who whispered to me that she was broken-hearted because she'd been having an affair with someone in AW's new office for five years but now it was over. She told me who it was, so now I will never be able to look at that person without thinking about this.

This is the first time we have ever arrived in a new posting and found such a welcome: there were flowers and champagne in our room at the hotel, then the party tonight, and Jean-Yves is giving a reception for us on Monday. We are bowled over. It's the total opposite of Kazakhstan.

16 March

It's Palm Sunday and AW's driver took us to the Catholic Church for Mass. It was packed and I sat behind a man with a shaved head, and ears exactly like Shrek's sticking right out from the side of his head. It was really extraordinary, the only difference between the back of his head and Shrek's was that his wasn't green.

After Mass, AW took me sightseeing. We drove out of Baku past grim Soviet-era apartment blocks in a bleak landscape covered with rubbish, on through old oil fields with rusty cranes and derricks, pools of scummy black oil, and more garbage, and then into the 'countryside' where there is not a living green thing to be seen, just rock and mud and railway lines and groups of more grey housing blocks. I never saw a more desolate landscape and I felt depression descending over me like a fog – AW had predicted I'd be crying by Sunday.

I looked up the area in the guidebook while AW was driving along, and it said 'arid wasteland'. I couldn't have put it better. The only attractive thing we saw was an old stone caravanserai in the middle of nowhere, with arches round a courtyard – but it was all graffiti and broken glass and rubble and ripped-out electric wires. Depression deepened.

Our destination was some caves with prehistoric pictures scratched into the rock – one of these could, at a pinch, be seen as a longboat with oars (could also be a woodlouse with legs) and we learned that Thor Heyerdahl of *Kon-Tiki* fame came to Baku to examine this ancient sketch, and became intrigued by the country.

At the foot of the hill with the caves are other marks on a rock, Latin letters this time, etched by a Roman centurion. The Romans tried invading Azerbaijan three times, and this is the furthest east that any Roman inscription has ever been found. The guidebook didn't offer a translation of his words, but after our day in this grim landscape, I know exactly what the centurion wrote, it was: I WANT TO GO HOME. I felt sorry for him, so far from Rome – but at least in his day there wouldn't have been plastic bags blowing around his rock. In the West we are all so careful about recycling our refuse, but when you see the piles of junk lying about here, you wonder what is the point.

On the way home, AW did a detour to another bleak brown area that looked as if it was covered with termite mounds – but these were the famous mud volcanoes. Each mound has a pool of cold liquid mud in its crater (looking just like melted milk chocolate) in which big bubbles form, expand and then burst, one after another, endlessly, to a soundtrack of burping, farting and belching. They are hypnotic; you could stand for hours watching them.

On the way home I marked the day out of 10: environs of Baku, -7; rock engravings, 4; centurion graffiti, 8 (because I had bonded with him); mud volcanoes, 10.

17 March

AW is a hero! He has arranged for me to have an empty room at the office where I can work, look at my emails and write every day. I don't feel lonely as I would by myself all day in the hotel, and if it wasn't for the sweaty-palm anxiety about Maisie I think I would feel okay.

18 March

Oh God I can't believe it! The hotel maid has thrown away the little plastic tray that holds the bleach for whitening my top teeth. It's my fault: I took it out yesterday morning, rinsed it, and then wrapped it in loo paper and left it on the bathroom shelf. She must have just chucked it out thinking it was a bit of old rubbish. This whitening treatment is so expensive and now I'll have to have another tray made. When she came in this morning I tried to mime, 'Have you seen the plastic mould of my teeth?' but she looked baffled. She obviously understood something though, because when I passed the English-speaking receptionist this afternoon he said, 'I am sorry to hear you have lost your false teeth.'

Perhaps it's Fate teaching me a lesson – I was becoming ever-more obsessed and grinning to myself in every reflective surface I passed to see if my smile had got whiter. Though the dentist did say, rather tactlessly I thought, 'Don't make your teeth too white or, *at your age* [my italics] people will think they are dentures.' It's quite shocking when professionals are frank – once, after an eye test, I selected some new frames for my reading glasses and the optician said, 'If I had small, rather close-together eyes, I wouldn't have chosen *those* particular frames.'

The last time I was so caught up with my teeth was when I was about fourteen – and with more reason. In those days, when I smiled only my gums showed – you wouldn't even have known I *had* teeth – and it took me about a year of training to get my upper lip to come down over my gums when I smiled. Now I have a very long upper lip but a better smile.

We met the whole Azerbaijan Dip Corps at Jean-Yves's party tonight. My sore throat was worse and I didn't really want to go, but just as we were getting ready we heard from Claudia that Maisie's brain scan didn't reveal anything bad and the doctor says she will grow out of the twitches. The relief was like being born again. We were so elated that we rushed to the party beaming and smiling.

20 March

Yesterday, after the party, I suddenly started to feel really ill so I went and got myself some antibiotics from the chemist – you just buy them over the counter here. AW and I were supposed to be going out to a UN reception but I went to bed and have stayed there ever since. Last night I woke up burning hot and I didn't know who I was or where I was, and I thought I was going to die – in fact, I wasn't sure if I hadn't died already. My mind was full of dark thoughts rushing round and colliding with each other and I was overwhelmed with fear that there would be an earthquake and my bed would fall out of the hotel room's huge window – which is only four feet away – and crash down fifteen floors. The whole night was a prolonged panic attack and I felt very far from home. Then I managed to tell myself that this was all because I had a high fever, and I took some Nurofen and after a while felt a bit better.

Woke up today still feeling panicky, and tried to read Nora Ephron's book about growing older, called *I Feel Bad About My Neck*, which is really funny. It may help my fear of flying too – in a list of things she wished she'd known when she was younger, she includes, 'The Plane Won't Crash'.

21 March

It is the Nowruz holiday – this is really an Iranian festival celebrating the start of spring but as Azerbaijan used to be part of Iran it's celebrated here in a big way. Everyone seems to have gone away and the streets are empty, which is a change. Before I came here people told me that you can smell the oil in the air in Baku, but all you can smell is exhaust fumes from the endless traffic jams. It takes hours to get anywhere. This is because there are no rules about parking: you can just dump your vehicle anywhere you find a space, or if you can't find one, you simply park in the road. The result is that all the streets are narrowed down to one lane. I never thought I'd long for traffic wardens.

There have been huge firework displays to celebrate Nauruz, which I've watched out of the hotel window. It was the same in ex-Soviet Kazakhstan: public holidays were celebrated with government-sponsored jollity, a sort of compulsory bread and circuses. Heaven knows what the fireworks cost here, they are spectacular, but I am sure people would rather have schools and hospitals.

22 March

We went out for a walk today and were told to jump over a little fire that someone had made on the pavement – this is a Nauruz tradition and signifies a new, purified beginning.

I wish it were: I still feel bad. What is going on? I can't sleep, instead waves of panic sweep over me every time I close my eyes. Why? I am living in a perfectly comfortable hotel, I don't have to cook or wash up or look after babies, I am in a new country with lots to explore, I have a great husband, I am the luckiest person on earth, why do I feel so anxious? It's as if I have lost my bearings. Am I getting Alzheimer's like my mum? Is this what dementia feels like? I feel so sorry for her in retrospect as it is the worst feeling I have ever had.

AW and I have been exploring the city. Mind you, it's lethal walking round here – manholes with no covers, metal rods poking out of the pavements, loose slabs, and holes everywhere. Yesterday I saw some men throwing down scaffolding poles without looking to see if there was someone underneath – and there was. Honestly, they missed two girls by an inch. It's not just traffic wardens you want here but Health and Safety too.

In Fountains Square, a big open area near the hotel, there is a playground without borders so the unwary pedestrian can be mown down by a three-year-old in an electric bumper car going at speed, or hit in the face by another on a swing. There are photographers there too, waiting to take your picture arm-in-arm with a giant pink bunny, or a man dressed as Mickey Mouse, and lots of I-Speak-Your-Weight machines calling out for custom in shrill mechanical voices. Apparently, the previous German Ambassador had to move out of his Residence because there was one of these right outside his building and it nearly drove him insane.

All the girls here are very slim, with long dark hair and pale gold flawless skin and exquisite hands with black nail varnish. Everyone seems to wear black too, so that from the hotel window every scene looks like a Lowry painting.

Later. We went back to our apartment again today to measure for curtains – Peter Jones is going to make them. We walked up six flights (159 steps) rather than take the terrifying lift. There is an odd thing here: people's homes are comfortable, but the common parts of every building – including ours – are a total mess. The staircases are broken, the walls have peeling paint, the corners have rubble and rubbish piled up in them, there are tangled wires everywhere, and everything is filthy. I can't understand how people can live like that, and it's the same on a big scale in the town: the façades of houses are being restored everywhere you look, but walk two yards round the corner and it's a dump.

We've just heard that my wish came true – Oka provided the cheapest quote for the furniture for the Residence, so I am hoping that Head Office in Brussels will give us the go-ahead to place the order soon.

We had dinner with the office landlord this evening, I liked him a lot. He is a Turkish Cypriot, married to a very attractive Azerbaijani woman (I don't think there are any unattractive Azerbaijani women actually), educated at Millfield in Britain and with a passion for Proust. He collects Azerbaijani art from the Soviet period and his beautiful modern apartment looking over the Caspian Sea is stuffed with wonderful pictures – but, once again, to get there you walk through a courtyard full of garbage and bits of broken machinery like a hillbilly camp, and up four flights of dirty cement stairs. We didn't get home till 2 a.m.

23 March, Easter Sunday

At church today, representatives of each of the fifteen nationalities at Mass wished everyone a Happy Easter in their own language, and who should step up for the Philippines but Shrek!

Chatting outside afterwards, I met an Italian who is restoring the National History Museum, once the grandest of the oil barons' houses, and he said he would take us round it sometime – it is not open to the public yet. These houses would make a great magazine story. What would I do without the people I meet at church on Sundays?

After all that we decided to go to some furniture shops and check out what sort of stuff is available here. It was extraordinary – I have never ever come across anything like the things we saw: huge silver beds in the shape of giant shells, bulbous bedroom suites in gold or leopardskin – or both. You couldn't tell if they were made of shiny plastic or varnished wood. We hurried away to look at the old Muslim rulers' palace, the Shirvanshah, to cleanse our minds. Just having a fifteenth-century monument in town makes Baku a zillion times more appealing than Kaz.

Baku, 27 March

We are just back from a three-day visit to a place called Sheki, in the mountains, about a six-hour drive from Baku (the nearest proper green countryside turns out to be about three hours away from the city). The weather was glorious and we made so many interesting discoveries on the way that I have to put them down in proper order.

For a start, as we reached the first hills, we drove through villages belonging to two completely different ethnic people from mainstream Azerbaijanis. Molokans seem a little like the Amish in the United States: they are Russians belonging to a Protestant sect who fled here from persecution in the nineteenth century, and live in charming traditional Russian wooden houses painted blue. They are farmers and have a shop in Baku for their produce (thinks . . . will I be able to get fresh milk there?).

Not far from the Molokans, we came into the territory of the other group, called the Udis, who are descended from the Christians of the old Kingdom of Albania (no relation to present-day Albania), which was powerful in Azerbaijan from the fourth century BC to the eighth century. AW and I had no idea that Azerbaijan, which has been Muslim for centuries, had ever been a Christian country; we'd never even heard of the Kingdom of Albania and were utterly astonished to find ancient Christian churches in various states of decay – some still being used – in the Udi villages. We were told there were ruined monasteries in the forests but we didn't have time to investigate.

(When we returned to Baku we found that not many other people knew about the old Kingdom of Albania either and we decided that this must be because when the Russians took over this part of the world, they put everything to do with the Albanian Church and its archives into the hands of the Armenians, who later became deadly enemies of Azerbaijan and not likely to be telling anyone the fascinating history of their rival country.)

In the Udi areas there are acres of plantations of hazelnuts, and these are sold in stalls all along the roadsides, along with Molokan, locally made wine in second-hand mineral-water bottles (about sixty pence each) and big glass jars of home-made pickles – plums, peppers, pears, cucumbers – looking like illustrations from the food pages of a glossy magazine.

The oldest church we saw was in a pretty mountain village called Kish, where, as if we hadn't learned enough for one day, we discovered that as well as the church (probably built in AD400 – though locals say it was built in AD74), there were ancient tombs in which archaeologists had found skeletons of men and women over two metres long and with blond hair. Amazingly, Thor Heyerdahl pops up again here because he developed a theory that some of these tall fair people in the Caucasus made their way to Scandinavia and became the ancestors of present-day Norwegians. Our minds were bursting, and that was only Day One of our tour, so we sat down in a tea shop to digest all our new information and were served in the traditional Azerbaijani way: glasses of tea accompanied by bowls of delicious homemade jam: mulberry, fig, cherry, and tiny saucers and spoons for you to eat them from.

Eventually we reached our destination, Sheki. AW and I had booked into a new hotel, which everyone in Baku raved about. Unfortunately it was built in marble and had a central atrium which made it a perfect sound box – you could hear people *breathing* in the lobby from three floors up; the problem was that as well as breathing they were shouting, noisily playing tric-trac, slamming doors and moving furniture. We decided to leave the next day and try to find something quieter. (It's a problem in newly rich places like Azerbaijan: developers want to build everything to impress, when what most tourists want are just simple comfortable hotels with bathrooms that work, as you might find in Europe. The government should be thinking on those lines: tourism can't get off the ground here because there is hardly anywhere in this pretty country to stay – instead of which they are wasting money building monstrous high-rise, un-needed office blocks in Baku.)

AW had been in Sheki before, and put up in the Olympic Village (don't ask – I have no idea why the government has built Olympic villages around Azerbaijan. Optimism?). He said it wasn't particularly comfortable but at least it wasn't noisy, so we went there and after much pleading (mysteriously they said it was full, though it was clearly empty) managed to get a little bungalow with twin beds and a tiny patch of green outside where we could sit in the sun. It was a bit primitive in a mauve-nylon-sheets kind of way, but the breakfasts were the best I have ever had: freshly baked flat bread with butter, thick cream and honey. This is not a country where AW and I are going to get thinner.

Next day we went round a past ruler's lovely little painted palace in Sheki, after that, directed by our brilliant guidebook to Azerbaijan, we found the grave of Hadji Murad, whom Tolstoy wrote a book about, and then best of all, we located Gabala, the ancient capital of the Kingdom of Albania, or at least the site of it because the town no longer exists, though every footstep on the lovely low green plateau where it once stood turns up shards of ancient pottery.

Pliny and Ptolemy and Strabo wrote about Gabala, the Romans tried to capture it several times, it was invaded by Tamerlane (among others), but it was eventually destroyed by Nadir Shah of Iran in the seventeenth century. The villagers we met told us that they had found huge amphora with skeletons in them. 'What did you do with them?' I asked eagerly. 'Oh the jars were broken so we threw them away and buried the bones,' they said.

There were a couple of visiting officials loafing about, dressed in wide-shouldered, shiny, pinstriped suits with not-meant-to-be-baggy trousers (just like the suit AW bought in a Turkish shop in Brussels before leaving), as well as a smartly dressed woman called the Director. She asked us for a lift back to her office in the museum in New Gabala a few miles away, and en route she told us that she was fed up, got very low wages, and that just getting to the site at old Gabala involved taking four different types of transport, so she only did it a few times a month. She also told us that lots of finds mysteriously disappear from the site, though some do find their way to the museum.

AW and I are so excited about Gabala and wonder if we could somehow organise a really expert Euro/Azerbaijani archaeological dig there. The trouble is, we don't get the feeling that the government, or whoever it is who calls the shots here, is keen on 'old' or 'history'. In spite of the fact that lovely houses feature in the glitzy TV ads for Azerbaijan, in reality a lot of them are being pulled down. Money is being utterly wasted here – spent on all the wrong, superficial things. It's heart-breaking because, away from the oil areas, this is a beautiful country that would thrive with development of the right sort. In the office is an old map of Baku showing all the significant oil barons' houses – I have tried to buy a copy of it, but it's out of print, I expect that's because they don't want people to notice how many gaps there are now where these houses should be.

AW and I have discovered that New Gabala is famous for its meatballs, which are so big that a whole chicken is hidden inside. Sadly, we didn't get to see one of these, and neither were we able to photograph ourselves beside the sign for a village we passed through on the way home – BUM – because we'd left the camera behind.

Whiling away the time as we drove along I looked through the guidebook and found some interesting nuggets: 'The most common cause of sickness among expats in Azerbaijan is alcohol-related' . . . 'Men in shorts here are the equivalent of men in Y-fronts in the UK' . . . 'British troops stationed here in the First World War were given caviar as a cheap way of providing nourishment. "This jam tastes of fish," said a British soldier.'

We got back to Baku feeling tired and rather as if we were returning to boarding school – even the Caspian Sea was black and sullen-looking. It is incredibly windy and dusty. I quite like the dust as it acts on my hair like dry shampoo, but AW may have to find some goggles like Biggles' to stop the dirt getting in his contact lenses.

We had dinner at Sultan (it's become our dining room now) and then watched the Daniel Day-Lewis film about the early days of the oil business, *There Will Be Blood*, one of our pile of locally bought, pirated DVDs.

Apparently Sandy rang from the UK while we were away and was told by the hotel that we were sleeping outside – she thought they meant in the garden and she couldn't imagine why.

28 March

Went in search of the Molokan shop and found it not far from the hotel. Asked for fresh milk but they don't have it, only homemade *Smetana* (Russian crème fraîche) and I don't need cream because Fikret, the kind-hearted giant who is the office receptionist, gave me a pot of *kaimak* which is the utterly yummy, not-quite-so-rich-as-clotted-cream they served for our breakfast in Sheki. (I had raved to him about our excursion into the country – especially the breakfasts.)

30 March

After church today we went off to see the famous Fire Temple of Azerbaijan. I'd mark this 6 out of 10 because it isn't very old (eighteenth-century, built by Indian traders who, we were told, were 'Zoroastrians' – but we guessed that means Parsees) and it is in a dismal area on the outskirts of town full of derelict oil fields. The oddest thing is that the natural gas that once fed the fire in the temple ran out a few years ago, and it is now fuelled by piped gas.

1 April

We were invited to a welcome party by the UNICEF representative here, a lovely Egyptian woman called Hanna. Her food was wonderful: Iranian chicken faisinjan, which is cooked with pomegranate and walnuts, with rice. As I said, AW and I are going to go home twice the size we arrived here.

2 April

My diplomatic career here got off to a bad start at the Greek reception this evening. I saw the guy from the British consulate, who has been really kind about getting me a second passport for my upcoming journey to Israel/Palestine for our Festival of Literature. He was chatting to a woman, but when there was a pause in their conversation, I said, 'Thank you *so* much for doing my passport so quickly, now I won't get any hassle about Arab stamps from the wretched Israeli immigration people.'

He looked green with embarrassment and then said, 'Brigid, may I introduce the wife of the Israeli Ambassador . . .'

Someone has come from the EU office in Georgia to sort out the furniture order for the Residence and the office, and a car. We are making progress. But the best thing that has happened is that I have tracked down a woman I found on the Internet when I was looking up Azerbaijan. This is Betty Blair, who runs an excellent glossy magazine, *Azerbaijan International*, full of fascinating stories about this country. She lives in the USA but has emailed to say she'll get in touch when she next comes here.

Sat next to a visiting Englishman at an official dinner in a restaurant a few days ago – he suddenly turned to me and said, 'You've got some sauce!' I couldn't think what on earth I'd said to bring on this accusation, so I asked him, and he looked bewildered and said, 'I just noticed that there is sauce for your fish and you haven't taken any.'

3 April

The Italian restorer I met outside church was as good as his word and took me round Taghiyev's former Residence, the National History Museum. Every inch of it is being restored, which is a bit of an issue with Alissandro, the restorer, and his assistant, Daria (who, of course, have to take instructions from the government), because *everything* is being redone – even things that don't need re-doing at all, e.g., the main front door was in perfect condition, but it has been replaced by a modern replica. Why?

The frustrating thing is there are no architectural salvage yards here to sell the lovely ceramic tile stoves and exquisite plasterwork they are tearing out of the old houses – everything just gets smashed up and thrown out. Perhaps AW and I should start one.

When we'd finished at the museum, Alissandro walked us through town to another of their projects, the Iraqi Residence, in a flat on the top floor of a pretty French-looking house that is in the process of being 'improved' with aluminium windows, a sheet-metal front door, and new stone carvings on its façade (the old ones are being sawn off and replaced by identical new ones). The Iraqi Residence is probably the only part of the building that retains its original, stunning, décor – though Daria has discovered that under all the paint in the hallway and stairwell, the walls are marble and gilt. I wish I was mayor here, and could set about properly restoring the oil barons' heritage in Baku.

7 April

I can't believe it – I am going home tomorrow (loaded with Russian dolls for everyone, including one that has all the past six Presidents of Russia fitting into one another). When I come back AW says he will have moved into the Residence with or without furniture.

9

Middle Eastern Adventures

London, 8 April

I am writing this on the plane going home to London, clinging to Nora Ephron's words, 'The plane will not crash.' I'll
be seeing the family in a matter of hours, and I should be so
happy, but all I feel is panicky and anxious, and not just about
flying. Is this to do with moving to Baku? I've enjoyed my
stay – I'd mark Azerbaijan 7 out of 10 (compared to
Kazakhstan which would be about 3 out of 10). I know I
could be happy living there, and I am wondering if that is
actually the root of my problem: in order to settle down in a
place you have to make a commitment to it, and not keep
wishing you were at home, but if I make this commitment
then I will feel I am abandoning my daughters and
grandchildren.

In the meantime, this flight is weird enough to take my
mind off my mental health: there are 170 men on board, all
oil workers from Aberdeen wearing only T-shirts over their
tattoos, even though it is really cold, and there are only eight
women (including me and the hostesses). The men have been
on oil rigs in the Caspian Sea for weeks where no alcohol (or
women, obviously) are allowed, and so they've been out on
the binge in Baku all night and haven't even had time to
develop hangovers yet. The plane smells of stale booze and

everyone is shouting out jokes and guffawing with laughter and trying to steal the hostesses' hats. I feel a bit like an outsider on a factory charabanc outing. Right now they are all knocking back beers with shots as if they were going out of fashion. My neighbour, Stephen, is one of them, but he's okay so far. He has his laptop open and I can't help noticing that his screen saver is of a girl in a very skimpy bikini sitting with her legs wide apart. I can hear myself talking to him and sounding just like the Queen, 'Oh, you've come orf an Oil Rig, how fascinating,' etc. Earlier I heard him telling a friend what a rough night he'd had, but now I can't seem to make any sense of his accent, and it reminds me of when I went to look after my sick sister in Scotland long ago, and the taxi driver in Edinburgh and I had to communicate with each other in writing since neither of us could understand a word the other said.

Later. I took a minicab home – except I can't stay in my flat because Hester and George are still there and I am in my kind neighbour Valerie's. I dumped my luggage there and then went upstairs to my own flat to make a cup of tea. There was no milk in the fridge and I couldn't find my emails on my computer because someone has rearranged the desktop, and I felt disembodied and weird so I went downstairs again and cried for the first time since leaving England a month ago. What with Hester's family being in my flat, and living in the hotel in Baku, I have not unpacked properly or slept in my own bed for weeks and it's really destabilising.

I felt much better after fetching Malachy from nursery. He gave me such a morale-boosting welcome, screaming with joy and throwing all the toys around.

6 April

It's snowing in London and all my winter clothes are in Azzers.

Went to the dentist's to get a replacement whitening plate for my teeth; it will be ready in a week. Speaking of which, I saw my cousin Frances yesterday and she suddenly said, 'You have the most wonderful white teeth, you know.' I had to tell her why, she was most impressed and I am too, actually.

Met up with my friend Chris, who had been to the Finnish Embassy to see his friend Bertie Lomas collect a poetry award. While the speeches were going on Chris and his wife Wendy leaned against the wall – and were suddenly aware that the whole dado rail, about twelve feet of it, had become detached and was falling off. They grabbed it behind their backs, lowered themselves into a synchronised squat, and left it on the floor. 'I couldn't move it anywhere,' he said. 'I would have looked like a pole-vaulter.'

16 April

I am feeling completely dislocated – that is exactly the right word, i.e., not located in the right place. I can't smoke in my flat because Malachy is there, I can't smoke in Valerie's flat, so I have to sit and smoke in the car. In a couple of days I am off to Holland for my *paid* talk to the Shell wives, which is terrifying, but at the same time I'm quite looking forward to having my own room in the hotel.

Holland, 22 April

My instructions from the Shell organisers were to go to the meeting point at Schipol airport when I arrived, and there would be a taxi waiting for me. I expected it all to go wrong, but there was the car with a young woman driver who told me that her usual job was taking elderly folk on excursions from old people's homes and I wondered if they'd chosen her specially for me.

It was very late when we got to the hotel, which was on a beach somewhere, so I just had a quick drink with the organisers of the conference and was on my way to my room when one of the team called after me that I could go nude bathing if I wanted – 'Men and women together!' she said enthusiastically. This had about as much appeal as an invitation to stab myself, so I continued on to bed and lay there in my usual state these days of barely controlled panic.

Later. The talk started at 9 a.m. (8 a.m. London time), an hour when normally I can barely speak to AW, let alone two hundred Shell wives, but it went really well. I asked them if they had any tips or hints from their own experiences to make life easier for the trailing spouse, and they all did, and the session could have gone on for hours. It was great fun.

London, 1 May

Shell wives is one dread ticked off, and now I am getting ready for the really big one: Palfest. I will travel to Amman in Jordan tomorrow and stay with Jane, an old friend who lives there, for a couple of days before I meet up with Ahdaf and the writers we have invited for the festival, and then we will all go together in a coach to the Allenby Bridge crossing into Israel, and then on to our various venues in Jerusalem and the West Bank. The Palestinians can't move from place to place, so we are taking the writers to *them* in a bus.

Why am I such a hopeless packer? You'd think that after all these years I would be an expert, but oh no, I always seem to have to take about twenty identical black outfits 'just in case'. Last night I tried them all on in front of Hester and she helped me hone the number to about eight. I have also packed my pillow, a bottle of gin, and a cafetière with two packets of coffee. Had to make a last-minute dash to Marks and Spencer to buy some comfy shoes.

Amman, 2 May

On the plane to Amman I sat next to a beautiful woman, she looked like Julia Roberts. She was on her way to meet her Jordanian boyfriend, she said, but there was a bit of a problem with their relationship because of the age gap between them. I guessed that she must be about thirty-two and that her boyfriend was a much older man, but it turned out that she was forty-five and her boyfriend was twenty-three. 'Do you think it's doomed?' she asked, and though I didn't say it, I thought yes, doomed, especially when she told me that he was keen to marry her so that he could get a visa to go to England. Hmmm.

I will never know the end of their story, but I really hope it worked out for her. She saved me at the airport in Amman: we queued together to get our Jordanian visas and it was only when we got to the counter that I discovered you could only pay for these with Jordanian pounds. I would have had to join the even longer queue to change money, and then come back to the end of the visa queue again, if she hadn't bought mine for me. 'You are not very well organised, are you?' she commented – not knowing the worst part of it, which was that Jane had said she would meet me at midnight when the plane arrived, but it was now 1.40 in the morning and I was in a total panic wondering whether our friendship was strong enough for her to have waited, and praying that it was, because I had forgotten to bring her phone number or address with me, and if she wasn't there I would have to spend the night at the airport.

She was. Good old Jane. We got to bed as the morning call to prayer was being sung out from all the mosques of Amman in a chorus.

Jordan, 6 May

Moved from Jane's into the hotel where Ahdaf and the writers will arrive late tonight. William Dalrymple was already here, and so was Ana, a political activist and amazing character who was a Tupamaros guerrilla in Uruguay when she was nineteen, imprisoned and tortured, and then deported to Sweden where she has lived ever since.

Jordan is plastered with pictures of the young King Abdullah with his father King Hussein; in Azerbaijan it's pictures of the current president, Ilham, with his famous 'Creator-of-the-Nation' dad, Haydar Aliyev, and in Syria you can't get away from pictures of young Bashar al-Assad with his father, Hafez. In all cases the fathers look tough and lean and unspoiled and you can see why they became leaders, and their sons look slightly pampered and weak and you can see why they will probably fail in the end.

Later. It is 3 a.m. The writers arrived not long ago and we all had a drink in the lobby of the hotel to 'bond'. We have to be off by nine, which means we'll only get five hours' sleep.

Jerusalem, 7 May

The first thing I noticed on the coach to the Allenby Bridge this morning was that the writer Esther Freud was reading

Dip Bag – a good omen I think. Everyone was chatty and friendly. There is an American woman with us who heard that the writer Roddy Doyle (one of our group) is a Chelsea fan, and thought that meant Chelsea Clinton, which caused some secret hilarity.

Laughter ceased at the Allenby crossing. All the people in our group with Arab names were stopped – in spite of the fact that they held US or British passports – and taken off for questioning; the Israelis said they were checking with the British Council to make sure they were all writers, but tonight we discovered they hadn't been in touch with the Council at all, it was just an exercise in power. It was four hours before our friends were released and we could continue on our way.

The drive to Jerusalem was a total shock: I had been imag-ining 'settlements' as small beleaguered outposts on the tops of some hills – but in fact they are *huge* towns with high-rise buildings that cover every single hilltop, all running into each other to make one vast urban sprawl dominating the country. Why don't we all know this? It seems like an incredibly well-guarded secret – I wish everyone could come here and see what is going on. As for the idea of demolishing any of them – dream on. No one is going to be able to dismantle any of these illegal towns. Maybe the most alien thing about them is their greenery: the trees of the Holy Land are umbrella pines, cypress and olive, but the settlers go in for plantations of Christmas trees so they have not only taken over the land, but the landscape as well.

I was already feeling nervous because I was to be part of our opening event in Jerusalem tonight, along with Esther Freud and Willie Dalrymple (moderated by the Palestinian politician Hanan Ashrawi), but after our experience at the Allenby crossing and seeing the settlements, I got into a real panic because I thought my contribution would be too lightweight and flippant. I needn't have worried: a Palestinian lady came up to Esther and me after the talk and said that it was the first time she had laughed for three years.

Ramallah, 8 May

This morning we came face to face with the hideous grey cement Wall (higher and uglier than we'd imagined) that we'd seen in the distance, snaking its sinister way round the country, and we went through our first checkpoint at Qalandia en route for Ramallah – and here's another thing: I'd always imagined the checkpoints to be sheds manned by a couple of Israeli soldiers, but they are more like airport terminal buildings. Soldiers you can't see yell at you through megaphones; you queue to go through tightly revolving barred gates, drag your suitcase across concrete for miles, and everything is fear, ugliness, hostility, hate. The only light relief was Banksy's paintings on the Wall at the checkpoint; he immediately became a hero to us all.

Next stop was Birzeit University where, after the writers' event, everyone went off to do workshops with the students, and I was suddenly told I would be teaching a class along with the journalist and human-rights activist, Victoria Brittain. *Teaching a class?* I have never taught anyone anything in my whole life. Where do you begin? Not only that, but my heated rollers have broken down and I can't wash my hair without them to curl it afterwards so now it's flat and greasy and I've had to tie it back and look like an egg with a face painted on it (as we used to taunt one of our cousins when we were children).

The title of our talk was 'The Effect of Political Reality on Journalism', and I was relieved to hear Roddy Doyle saying he didn't understand what 'reality' meant, as I didn't know what *any* of it meant. When Victoria and I turned up in the classroom we found that our pupils, six charming girls in headscarves, had written VICTORIA AND BRIGID OUR HEROES! on the blackboard, which was very sweet. I watched Victoria like a hawk to see if I could pick up tips about teaching. First she asked them their names, and then suggested that they put some questions to us. Their main concern was how to get their voices heard in the world outside Palestine. That led to all of us joining in to make suggestions and in the end it was agreed that the girls should do a Birzeit Blog and put themselves out there on the Internet.

Bethlehem, 9 May

Back to the Qalandia checkpoint this morning (en route to Hebron and then Bethlehem) where we were made to queue up and go through *twice*, once by ourselves and the second time with all our heavy luggage from the bus. I don't know why we had to do this, but you very quickly learn not to ask questions because things will get worse if you do. As we were queuing to go through the gate for the second time, a Palestinian couple with a toddler hobbled slowly towards us: they'd obviously wanted to go through the checkpoint and been turned back. The husband was young but clearly very ill – there was a tube with blood in it coming out from his clothes, and his wife was practically carrying him. Her face was shiny with tears and the toddler was clinging to her legs as she walked.

I think we all had the same thought: in any proper society this man would be on a stretcher or in a wheelchair, and people would be coming forward to help his wife. We didn't know what to do: should we try and speak to the soldiers at the checkpoint and persuade them to let her pass? With the

Allenby Bridge crossing fresh in our minds, we feared that any action we foreigners took could make it worse for her, and decided to do nothing. But I can't get the image of the couple out of my head.

Later. A new image has lodged in my mind. As we drove through the outskirts of Jerusalem our bus stopped at a red light and we saw, sauntering along the pavement, a young hippy in T-shirt and jeans with long blond hair and a gun on a strap slung over his shoulder. 'Who is that?' we asked our driver. 'Why is he carrying a gun?' This is when we learned that all settlers are allowed to carry guns wherever they go.

Hebron has been a terrible shock to all of us. This city, which used to be the busiest on the West Bank, where 160,000 Palestinians live and where there was once a huge market serving the surrounding area, is like a ghost town. There are only five hundred Israeli settlers here, but with two thousand soldiers to guard them. The market is closed, the shops are closed, the roads are mostly closed to Palestinians, and on rooftops you can see Israeli soldiers with their guns pointing down at you. We walked along one of the few streets that Palestinians are allowed to use, but even here they have to keep behind a barrier at the side, while macho Israeli settlers jog down the centre of the road carrying guns.

One of the settlements in Hebron is above a narrow street in the old part of town still used by Palestinians. They have had to put wire netting over the top of the street to catch the missiles that the settlers throw down on them: you can see the big things caught in the net: bricks, bottles, rubbish – but of course it doesn't prevent poo or pee – or acid – coming through. We walked through, slightly warily, on our way to the Mosque of Abraham, which was once accessible to every-one, until in 1994 an armed settler walked into it, and shot dead twenty-nine Muslims at prayer, and injured over a hundred. Now it is divided in two, with a synagogue in the second half. We joined Muslims going to pray in the mosque: we had to pass through *three* checkpoints in the space of a hundred yards before we could enter. Once there, the women in our party were given hooded gowns that looked a bit like Ku Klux Klan outfits, and then we were free to wander round this holy of holies, some of us moved to tears.

None of us had experienced anything like Hebron before, and we grew more and more appalled and uncomfortable as the day went on because we were witnessing the deliberate humbling of a people.

Tonight in Bethlehem we watched a local dance group leaping about on stage full of energy and good humour and we sat there wondering how on earth the Palestinians keep their spirits up. We are all impressed and admiring.

I was telling someone we met that I couldn't bear the arrogance of the settlers in Hebron and the way they strut around, and I inadvertently coined a new word, struttler, a rather better description than settler.

Bethlehem, 10 May

This morning we were taken on a bus tour to see the wall that nearly surrounds Bethlehem now. We were as shocked as we had been in Hebron. Bethlehem is on a hill with carefully tended olive groves on terraces down the sides. The route of the wall is not at the bottom of the hill – no, it presses against the last houses in the town, it is the view at the end of the street, its watchtowers loom over the houses. When it is complete it will cut the land off from its owners, and here is the catch: there is an Israeli law which says that if land lies untended for seven years it can be confiscated by the

Israeli government. Everyone knows in advance their land will be taken because, when the wall is finished, no one will be able to get through it. We passed an old monastery where, for centuries, monks have been making communion wine from their vineyards for the Christian churches of Bethlehem; when the wall is finished it will lie on the Israeli side, what will happen to them?

Jerusalem, 11 May

We had a few free hours today so I begged Ana (the ex-Tupamaros guerrilla), who is an IT wizard, to let me talk to AW on her mobile because my Jordanian SIM card doesn't work here and I am desperate to tell him that all is well.

Then Hanan al-Shaykh and Esther and I visited the Church of the Holy Sepulchre with one of our Palestinian volunteer guides, Hamada, who is a theatrical costume designer. As we went into the church I said to Hamada, 'I feel so moved that I am going to pray by the body of Jesus.' He gave me a funny look, and said, 'What do you mean? Of course it isn't here!' I had just forgotten the whole central tenet of my Catholic faith which is the Resurrection . . .

Hamada led us through crowds of pilgrims carrying crosses (he says there's a roaring trade in renting out crosses) and on to the most famous pastry maker in Jerusalem. The small shop was tucked away in a corner against the Holy Sepulchre building and didn't look at all promising, just a couple of Formica tables and plastic chairs, no food to be seen. But the cook took a small lump of dough (one he'd prepared earlier) from a fridge and flung it around in his hands until it became paper thin (*tissue* paper thin) and then folded it round some cheese, then he did the same with some nuts, then he poured a few drops of rosewater and syrup over the top of the pastries, baked them for a few minutes and then we ate them, sweet and crisp and light. Possibly the most delicious things I've ever tasted.

Tottenham Hotspur beat Chelsea in the English Premier League yesterday – Roddy Doyle told us that he was woken in the middle of the night by a call from a distraught friend in Ireland saying, 'Chelsea lost – for God's sake get to the Wailing Wall.'

This evening was our last event. There were speeches of thanks and then the writers read out passages from their favourite books. I read from the love story *Ali and Nino*. Then we all went to dinner in a nearby restaurant and danced. Arabs are genetically programmed to be able to shimmy their hips; Brits are definitely not – I was so aware of looking like a cartoon of an English person doing Arabic dancing that I gave up. But it was a great evening – and to think that only a few days ago we were all at the Allenby Bridge full of fear and trepidation and worrying about all the things that could go wrong – and *none* have.

I came up to my room last night, opened the door (which wasn't locked), turned the light on, threw my bag on to the spare bed in my room – and only then to my absolute *horror* I saw that there was a man in the other bed. I was in the wrong room. Worst of all I could see the back of his head and it was shaved like Roddy Doyle's and I thought *Oh God*, please, please don't let him wake up because he will think I have crept into his room on purpose. I could hardly breathe with fear, but I managed to pick up my stuff, and tiptoe to my own room next door, also not locked. (I later realised it couldn't have been Roddy in the bed as I had seen him downstairs at the bar before I came up.)

Amman, 12 May

Esther dreamed last night that she was in a sex education class and all the pupils were given an egg to hold. I dreamed that they'd demolished the Wall and that I was put in charge of getting rid of all the concrete rubble and I couldn't think of anywhere big enough to dump it.

We had a few hours in Jerusalem this morning before leaving by bus for Jordan again. Some of our party, including Ahdaf and the others of Arab origin, went to the Haram al-Sharif, the Holy Mount, to visit the Dome of the Rock and the Al-Aqsa mosques (the Israeli guards wouldn't let them in until they had recited verses from the Koran to prove they were Muslims – though this is supposed to be an area anyone may visit) and I went to chat to Munther who runs a wonderful bookshop next to the famous American Colony Hotel. Then I took a look at the hotel itself which is the prettiest place, only ruined (for me) by the fact that Tony Blair keeps a whole floor in it for his ineffectual peace mission. Grrrr.

When I was packing this morning I realised that though I'd used my pillow every night, I had never had time to make coffee with the cafetière or even drink my gin, so I gave them to a Palestinian friend. Just as well we are nearing the end of the trip – my floppy jersey trousers which I have worn nearly every day are growing longer and longer and pretty soon I won't be able to walk in them.

On the coach back to Jordan I sat next to the writer Ian Jack, a good friend (we used to be colleagues on the *Sunday Times*). I mentioned Jordan, meaning the country, but he thought I was talking about Katie Price, so we had a peculiar conversation.

London, 18 May

Ian wrote a good piece about Palfest in the *Guardian* yesterday. He used a Palestinian joke I told him – that the reason Ariel Sharon has been in a coma all these years is because God is making him go through all the checkpoints that he put up for the Palestinians, before he allows him across to the other side.

10

Settling In

London, 20 May

I feel as if I've lived about thirteen different lives since returning from Azerbaijan six weeks ago. I have certainly slept in
twelve different beds and will sleep in more now because
Valerie wants her flat back tomorrow and Hester and George
are still in mine. Apart from that though, all the things I had
been dreading are now successfully accomplished and even
the horrible panicky feelings I had in Azerbaijan have disappeared without me noticing.

21 May

My grand finale in Valerie's flat was locking myself out this
morning. Actually, it was all Hester's fault as she slammed the
door without thinking as we came out into the hall together.
I had to call a locksmith and he said it would cost a minimum
of eighty pounds. He arrived about an hour later and opened
the door in two seconds with a piece of plastic. 'I could have
done that,' I said grumpily as I paid out the money.

'Not without this you couldn't,' he replied, waving the
plastic.

'Well, I am going to buy one of those and keep it here for
emergencies,' I retorted.

'No you can't do that,' he said triumphantly, and showed me where, stamped on the plastic, it said ONLY FOR SALE TO BONA FIDE LOCKSMITHS.

28 May

I have been staying with Claudia and with Chris and Wendy (which makes fourteen different beds I have slept in now) but today Hester and George have moved back into their re-done flat – which looks wonderful – and I have moved into my own place again.

29 May

Ana (ex-Tupamaros guerrilla) has just sent a picture she took of me in the Mosque of Abraham. I look like Death, literally: pale blob face under the pointed hood of the black Ku Klux Klan-esque robe – all I need is a scythe in my hand and I would be the Grim Reaper himself.

Had my annual cancer check at the Royal Marsden; all seems to be fine. I didn't tell them about the pain in my knee which has suddenly started, and which is helping detract from the pain in my back.

2 June

AW has been in Brussels for work and came home a couple of days ago to see the family en route to Azerbaijan. Without telling me, he altered the ring of my mobile phone so that it sounds like a cock crowing. I keep my phone in my bra so the sudden *cock-a-doodle-doo* coming from my chest gave me the fright of my life – and not only me but all the passengers on the bus I was on.

4 June

Have cough, streaming cold, bad knee, bad back and am on antibiotics. An Ambassador friend, older than us, once advised AW not to retire too late because after the age of sixty-five, everything suddenly falls apart. I see what he means. Am off to Azerbaijan tomorrow, perhaps the oily air will make me better.

Baku, 6 June

AW met me at the airport and we arrived at the new Residence at 2.30 a.m., and sat admiring it over a glass of wine. It is wonderful – there is no furniture, nothing in the huge room except carpets (two big ones that we bought at auctions in Brussels especially for this apartment) and views over the Caspian Sea. We are so lucky. AW is brilliant to have found this place, and a hero for unpacking the boxes of our personal stuff – bed linen and all our greasy old kitchen equipment – sent from Brussels. He has borrowed two beds from Eran, the office landlord, and a table and chairs from someone else, and so we are very cosy. It's so much better than being in the hotel.

8 June

AW has hired a Russian woman who is cooking and cleaning for us while we work out what sort of help we will need in the house. Today she put *ground* pepper into the pepper grinder. This is not promising. Her name is Valia – as in Valium, which I might need at this rate.

Rovshan, AW's driver, came today to show us the big general market in Baku where I saw leopard-patterned saucepans – shall have to go back for those – and then on to some plant shops where we bought two palms for our lovely room.

Jean-Yves, the French Ambassador, came to lunch and loved the apartment, and gave me some nicotine chewing gum to help with my new effort to give up smoking because of my cough. (It failed by this evening.) When he left he refused to go in the lift. 'Oh go on,' said AW. 'It's good solid Soviet stuff.' It turned out that J-Y was in a good solid Soviet lift in Moscow that fell four floors before it was caught by the safety cable.

AW and I went for a walk this evening to buy some cherries, which are in season now. In our short stroll we counted one Humvee, one Rolls-Royce, two Lexus jeeps, three Mercedes jeeps and loads of BMWs and other Mercedes. They all seem to be driven by teenagers who love hooting the horn to give you heart failure as you cross the road.

9 June

AW went to the office this morning, and I decided to wash my hair, but just as I stepped into the shower the water went off – there was a power cut and, as our water is pumped up by electricity, no power means no water either. I hadn't thought of keeping a bath permanently filled as I have always done in postings abroad because I thought Baku would be like London. It was just as well I hadn't got as far as using my blonde shampoo – without being able to rinse it off, I would have ended up with orange hair.

Tried to discuss the electricity cut – how often do they happen? how long do they last? etc. – with Valia, but she doesn't speak a single word of English and my Russian is non-existent; even the words I learned in Kazakhstan seem to have vanished. So . . . no communication, no water, no electricity, and, as yet, no telephone, mobile, computer, radio, or TV, and, of course, no newspapers. I feel like crying.

Before I left England, I read in the papers about Steve Hilton, David Cameron's political adviser, taking a sabbatical from his job (on full pay) to accompany his wife to the US where she has a senior position with Google. There was also a story about a man from Norfolk County Council who has gone to live in Australia with his wife but is continuing his job somehow, and another about a British High Commissioner and his wife who *share their job* . . . Men get a totally different deal when they have to trail behind their wives. On the other hand I can't imagine sharing a job with AW – one of us would not survive.

10 June

It's Malachy's birthday. He is two and I am not there. I feel so sad.

11 June

Things are become surreal. Yesterday Valia had a long 'conversation' with me in which I thought she was telling me that there was a very good butcher near her house and that she was going to bring beef fillet in today in order to make beef stroganoff. This seemed to show great initiative, and I was really pleased, but just to be sure we were talking about the same thing, I drew a cow and then a beef fillet cut in slices, and she nodded vigorously and smiled and kept saying, 'Da, da, beefstrogonoff, da.' When AW came from work I told him about the beef stroganoff, and we felt quite excited about the whole thing.

Then, this morning, while I was dressing, AW came in and whispered that there was no beef fillet in the kitchen, but there was a packet of chicken breasts.

This made me ponder: yesterday, during the conversation about the beef fillet, I had wondered vaguely why Valia was flapping her arms and looking at me questioningly – but I thought it was part of her having the menopause. (The day before she had come into the room and sort of swooned on to a chair, fanning herself and groaning, and I decided she must be having a hot flush.) Now that AW has told me about the chicken breasts it's beginning to dawn on me that she wasn't airing her armpits during our conversation, but being a chicken. If I imitate a chicken (as I had to in Kazakhstan when I wanted Nina to cook one), I don't flap my arms, I cluck, so I had misunderstood everything.

This whole incident puts me in mind of my grandmother's children's parties. To break the ice she used to pair off the little guests: you were told when you arrived that you were a dog or a cat or a pig and you had to go and find your partner by barking or miaowing or snorting, etc. This was always a huge success, but one year there were two kids left looking for each other after everyone else had found their partners. They were an English boy going *hiss hiss*, and an American saying *rattle rattle*. That's Valia and me being chickens, one flapping her wings, one clucking.

Anyway, back to beef stroganoff, it is obvious that in Valia's book, beef has got nothing to do with this recipe – it just happens to be called beefstroganoff and can be made with anything you like.

12 June

Today Valia washed the new white duvet covers together with a yellow duster so they are now saffron-coloured. Then, when I showed her how to make mayonnaise, she shrugged and indicated that it was okay two of us doing it together, but she'd never be able to manage it by herself. Then she plonked a bottle of tonic on the table at lunch when I asked her to bring the water jug. She is driving me mad.

I went to the Russian takeaway restaurant today – this is where everyone in the office gets their lunch. There were about twelve different Russian dishes, all made up of finely-chopped-something-red, and all looking more or less the same – a bit like uncooked mince. Everything Valia cooks, from beetroot salad to the famous beefstroganoff, looks the same as well. I don't remember this being the case with Russian food in Kazakhstan. AW has taken to calling all these red Russian dishes with unknown, unrecognisable ingredients, chopped cow's udder with dill.

I met a shabby old man with one eye on the way back from the office today; he seemed to be collecting plastic and glass bottles. There is no recycling here, everything just goes into the garbage, so we are going to start collecting them for him.

This morning I was sent some flowers and Valia put them in the basin in the spare room with their *heads in the water* and their stalks sticking out in the air. It looked weird, like flowers for a Witches' Sabbath or a Black Mass or something. I think she probably dislikes me as much as I do her.

13 June (Friday the thirteenth)

AW's driver, Rovshan, took me to the Green Market today to do the shopping. It was wonderful – mountains of fruit and veg – but less sophisticated than Kazakhstan where, by the time we left, you could buy everything from asparagus to out-of-season strawberries. People say Azerbaijan is behind because no one wants to invest in anything here since, if it is success-ful, the President or his wife will take over your business.

AW's gorgeous assistant Nigar came round later to help me communicate with Valia, and show her how to make a bed, lay the table, clean the house, and try and establish a routine and get off to a new start. Then I taught Valia how to make a delicious tomato soup so AW and I have something to eat over the weekend.

14 June

Howling hot wind blowing today – apparently Baku is known as the Windy City. Valia came in this morning and made the bed exactly as she had *before* Nigar and I gave her the bed-making lesson yesterday. (It's not that I can't make my own bed, but I am trying to train her so she will always have a job.) This is not going to work.

Later. Valia has gone off for the weekend. She seems to have eaten most of the soup we made . . .

It was the Greek Ambassador's party this evening: by the pool at the Hyatt Hotel and with a Force 10 gale blowing. I sat next to the President of the Azerbaijani Gymnastics Federation; he was nice, but I have never even done Pilates, so we did not have a lot in common. I wanted to ask him if Azerbaijan had anyone who could match the amazing Russian gymnast Olga Korbut, who wowed the world in the 1972 Olympics, but I realised that he probably wasn't born when she was a star.

On my other side was my friend Jean-Yves, the French Ambassador. When the inevitable Greek male dancers wearing very short tutu skirts and white tights and shoes with pompoms came prancing out in a line, I asked if he fancied them. 'No,' he said, 'their thighs are too fat.'

Lessons learned from today's party: never hold an outdoor reception in a place with an unreliable climate. Never play 'Never On a Sunday' (or any other music) so loudly that no one can talk. Avoid national dancers unless they are spectacularly good.

15 June

Went to church and could hardly wait for Mass to be over so that I could start recruiting staff. I have become a stalker, hanging around outside church, following any likely-looking Filipino or Sri Lankan who might know someone who wants a job . . . Today I latched on to an Indian, his name is Herman, and he says he will help me.

Later, Herman rang to say he is sending over a young Indian from Goa who works for a catering company, as well as an Azerbaijani woman and her daughter who could do cleaning. Am over the moon.

17 June

Oh my goodness, this is so exciting: two calls today, one from Sushant, who is the Goanese man that Herman suggested, and the other from Rebecca who is the daughter half of the Azerbaijani family duo. She sounds extremely nice *and speaks English*.

Later. Disappointment. Sushant came for the interview: he doesn't work as a cook in the catering company, but as a supervisor. He told me something shocking that has redirected my worries from finding a cook to the planet:

every day his team serve meals to the 75–100 staff of an oil company, and *everything* they use – plates, cups, bowls, cutlery – is *plastic* and is not recycled but just thrown away. I am wondering how long it will take for the Caspian Sea to be entirely clogged up. (Which reminds me – last week the Caspian Sea was *closed* for swimming because the water was too polluted. Imagine, a whole sea, shut.)

Actually, we wouldn't have hired Sushant even if he had cooked like Escoffier himself because a) he was chewing gum, b) he never took off his baseball cap and c) he answered his mobile phone whenever it rang during the interview, which was six times. (After the third time AW got up and left and I knew that was the end of Sushant and us.)

18 June

The mother and daughter were due for an interview at 5 p.m. today, but got lost (not easy as we live next door to the Maiden Tower, the most famous sight in Baku) and turned up more than an hour late, by which time I'd decided they must be daft and I didn't want them anyway. However, Tarana and Rebecca won my heart when they arrived – they were sweet and shy and gentle, with nice manners, full of enthusiasm about the job, and keen to learn to cook (Tarana said she would be the cook and Rebecca the cleaner). And I would be able to communicate with them because Rebecca speaks English. The only problem is that they work for the Catholic priests and I would be stealing them away – would I go to Hell?

I rang Herman and he said the Fathers know all about it and are happy for Tarana and Rebecca to get a better-paid job with us. (Tarana is a Muslim, and Rebecca is a convert to

Catholicism, and was chosen to meet the Pope in Rome on an Azerbaijani Catholic Youth trip.)

19 June

Jean-Yves, the French Ambassador, is leaving, which is very sad for us. The Italian Ambassador gave a farewell party for him this evening. The Israeli Ambassador and his wife were there – they are Americans who have *chosen* to go and live in Israel. I am extra-sensitive on the subject of Israel/Palestine since I went to the West Bank, so I decided to stay out of their way.

Valia was incredibly annoying today, but I won't go on about it because Claudia says having any help in the house is incredibly spoilt and I should stop complaining. Actually, in spite of Valia, I am really enjoying this week – but I realised today that I still have my watch on British time, which is definitely a sign of non-commitment.

20 June

I am obsessed with making jam. In England it never crosses my mind because where's the temptation in a plastic pack of under-ripe apricots from Sainsbury's? But here in the Green Market there are huge heaps of fresh blackcurrants, redcurrants, apricots, raspberries, strawberries, mulberries and fat black cherries. Over the last couple of days I have made quince paste, plum jam, redcurrant jelly and black cherry jam, as well as bowls of blackcurrant and strawberry sorbet for the freezer. My enthusiasm was nearly thwarted by not having any jam jars – I haven't lived here long enough to accumulate any, but Valia – yes Valia! – saved the day, bringing in a whole lot yesterday morning.

When I got back from the market laden with all my bags of fruit, I found the lift wasn't working, they are repairing it and it won't be ready for two weeks. Perhaps walking up the 159 steps three times a day, loaded like a mule, will strengthen my back muscles.

A farewell dinner for Jean-Yves at the British Ambassador's this evening. AW very upset because all the other Ambassadors had place cards saying 'His Excellency Mr X, Ambassador of X' in front of their places, but AW's said, 'Representative', as though he were a travelling salesman of some sort. But British Ambassadors will do anything to avoid using the A word for their colleagues from the European Union, even though, officially, they are proper Ambassadors too.

Before the party Rebecca and Tarana came to meet AW. He liked them as much as I do, and we have agreed they will start next week and we will try and find a good job for Valia.

22 June

Went to church today and apologised to the priest for taking away his staff; he was charming and said the Fathers knew it was a good opportunity and were pleased for them. He is from the Czech Republic, a really nice man. I admire the priests here – and the Mother Teresa nuns – they do a lot for the poor who are totally ignored by the new oil-rich government. No wonder there are many people who mourn the old Soviet days.

Lots of diplomatic welcome and farewell parties at the moment, the nicest one was given for us by the office landlord and his wife. They broke the rule of not having an outdoor do, but it wasn't too windy and in the middle of the evening the full moon came out from behind some clouds and made a river of light on the Caspian Sea. It was spectacular.

23 June

Good news: AW has found someone in the office who speaks Russian and wants Valia to take care of his children. Everyone is happy and today I realised that I was right to hire Tarana and Rebecca. I invited Betty Blair and Nicole, head of the British Council here, for lunch. I made a nice French onion tart and we had that with salads, but I couldn't really talk to them as I was dashing to and fro, laying the table, bringing drinks, carrying in the dishes, clearing the plates etc. It's not that Valia didn't want to help, it was just that she didn't know what to do, and I can't explain.

After lunch I took Betty and Nicole downstairs to see the apartment on the third floor. A few days ago I got chatting with the owners of it, and they showed me inside where there are fantastic Chinoiserie wall paintings and elaborate plaster mouldings, which give an idea of how our building looked before the Soviets came. But here's a mystery: apparently not so very long ago, say thirty years or so, the wife downstairs used to play with the little girl who lived in part of our apartment and she remembers it still had all its fancy plasterwork and wall frescos in those days – so perhaps it wasn't the Soviets who stripped everything out – perhaps it was the developers who created our flat.

In fact, all in all, I think the government/President/real estate people in Baku are probably far more destructive than the Communists used to be: for instance, the Old City here is a UNESCO site, but that didn't stop the President's wife knocking down a whole huge corner of it to build the new Hilton Hotel. Now there is a charming old two-storey house opposite our apartment which seems to be under threat. What happens, we're told, is that the house 'they' have their eye on receives a visit from the Ministry of Emergency

Situations, which then comes up with a report saying the building is structurally dangerous, and after that it can be demolished 'legally'. A huge kilometre-long section of the town behind the Lenin Concert Theatre (the Respublika Sarayi) – an area that is rather cosy, with trees and two-storey stone buildings and a nice community spirit – is in the process of being knocked down for a vast, flashy, high-rise development. Tragic.

23 June

Valia left today. She is pleased about her new job but still gave me a hostile look as she went. I think she could have been a bit more gracious considering I've just discovered she walked out of her last job giving one day's notice. Still, who cares? I am *freeee*.

AW and I are finding it very romantic living in the apartment with no furniture. When our Oka order finally does come we are going to hate it.

24 June

Woke up feeling apprehensive and then remembered it's the day Tarana and Rebecca start work. I asked AW yesterday, should I sacrifice writing and teach Tarana to cook instead? And he said yes, definitely, it could change her life for ever (all very well for him though – no one is asking *him* to give anything up).

As soon as they arrived Tarana said she had to clean the whole flat from end to end, so I hardly saw her as she disappeared with a bucket and mop and window-cleaning stuff. I did manage to get my first cookery lesson in later though: I showed her an aubergine dish we learned in Syria (aubergine, tomato, garlic, and lamb meatballs, all cooked together in the oven) plus mayonnaise, lentil salad, green salad, and tomato soup (the one that Valia ate). She wrote everything down in a notebook she'd brought specially. I am impressed.

Rebecca is sweet and inquisitive: she asks things like, 'Is this table very expensive?', 'How much is the rent here – is it very expensive?', 'How much did your make-up cost? Was it expensive?' Normally this would drive me raving mad, but I don't seem to mind. I feel motherly towards her and am already worrying about why she is so thin.

25 June

Today is a public holiday to celebrate ninety years of the Republic of Azerbaijan. The harbour is full of warships; it looks like a huge painted naval panorama outside the window. I was really impressed until AW pointed out that the ships are actually quite small and there are only about ten of them.

Later. AW went off to watch a military parade with the other Ambassadors. They all sat together in the Diplomatic Stand facing, across the square, two thousand soldiers in disciplined ranks. AW said all he could think of was the assassination of Anwar Sadat in Egypt at just such a parade. He mentioned this to the Egyptian Ambassador who happened to be sitting beside him, and he said exactly the same thought had gone through his head.

Apparently the Ministry of Foreign Affairs has a duty-free shop here – imagine the Foreign Office having a shop selling cheap fags and booze?

Another huge firework display this evening – this is the second since I arrived here at the beginning of the month. Bruno, our friend in the UN, estimates they cost *millions*.

27 June

No time to write my diary any more as I spend most of the day cooking with Tarana. The thing is, though, we never seem to have anything to eat. This is because I have become a hoarder. I think it's to do with being away from home: stocking up the freezer is my security blanket. Today, as I wrapped up yet another quiche to freeze, Rebecca said, 'Azerbaijani people like to make food and eat it on the same day.' And I said, 'British people like to do that too, but I can't seem to cope with that idea right now.'

Tarana and Rebecca smile and are friendly and they want to learn. I am beginning to love them.

29 June, Feast of St Peter and St Paul

My parents' wedding anniversary. Before he died my father was really worried about what was going to happen to him and Mum in the afterlife because my mother's first husband (who died a very short time after she married him) would be there too. I used to smile at Dad, but now I find myself being jealous of AW in advance: as a Buddhist he believes in reincarnation, and it really upsets me to think that in his next life he is probably going to go off and marry someone else.

After church today AW and I were exploring Baku and discovered a roadside stall making *qutab*, which is a thin flatbread with herbs in it. Utterly delicious. As we ate, we got talking to the elderly woman making the bread and she told us that she and her family are refugees from Nagorno-Karabakh, which is the big chunk of Azerbaijan that was invaded and annexed by the Armenians in 1992.

There are still more than half a million internally displaced refugees here from that conflict, which has never been resolved.

Suddenly the old lady began to cry and through her tears she told us that before the Armenians kicked them out of their home, she and her family had a farm with twenty cows and a good business producing milk and cheese and cream. Now she lives in the homemade shack behind her stall. I felt so desperate for her that after we got back in the car I asked AW for all the money he had on him, which was quite a lot, and I rushed back to give it to her. She absolutely refused to take it, and I felt so foolish, as if I believed that a few quid could solve her problems, but I just wanted her to have one nice thing happen.

30 June

Today among several other dishes, I taught Tarana cold cucumber soup, and then I remembered that I served this at a dinner party in Delhi once and a guest had said in a loud voice, 'Excuse me, but is this soup supposed to be hot?'

I forgot to mention that a small miracle has taken place over the curtains for the Residence. I measured them the first time I came out here, chose the fabric at Peter Jones (white) when I returned to England, and placed my order. I went to collect them before leaving for Baku the other day and to my fury they hadn't done them because they'd run out of the material and forgotten to tell me. I stomped out of the shop, but now I've discovered that I'd given them the wrong measurements – I measured the actual window instead of the window embrasure – so the curtains would have been far too narrow. I am thanking my lucky stars for PJ's inefficiency.

4 July

I am closing down my computer here till September. Hester's new baby is due in three weeks and so I am off to England tomorrow. What a thought: what will have happened in two months? A new and healthy grandson for a start, please God.

11

Fully Furnished

Baku, 14 September

There was no time to keep my diary over the summer, so I'll just recap.

Leaving Baku, or rather leaving Tarana and Rebecca, was touching. As I set off down the stairs they brought a bucket of water and started sprinkling it behind me. 'Oh don't bother to wash the steps *now*,' I said. 'We are not washing the steps,' Rebecca replied. 'We are throwing water after you, which is our custom; it means you will come back safely.' I nearly cried.

I wasn't scared on the plane because I am following Hester's new theory which is that fear of flying is all to do with Catholic guilt – we believe that if we don't feel fear, God will punish us for taking everything for granted, so we *have* to be afraid in order to stop the plane crashing. It makes sense. I am no longer to be found kneeling in airport lavatories or in the backs of minicabs en route for Heathrow feverishly mutter-ing prayers. Now I say them calmly beforehand, and then read the paper on take-off. So far, it is working.

Back in England I went to see a skin doctor about remov-ing broken veins from my cheeks. He said he could easily do that, but what about the lines around my lips and my frown mark? '*Those* are the first things I notice about your face.' Oh dear. I don't think I'll bother with any of it now.

Esther Freud gave a party, but I was an hour late as my minicab took me to Wood Lane in White City instead of Wood Lane, Highgate. When I eventually got there she told me a story that was in the papers while I was away, about a couple who took a cab to Wembley, London and ended up in Wembley, Yorkshire. Her father, Lucien Freud, was at the party. I shook hands with him but was too much in awe to talk to him.

AW rang to say that Tarana was cooking really well – though I was a bit worried about the menu for a party he was giving: it seemed to be mushroom tart, followed by onion tart, followed by cherry tart (tarts being the main thing I taught Tarana before I left), but later he told me she'd done a Persian feast from her own recipes and it was great.

I bought my first purchase on eBay: an ice-cream maker, which ended up costing quite a bit more than a new one from Peter Jones because I got locked into a bidding war for it, and then had to pay for a minicab to deliver it.

But the big event of the summer was the birth of our third grandchild, Jackson, on 30 July, after which the family spent August all together in Somerset, where I had installed a climbing frame and a sandpit, which proved useless as it rained every day.

Why is it that children do not play with their toys? Our house is crammed with fascinating plastic things that bleep and ring and have flashing lights and move, and yet the babies are far more interested in fiddling with the knobs on the TV or DVD player and the computer and the mobile phone. Am thinking of going into business making exact replicas of all those items, but even then I bet the babies would somehow know that they weren't real and go back to wrecking everything you own. It's all very exhausting: I used to pretend that I am younger than I really am, but now I find I am exaggerating my age and saying things like, 'I don't think I can cope with doing that because I am *nearly seventy-four*.'

Another, milder, excitement was the voyage of the furniture for the Residence. I wasn't there in Baku to hear about this, but I might just as well have been because AW rang me from Azerbaijan five times a day to tell me its movements. This was because the boat carrying it arrived at the port of Poti in Georgia at exactly the same time as the invading Russian army which set about looting and destroying Georgian ships. It was touch-and-go for a few days and AW and I decided that all our stuff would be blown up or stolen and then there would be a row about the insurance that would last for years, and we would *never* get the Residence furnished. But we underestimated our ship's captain: he managed to get out of Poti unscathed, and into Batumi port from where our container eventually arrived in Baku. (It helped, apparently, that our stuff was on the same boat as a container for the President – no wonder the captain reversed out of Poti so quickly.)

There was one aspect of our furniture delivery which didn't make me happy: the news that when the four removal men had finished in our flat, they got into the lift to leave and it didn't stop at the ground floor but sunk into the basement where they were stuck for more than an hour. Before I left Baku, Patrick, our Irish office admin man, told me that my namesake, St Brigid of Ireland, is the patron of tunnellers and engineers and *lifts*. (Apparently when they were digging the Channel Tunnel and the labourers from the French and British sides met in the middle, the Irish among them put up a shrine to St Brigid in thanksgiving.) Patrick knows how I feel about our lift and suggested putting a picture of St Brigid in it.

But the truly most amazing thing about the summer is that it passed without one single family row, even though we were all together. No one threw plates, no one slammed out, no one shouted. This has never happened before.

I had a stressful departure from London. My suitcase, stuffed with things you can't buy in Baku (though not the ice-cream maker, I sent that separately), was so heavy that the ground hostess at the BMed check-in made me go to the other end of the airport, buy another case and then repack them both kneeling on the dirty floor. I nearly cried – and what with that and my definite premonition that this time the plane would crash (I always have a definite premonition before flying) I decided to go and have a cigarette – and discovered that you can't just stand and smoke outside the door of the airport building, you have to go to a special 'Designated Area' in one of the car parks.

Luckily my bracelets set off the alarm in security so I had to be patted down. (I love this, it's soothing – a bit like having a very short massage. I read somewhere that Ruby Wax loves it too and makes sure to wear something that will set the alarm off.)

The man next to me on the plane, an oil worker, drank eight whisky miniatures and then fell into a coma, and I read one of *The No. 1 Ladies' Detective Agency* books – in times of stress, they are better than Valium, but in a nice way, making you feel full of happiness and love, even towards the woman at BMed check-in.

15 September

I nearly had another meltdown when I saw the Residence at 2 a.m. this morning. Our beautiful empty room looks like a furniture warehouse. All my mental pictures of how perfect it would be with the furniture I had chosen went out of the window. I lay awake all last night wondering what to do. My confidence is severely shaken.

16 September

Rebecca and Tarana arrived this morning and we spent the whole day trying to sort out the flat. Rebecca was ill early in the summer while AW and I were both away. She had an operation to remove an ovarian cyst, and then got an infection. When she told the doctor about her high temperature he said, 'It is usual to have a fever after an operation, stop bothering me.' It was only when the wonderful Nigar telephoned and said that Rebecca was really ill and that she was working for an *Ambassador* that the doctor got on to the case. 'If you are a poor person here, nobody cares,' said Rebecca sadly.

She is better now, but AW is sending her to another doctor tomorrow to be checked out.

17 September

We finished the room today. I sent back the table and chairs we'd borrowed before the shipment arrived (at one stage I counted the chairs in the room and, with the new ones, there were thirty) and I passed on a sofa and armchair to Patrick who hasn't enough furniture in his house, and we put up our pictures – they came from Brussels ages ago but we couldn't hang them until the furniture was in place. (AW sent the handyman from the office to help do this – what bliss not having to do it with AW himself: putting up pictures together has almost caused divorce in each of our postings.) Now the room looks fantastic and just how I dreamed it would. It is the most beautiful place I have ever lived in.

AW came home this evening and loved it all. We went for a walk together – everyone turns out and walks on the Boulevard by the sea in the evening, it's very pleasant. I saw a poor old beggar woman sitting on a chair at the side of the road so I pressed some money into her hand – at which point she screamed at me because she wasn't a beggar at all, just an old lady taking the air.

23 September

AW invited a Minister and his wife to lunch tomorrow. Starting four days ago, I have told Tarana every morning what the menu will be, but today she asked, via Rebecca, 'What will we give the Minister to eat tomorrow?' When we'd gone through it again – cold chicken curry and rice (my mother's secret recipe – a bit like Coronation Chicken actually, but nicer) with homemade chutney and other delicious side dishes – it turned out we didn't have half the ingredients so Rebecca and I had to dash to City Mart to get them.

City Mart sells all the things you can't get in the Green Market but at astonishing prices – leeks are a pound each, a head of celery is about a fiver, and a bottle of olive oil is twenty quid because it is imported, even though Azerbaijan is full of olive trees. We don't do much shopping there, though all the other ex-pats do I notice.

24 September

There was another electricity cut this morning, so frantic phone calls to the landlord's agent begging him to do something about it so that the Minister wouldn't have to walk up six flights of stairs. The power came back on again just in time, but then the lift wouldn't work so he and his wife had to walk anyway.

The good thing was we had lots to talk about at lunch because it had just been announced that President Bush is giving Wall Street $700 billion; the Minister said it was like giving a heroin addict a sack of heroin and telling him to get clean. They were charming people and Tarana's food was great – we were eight but there was enough to feed about twenty – and it all went well.

25 September

We had another lunch party today using the leftovers from the Minister's lunch. The bad news is that the curtains (now made to the correct measurements) have arrived at the airport. I have been dreading their arrival as they are all four metres long and I don't know how on earth we are going to put them up.

Later. I was moaning about the curtains to the UN wife, Catherine, and she has given me the number of some professional curtain people in Baku I didn't know existed.

I have got over my hoarding obsession, and now the problem with teaching Tarana to cook is that we have to eat all the dishes we make, so instead of a light salad at lunch we are eating pork with prunes in a cream sauce or chicken pie, plus chocolate cake or vanilla ice cream. We are going to be *enormous* by the time we leave here. I shall have to get out my special tummy-flattening roll-on again. I last wore it in Syria, at a cocktail party, and looked wonderfully slim, but we were unexpectedly asked to stay for dinner and when I sat down at the table all my constricted flesh suddenly popped out at the top, giving me a double layer of bosoms. It was a nasty shock for everyone.

29 September

I've discovered that Tarana and Rebecca have no sense of timing at all. The British Ambassador was coming to lunch today and twenty-five minutes before she was due Tarana asked me to show her how to make a cheesecake.

2 October

The Minister and his wife invited us to their dacha last night. It was astonishing: a cross between a Roman temple and a large mosque set in a lovely garden of palms and willows and water. We sat down to eat at 6 p.m. and continued until ten; there were *seven* courses of lamb done in different ways. First a *qutab* with minced lamb in it, then barbecued lamb, then lamb cutlets, then lamb kebab, then a kebab of minced lamb, then lamb cooked in the fat from the tail, and then, phew, lamb with rice. The meat was lean and meltingly tender and utterly delicious – lamb here seems to be a different creature to the one we have at home. Then there was homemade mountain sheep's cheese, fresh figs, cherries, pumpkin pancakes and the lightest crispy pastry rolls filled with nuts.

AW has discovered there is a local airline called Kras Airline, pronounced *Crash*.

4 October

Great excitement. The American Ambassador and her husband came to lunch today. The food didn't go quite right (pork with prunes came out more like pork in porridge) but they drank loads of wine and they came in two cars, one with bodyguards who sat in our hall the whole time. Rebecca was thrilled.

5 October

We had a glorious day today out on the peninsula, Absheron, that juts into the Caspian Sea. It's all islands and water and miles and miles of empty beach. Every now and again a helicopter would take off from somewhere nearby and head out over the waves to the Oil Rocks, which is a whole huge oil town built on stilts in the sea. You can't see it from the land, but it appears in the Bond film, *The World is Not Enough*. The only way to get there is by helicopter and with the permission of the Azerbaijani government.

Then Rovshan drove us to the other side of the peninsula where we found a nightmare scene of ancient oil wells and pumps and cranes sticking up out of an oily sludge covered with rubbish. All ex-Soviet countries seem to have unexplained hunks of concrete and metal sticking up out of the landscape, and desolate industrial areas, but here they reach an art form. The town of Songat, just outside Baku, has acres of abandoned chemical factories and is so astonishingly ugly and polluted that it is utterly fascinating – it could be a tourist destination in its own right. I am reading a book called *Blood and Oil in the Caucasus*, which tells of the appalling conditions that the early oil workers here suffered – going down the wood-lined shafts (as they do in the film *There Will Be Blood*) and working up to their necks in the oil. Dozens of them died in places like this.

On the way home we did a detour to see the Eternal Fires of Baku. This is a place where there are flames coming out of the side of a hill. There is a café there where you can sit and watch the earth on fire as it were, but it seems the flames are not nearly as ferocious as they used to be and the café owners fear the gas is running out. My parents had never been here, but they told me long ago about the Eternal Fires of Baku and I felt quite tearful thinking how amazed they would be if they knew their daughter was actually looking at them.

8 October

There is the presidential election coming up here in a week. Everyone says the President will win this election and then his wife will win the next one, and the one after that, and then his son will be old enough to win the one after. Or, as someone commented the other day, the votes are already counted.

9 October

Total panic today. It was all my fault. For some idiotic reason I decided to wash my hair before embarking on cooking lunch for the new French Ambassador and his wife, and I didn't leave enough time. We were to have a nice-looking salmon I found in the market, which we baked in foil with lots of herbs and butter and lemon and it looked great but tasted disgusting – just like solid pink castor oil. I tried to make a hollandaise sauce which curdled *twice* (I swear it's nerves that affect it) and I was beginning to panic.

Then AW arrived unexpectedly early with Claire, a charming French girl who works in his office (she was one of the guests), and I nearly died of embarrassment because I hadn't put on my make-up and nor had I brushed my hair and I looked like a mad witch. Claire calmed me down and told me to go and get ready and she would do another hollandaise sauce, and in the end we did get a reasonable meal on to the table. AW says I should chill out, and that nobody says to themselves, 'I will never forget the appalling meal we once had at the European Ambassador's Residence,' but I think they probably do.

Afterwards we wondered if the salmon tasted bitter because of the pollution in the Caspian Sea. It might be closed to humans but the fish aren't so lucky.

12 October

A friend from England, Georgina, has arrived in Baku as an election monitor. We first knew her in India where she had a cook called Gopal who was often drunk and would try and serve the courses at dinner the wrong way round, e.g., Coq au Vin as a starter and pâté as a main course. He once excused himself for being late by saying that his bicycle had slipped on a banana skin.

I am going to try my new eBay ice-cream maker out on her. I am becoming completely obsessed by cooking; I must try and think of something else.

14 October

The day I have been dreading – the day we are going to hang the curtains. Nigar made an appointment with the professional curtain man, Kamil, and he arrived on the dot with three helpers – they instantly became a small whirlwind of efficiency, rushing about the flat, ironing, putting up ladders, twitching, tweaking, and doing a fantastic job. I can't believe it: the room is done and looks incredibly elegant, a lot more ambassadorial, but still really pretty. The only thing is that the English firm who made the white curtain poles for the bedrooms threaded them with *black* cord. It's just like when the upholsterers in Kazakhstan put buckles on my chair covers – it's not something I would have warned them not to do because it wouldn't ever have occurred to me that it was a possibility. I think this is what Donald Rumsfeld meant by an 'unknown unknown'. There is nothing I can do about it, short of sending them back to London, so we'll just have to live with them.

Last night AW took some of the election-monitoring people out for dinner. There was a British Euro MP who actually likes Sarah Palin, our friend Georgina, a man who was introduced as 'the former failed presidential candidate from Slovenia', a Minister from Bulgaria, and various others. I liked the failed presidential candidate: he held me spell-bound with a story about being cured of cancer by a faith healer, then, towards the end of the evening, we *all* fell in love with him because he suddenly whipped out a mouth organ and gave us a beautiful little concert ending with 'Ode to Joy' (the EU national anthem).

AW and I decided that this was exactly the kind of evening, and precisely the types of people, that we will never again experience once we retire to Somerset, and that we will miss more than anything (even the Euro MP).

15 October, Election Day

There is not the slightest tension or suspense around as every-one knows what the result will be. I get the feeling though that people don't mind about the lack of democracy here, so much as the corruption – even the curtain people said that made life difficult. Here you have to pay to get a job, pay to get into school, pay to pass your exams . . . (AW says that the word for 'corruption' and the word for 'gratitude' are the same here). Someone told me that if you don't bribe the anaesthetist before an operation, he/she will wake you up in the middle.

The sceptical election mood here reminds me of a joke that was going around in Syria when we lived there and Hafez al-Assad, the father of Bashar, won a presidential election with an enormous majority. In the joke, Assad's staff are congratulating him on his tremendous victory: 'This is a magnificent result, Mr President,' they say. 'Ninety-nine-point-nine per cent of the Syrian people have voted for you – only point one per cent did not. What more could you ask for?'

'Their names,' says the President.

We joined more election monitors and observers for supper tonight; among them were two middle-aged Finns and a Swede who were all extraordinarily handsome – what is it with the Scandinavians? They make most Brits of the same age look red-faced and fat.

Frantic cooking at home all day as AW has invited twenty-two journalists for lunch tomorrow. They are all Azerbaijanis so, apart from the puddings (mine), Tarana is doing local food and I am not involved except to learn. Everything she is doing is stuffed and incredibly labour-intensive: stuffed cabbage leaves with quince; different stuffings for aubergines, tomatoes and peppers; stuffed vine leaves – and the main dish is chicken stuffed with nuts. It is all wonderful to taste and look at.

16 October

Found Tarana on her knees in the kitchen this morning kneading *qutab* bread on a board on the floor; the *qutab* is also stuffed, with herbs.

Later. Tarana's lunch was a real feast and the journalists tucked in as though it was their last meal on earth. She was so proud and happy.

24 October

I tried to show Tarana a seafood filling for pancakes today. Turned out she had never seen frozen prawns before and was as repulsed by them as I would be if someone showed me a packet of frozen caterpillars and tried to make me cook them. I had to do the filling while she stood in the corner making sick noises. When I went up to her with a spoonful and asked her if she'd like to taste the mixture (delicious) she screamed with horror. She'll never be able to do this recipe, that's for sure.

29 October

This morning Tarana grabbed Rebecca and pulled her clothes aside on her arms and legs to show me how she has padded herself, wrapping bandages round her limbs, so as not to look so thin. I nearly cried it was so sad. Why *is* she so thin? The German Ambassador's wife has told me of a clinic run by a Finnish doctor. I have made an appointment for Rebecca there, as the doctor AW found to check her could not discover anything wrong.

3 November

Went to the clinic with Rebecca. The doctor is going to run some tests.

AW is back from Brussels where he has been for a few days' training. Some time ago he complained to his boss about something and got a letter back saying, 'Please feel free to come and see me any time you are in Brussels. I believe in an open-door policy towards my valued delegates.' So while AW was there he tried to make an appointment with him but was told he was unavailable. We can't stop laughing about it.

5 November

Hurrah hurrah. Barack Obama is President of America! It feels like history – I want to rush out and embrace every black person I can see, but sadly there don't seem to be any in Azerbaijan – I've only ever seen one or two at the Catholic Mass on Sundays.

9 November

The weather has turned horrible, very windy and wet. I was thinking again of getting goggles for AW, when I read in an old book on Baku that in the oil barons' day people here *did* wear goggles because of the wind. Thinking of the past, apparently the Caspian Sea has so much oil in it that in the old days, people used to take a rowing boat out at night and set light to the water to amuse themselves. I am longing to go out and drop a match into the sea, but AW won't let me in case there is a giant conflagration which consumes the whole Bay of Baku.

AW and I went to the Armistice Day service organised by the British Ambassador. A Scottish ex-pat had volunteered to play the bagpipes – I am tone deaf so I couldn't judge, but the German Ambassador's daughter whispered, 'I don't know what bagpipes are supposed to sound like, but I am sure it isn't like this.'

In the evening we went to a talk given by Mark Elliott, who wrote the guidebook that took us around Azerbaijan so successfully earlier this year, and then it was dinner with the US Ambassador and her husband. They gave us a roast beef fillet that was incredibly tender. I've been round and round the market here trying to find beef that can be eaten without being stewed for ten hours, and given up, so I asked them where they got theirs, and they took us down to the kitchen to meet their chef who told me to talk to the butcher at City Mart who is a good friend of his. This could change my life.

10 November

Rushed to City Mart to find the butcher. He is called Ronaldo and is from the Philippines. He'd never heard of the American chef but was very helpful and I bought a whole beef fillet for much less than it would be in England.

13 November

Tarana yawned all through the cheese soufflé lesson this morning. We had to do it twice − not her fault − as it came out like a solid cake the first time (actually Tarana liked that better than the correct, lighter version). She is tired as they have rented out most of their house to make some money, and she and her five children (four girls, one boy) are sleeping in one room.

14 November

AW often has to go off in the middle of the night to meet and greet bigwigs from Brussels. Last night it was the EU Commissioner for Energy. AW got to the airport at 1.30 a.m. only to find that the commissioner had arrived forty-five minutes early (in a private plane) and was already en route to his hotel in the official government car with a police escort. This could have been really embarrassing for AW but Rovshan somehow got the mobile number of the police car and rang them to say 'slow down so that we can overtake you'. They did, and AW was able to step forward and greet the commissioner as he arrived at the hotel as though he'd been waiting there all evening instead of risking life and limb hurtling in from the airport at 110 miles an hour.

15 November

The car parking has got worse. There are more vehicles on the pavements than on the roads these days; yesterday Rebecca and I had to literally climb over a car with all our shopping to get to the front door.

I taught Tarana choux pastry this morning, but our little eclair puffs came out solid and looking like pale dog turds, so we did them again and they were perfect. I hate not knowing why something doesn't work; now that I am a cookery teacher I really *need* to know.

I walked to the office this afternoon and passed a new shop with the most elaborate fur coats I've ever seen. One had chinchilla, fox and mink all in the same coat. I had my nose pressed to the window because I thought I saw a leopard-skin coat at the back of the shop and was trying to see if it was real fur because, if so, I ought to report it to someone, but then the security guard came out of the shop and stood against the window giving me a hard stare so I left.

17 November

Rebecca went to the doctor again today. The blood tests didn't show anything wrong so we are all baffled about why she is so thin. I have given her a diet to follow but she hardly eats a thing. Maybe she has a secret eating disorder.

18 November

Someone in the office today told me that Fikret, our adorable gentle-giant security man/receptionist, has some leeches which he is going to put on his feet this evening. I asked Fikret if I could look at them and he showed me a jam jar with five horrible wriggly wormy things in it about five inches long, all frantically trying to get out of the jar – I can't stop imagining how *huge* they will be when full of blood. Aaargh. He bought them from his local chemist and they cost two *manats*, which is two euros. Apparently they are good for high blood pressure. Maybe we should get some for AW. I wonder if they are reusable.

21 November

It's my birthday today. I came out of the bedroom for breakfast and found Tarana and Rebecca waiting beside an *enormous* cake with a huge, pink plastic candelabra on it which played 'Happy Birthday'. I was so touched. I do love them.

The Belgian Ambassador came to lunch – we knew him in Syria when he was married to a fiery, unfaithful Colombian beauty who made him miserable, but now he has a sweet, gentle North Vietnamese wife, Phuong, who is an acupuncturist. She told us about her childhood spent in underground tunnels. Everything happened in those tunnels – school, eating, sleeping, playing – all in an effort to keep safe from the US bombing. Once, she left her tunnel to visit her sister in another one, and while she was away hers was blown up and all her friends were killed. She found their body parts in the trees around the crater. People in the West never thought about how the Vietnamese in the North lived – I certainly never knew that ordinary civilian families had to live in tunnels for *years*, and neither did I realise that two and a half million Vietnamese (soldiers and civilians) died in that pointless war, because we were only ever told about American casualties. Then I suddenly realised that Phuong must have been living in a tunnel in the North at the same time I was rather naively trying to be a war correspondent in the South and I felt humble.

The office gave a party for me this afternoon with *more* cake – I am now so fat that I am past caring. All my hopes rest on the Ayurvedic spa in Sri Lanka where AW is taking me for Christmas. He has planned this terrific treat because a) this is the first year *ever* that our children will not be with us since they are both going to their in-laws', and b) it is our thirty-sixth wedding anniversary in January and this is to be our celebration and present to each other.

Actually, to tell the truth, remembering the ferocious masseuse Tamara in Kazakhstan, I am not sure I am going to enjoy being massaged, but maybe it will help my back, which is still painful, not to mention my neck and shoulder and knees and feet . . . It's extraordinary how when one thing gets better something else goes wrong – right now it's watery eyes and cramps that are bothering me most. In *Bridget Jones's Diary* she wrote down her daily cigarette and alcohol consumption – at our age it makes more sense to list the new things that are hurting each day, and how badly on a scale of ten: Neck, 4½; Back, 8; Knee, 5, etc.

London, 2 December

I came back to London two days ago to get ready for our trip to the spa in Sri Lanka. Our last social engagement in Baku was dinner with the boss of a French oil company – he and his wife told us they were really worried because their son is going out with a girl who has feet two sizes bigger than his. Surreal: both the feet and the worry. Then I was in the office tidying up my things, when a strange man put his head round the door and told me he was reading *Dip Bag* in *Estonian*. I didn't even know it had been published in Estonia.

It was Malachy's nativity play at nursery this afternoon. I asked him what he was going to be in the play and he said, 'A digger!' (Why are all boys obsessed with diggers? How do they know about them? I don't think I knew they existed until I was a grown up.) When I told this to my friend Lesley she said, 'Ah, then it's not a nativity play; it's *Hamlet*.' Ha. Ha.

The thing that makes me laugh is that whenever Malachy or Maisie do *anything*, e.g., stand shyly on stage in the school play, do a poo, splosh some paint on a bit of paper, put a brick on top of another brick, or eat something – we all fall over ourselves saying: 'Wow, Malachy/Maisie! That's *brilliant*! That's the best acting/poo/picture/building/eating that has *ever been done, ever*! You are *amazing*!' I can't help thinking that perhaps they are going to feel failures later in life when they don't get this kind of response every time they go to the lavatory or swallow a forkful of spaghetti.

3 December

I could weep – none of the sweet pictures of Malachy *as an angel* in the nativity play that I took on my mobile phone yesterday came out. Instead there's a message on it saying MEMORY FULL. I know exactly how that feels, and wish I had a display screen on my forehead to tell everyone.

I am beginning to feel nervous about the Ayurvedic spa: you can't drink or smoke or have coffee there, and all the food is vegan. I have *never* not drunk or smoked for more than a day or two since I was about seventeen, and we are there for two weeks. I am wondering if I will have to be medevac-ed out. (AW has been saying that he is so exhausted he will probably have to be medevac-ed in.) Also, this whole expedition to a health spa is so unlike AW that I am beginning to suspect an ulterior motive. Will he spend the whole time doing Buddhist meditation? Is he going to take a vow of perpetual silence there? Or celibacy? What's going on?

7 December

Judging by AW's snoring last night I am setting off for two weeks of no smoking, no alcohol, no eating and *no sleep*.

12

Trouble at Spa

On plane to Sri Lanka, 8 December

I was woken up in the middle of a nice snooze by the membranes in my nose tingling – or cringing more like. It turned out AW had been to the loo and slathered himself with some sort of overwhelming Brut-type prizefighter's perfume. He cannot resist anything that is free.

On the last leg of our journey my fear of flying came back in a terrible rush because it suddenly occurred to me that if the plane crashed into the Indian Ocean we would be eaten by sharks.

Sri Lanka, 9 December

Very hot and sticky at Colombo airport, so I popped into the ladies' and changed into a 'loose' summer frock. I hadn't worn it for ages and it is as tight as a sausage skin. What an awful shock. Thank goodness we are going to lose weight here.

We are making our way down to the spa in a hired car with a nice driver called Somi, stopping off at Sri Lankan sites/sights en route.

It was a beautiful drive today, though it poured with rain most of the time: small villages, lovely green countryside, and we went to Dambulla caves and Sigiria and the Sri Lankan architect Geoffrey Bawa's famous hotel.

Kandy, 11 December

Today we drove to the truly beautiful Buddha stone statues at Polonnaruwa. Sri Lanka reminds me of India before high-rise developments and shopping malls took over. At one stage we passed some elephants bathing in a river. Somi pointed them out and commented, 'Those are working elephants taking a rest.'

AW said wistfully, 'I'd love to have a working elephant,' and I said, 'You have, me!'

Last night the man in the hotel room next to ours switched on his telly – volume on high – at midnight. He didn't turn it down when I asked him on the phone, so I had to get the hotel night manager to intervene, and by that time I felt utterly depressed and couldn't sleep anyway. It's the rain that is getting me down. I wasn't expecting it to be pouring all the time.

Weligama, South Sri Lanka, 12 December

We arrived at the spa in the dark and rain last night. I nearly got off to a bad start by falling into one of the trendy shallow black pools around the reception area. Geoffrey Bawa invented these for his own hotel and now everyone is doing them; they are lethal.

We had to be 'admitted' to the spa, as in a hospital, rather than 'registering' as in a normal hotel; frangipani garlands were put round our necks, and then we were shown our room where they'd given us a double bed instead of the two singles we'd asked for. My heart sank because of the snoring, but within minutes they'd wheeled in another. Then we went back to the charming receptionist to find out what we were supposed to do next. 'Would you like to see Dawn?'

she asked us. We wondered who that was and why we should see her, but it turned out she meant sunrise. Apparently lots of patients (guests?) like to do yoga outside at dawn. Not us.

We smoked our last cigarettes (for the time being anyway, I am telling myself) on our little veranda at 7 p.m. and then we wrapped the butts in loo paper and hid them in the wastepaper basket so no one would know our guilty secret.

We were shown to the restaurant for supper; it's a lovely room on the top floor with no windows, looking out over the sea. We were amazed to find that all the other people here are young and slim and good-looking – we'd expected them to be old and fat like us. But probably they are slim and good-looking *because* they come to places like this. They seem to be mostly German, which is not surprising either as Germans take health very seriously. There were bottles of yellowish-coloured liquid on their tables. 'What do you think is in those bottles?' whispered AW. 'You don't suppose it's urine?'

The starter course at dinner was a few thin slices of green beans, but we will know what our diet is to be after we see the doctor tomorrow.

13 December

The doctor was a nice plump lady in a sari who took our pulses. As she held each of our wrists she did a kind of low hypnotic chant which made us feel better already. Then she asked lots of questions. Do you have haemorrhoids? Do they bleed? What colour is your phlegm when you cough? How many motions do you pass a day? Are your stools loose or firm? (You only really hear that stool word in the subcontinent these days. When we were posted to India I had a permanently bad stomach and was constantly taking samples to various labs. As I set off with a new batch one day, AW said, 'You must be careful not to fall between two stools, ha ha ha.')

We wished we could have seen the doctor separately because we didn't know whether to lie, or answer her disgusting questions truthfully and reveal secrets we had attempted to hide for thirty-six years in order to keep some mystery in our marriage.

The one thing we should *not* have told her was that we both have a cholesterol problem, because she has put us on a *no fat* diet. Luckily we don't have to start this until tomorrow, so we were able to tuck into the buffet lunch with all the weird and wonderful veg cooked in delicious coconut milk, plus rice and hoppers (the most delicious Sri Lankan pancakes). Then we collected our Ayurvedic medicines; we have seven *each* – pills, liquids, powders, all of them absolutely disgusting.

This afternoon it wasn't raining and we went swimming and even though we sunbathed for only ten minutes, I got burned and by evening was bright red except for circles around my eyes, which, for some unaccountable reason, have stayed white so I look like a baboon – I didn't wear my sunglasses so it wasn't that.

AW bought a terrible red baseball cap in the bazaar when we first arrived in Sri Lanka. I told him that plump elderly men in caps look awful (e.g., Michael Moore) but he is wearing it doggedly. I don't know what the peak is made of – titanium? – but this afternoon he leaned over my deckchair to give me a kiss and the peak jabbed into my forehead really painfully – it was like being pecked by a giant parrot.

I bought my usual twenty identical black outfits to wear here but in fact you hardly ever put on normal clothes, everyone goes round in sarongs and flip-flops supplied by the hotel; in fact these are compulsory during the *two and a half hours* of treatments every day.

14 December

I slept really badly last night. I don't know if it was giving up cigarettes or alcohol or both but I lay there awake most of the night. Still, it's not as if we have anything very arduous to do.

We started our treatments today: they consist of acupuncture, body massage, face massage, head massage (quite painful as it pulls your hair), inhalations of hot steam with herbs. After all that they put oil pads on achy bits of your body (in my case that meant more or less all over) and then you lie, absorbing the oil for half an hour. (Just as I was drifting off to sleep a fly came and sat on my nose and I couldn't bat it off because of my hands being covered with the pads.) Then you have a shower to wash off all the grease, followed by a herbal bath. It sounds wonderful but I didn't really enjoy the treatments because I kept thinking of all of us reasonably well-off Western people coming here to be massaged and pampered by poor people and I thought how decadent that was. Plus, I am not sure I wouldn't be happier reading a book in the lovely garden. But you can't opt out, apparently – this is a treatment hotel, not a hotel with treatments.

Later. I have been reading about some of the schools and hospitals that the hotel and its guests support, not to mention the good things they did after the Tsunami, so maybe it's not so decadent after all. And of course it provides masses of employment and training for the locals – there are 120 staff from this town.

15 December

No sleep again last night. I just lie there with horrible surrealist thoughts spinning round my head and quietly panicking because I can't go home from a health resort and tell everyone how tired I am.

At breakfast today I was looking at the huge container ships passing on the distant horizon – I suppose there is some great East/West shipping lane out there. Then I thought about pirates, how easy it would be for them to capture these ships. So I asked the waiter if they had pirates in Sri Lanka and he said, 'Oh yes, madame, they are living down there by the beach and you can hear them at night.'

How extraordinary, I thought, fancy the hotel tolerating pirates on their land, and why can you hear them at night? I imagined them all sitting around wearing their eye patches noisily singing, 'Sixteen men on a dead man's chest, Yo Ho Ho and a Bottle of Rum' . . .

Then the waiter added, 'Yes, they are nesting in those trees and making a big noise in the evenings.' He thought I'd said parrots, not pirates – it's a good thing that's been cleared up, or I would have been puzzled all holiday.

We've been studying our fellow patients/guests. There is a poor mute man with his wife (AW says he doesn't think he's deaf as well because he can feel him listening as his wife talks); a handsome German who looks like Ralph Fiennes, so we call him the English Patient, with a glamorous partner, and then there is a fitness fanatic we have named the Red Baron. He looks like Leonardo da Vinci's famous drawing of the perfect man with arms stretched out in different positions. The first time I saw him he was doing a headstand with his legs folded in the yoga lotus position in mid-air, and I didn't recognise him as a human being at all, but thought I was looking at some kind of huge wide-headed beast that had got into the hotel gardens. I was quite shocked.

AW has to have an enema today. Before we set out from London he said I can take anything – no cigs, no booze, the diet, but I just couldn't handle having an enema, not ever. 'An *enema*?' I'd said. 'Don't be silly, who on earth is going to make you have an enema?' Now he has been *ordered* to have one by the doctor. See what I mean about the mystery in our marriage.

I felt slightly less homesick this afternoon when I discovered that you can do emails at the hotel, so I have managed to tell Hester and Claudia that we arrived safely and are okay. I found a message in my inbox from someone called Ninni who is a friend of a friend in London, inviting us for a drink at her house in nearby Galle. We will go and just have water.

16 December

We were weighed today and have hardly lost anything even though the Enforcer in the restaurant actually checks our plates at meals to make sure we haven't secreted some fat under a lettuce leaf. Are we going to be the only people in the history of health farms who spend two weeks dieting and don't lose weight? I can't bear it.

I had to have *Vashi* treatment today – am not sure what it was supposed to do, but it meant lying on my front while they built a sort of Great Wall of China in *pastry* around the edge of my back and then poured warm oil into the enclosure. (As I lay there I thought I must look just like some great pink lizard with a frill along its back.) It was very relaxing but hasn't made my back less painful.

17 December

I still can't sleep and am getting desperate. Is this what cold turkey feels like? I don't miss smoking or drinking during the day, but these awful nights with their surreal thoughts make me miserable and I want to go home. (I must have slept at some stage last night because I dreamed that Hester got married to her friend, Ramsay, and they made their home in the bottom of a swimming pool. This hasn't helped my mood.)

AW loves it here – he says he hasn't been so clean since he was a baby.

At lunch today the mute man *spoke* – turns out he was only keeping silent because he was having – or should it be doing? – *Shirodhara*, whatever that means. But on the other hand the handsome English Patient really is a patient, he has a motor neurone disease, like Stephen Hawking, and his wife has to feed him; it is so sad.

I love the newspapers here, though Sri Lankan names make the going tough – Balamugunthan, Tammraparnee, Paashavimochaka – by the time you've figured them out you've run out of newspaper-reading time. When we lived in Delhi I used to worry about reading Indian newspapers in the morning because I was brought up not to read novels before lunch and almost every story seemed so outlandish that it could have been fiction: MAN BITES SNAKE TO DEATH; STRAY DOG STEALS NEWBORN BABY FROM HOSPITAL; YOUNG GIRL KIDNAPPED FROM HER HOME TWELVE YEARS BEFORE TURNS UP ON DOORSTEP AS A BLIND BEGGAR AND IS RECOGNISED BY AN OLD SERVANT AND SAVED. There are not quite as many lurid items in the papers here. So far my favourite is about a group of people in a Sri Lankan town who have formed a Laughing Club. They meet every morning for half an hour and just stand there laughing. There was a photograph of them all doing this, which made me burst out laughing too.

18 December

We had a great day out today. We hired the hotel car and went to Galle to have a look around and visit Ninni. She has a beautiful merchant's house within the old fort, which she has restored from scratch, and she spends her winters here. It is my dream come true really, but then again AW and I couldn't live half the year so far from our family in London. Also, I imagine there's a very small ex-pat society here and I would spend my life worrying about why Geoffrey Dobbs (he is the big cheese who organises the Galle Literary Festival) hasn't invited us to dinner and things like that. Also, not sure I could live in a hot steamy climate where it rains every day – my hair is always limp here, and my eye make-up smudged. Ninni offered us wine but we stuck to water and funnily enough we weren't even tempted to smoke or drink.

19 December

I slept so badly and wanted to go home so much that AW let me have a lie-in until 7 a.m. This is one of the weird things here: I quite happily go to bed at 9.30 or 10, lights out at 10.30 latest, and then up with AW at 6.30 a.m. If only I can keep this up back home my life will be changed for ever.

AW says he is sick of me rushing up to people saying, 'Hello, I am Brigid, I haven't slept for four nights and I can't stop crying. Is this normal?' But today I blurted all this out to a nice woman who had just arrived, and she said she would give me a sleeping tablet at dinner. I feel better already.

I think AW has developed Stockholm syndrome: he is completely besotted by the acupuncture lady as well as the lovely Dr Pushpa, who asks all the embarrassing questions. I've noticed that during the acupuncture sessions, when he is lying there with the needles sticking out of his body, he follows the acupuncturist round the room with his eyes, and last night at supper when he spotted Dr Pushpa in the restaurant he said, 'Do you think I should go and tell her about my enema results?' (I advised not.)

In the afternoons here they serve herbal teas in the living room and this has become a sort of parish-pump or office water-cooler assembly point for chatting. Today I poured myself a cup, and the man next to me in the queue said, 'Black tea gives you constipation.' I said, 'You would never say that to me in London.'

True to her promise the nice new woman slipped me a sleeping tablet this evening while we were having dinner.

20 December

I took my pill last night and was asleep before my head crashed on to the pillow and I woke up this morning feeling miles better – in fact I am now feeling quite sorry that we have only a week to go.

Today I rang the Catholic priest in town to ask about Christmas services. He said he would do one in English at 8 a.m., if we can get enough people to come. The hotel manager says she will put up a notice. We have made a friend, a very nice young woman called Adrienne who is Chinese-American, descended from one of the Chinese 'coolies' taken to the US in the nineteenth century to build the railroads. Her ancestor should have been shipped back to China, but in the Great San Francisco Earthquake of 1906, records were destroyed and he was able to assume a new identity and stay on.

Adrienne told us that she was offered drugs the very first time she set foot on the beach outside the hotel. AW and I feel a bit disappointed that no one has offered us any . . . we don't want them, but being excluded makes us feel old. It's how I felt when a new girl in the office in Azerbaijan complained about being sexually harassed in the streets of Baku – something that has never happened to me.

22 December

We have been asked to a party! Ninni, the nice woman who lives in Galle, has invited us to her Christmas revels. We can't accept though as a) it's the day AW is having oil poured up his nose and I am having oil poured on my head, and b) because we don't remember how to behave in the outside world any more and I might find myself asking Geoffrey Dobbs about his bowel movements or phlegm colour.

AW is reading a very serious book on *Ayurveda for Health and Family Welfare*, and has found this sentence: 'If one wants to attain salivation by means of correct living . . .' We attain salivation every time we go into the dining room.

23 December

I woke up this morning thinking there is no point in living if I can't have a cigarette, but a) we are not *allowed* to smoke here, which helps, and b) I haven't got any.

The hotel is filling up for Christmas: a party of ten friends has just arrived. Strange: I can't imagine AW and I suggesting to eight of our pals that we should all go to an Ayurvedic spa for Christmas. It is weird being in the tropics at this time of year and watching the tinsel swags and cardboard Santas going up to background music of 'Rudolph the Red-Nosed Reindeer' – it's like spending Christmas in Oxford Street.

Talking about weird, I went to reception today to ask about shopping over Christmas. 'Please could you tell me,' I asked the young man behind the counter, 'whether the shops in Galle will be open on Christmas Eve and on Christmas Day, because I need to buy some things, but I don't want to order a taxi and go into town if everything is going to be shut.'

There was a long pause while he tried to work out what I'd said, and then he replied in a voice of puzzlement tinged with hope, 'Elephant, madame?'

AW and I went over my rather rambling question several times this evening, wondering at what point in it the receptionist could have imagined I was ordering an elephant. Now every time I think of it I get the giggles.

25 December

Today the hotel gave us each a T-shirt for Christmas. AW's was XL and mine was L, so you can see what they think of our shapes.

I had the oil-dripped-on-forehead experience yesterday morning (while AW was having oil poured up his nose, yuk). It is meant to be the most relaxing treatment of all, but the clay pot that holds the oil is placed on a tripod just above your head and I kept imagining it crashing on to my face if the tripod gave way. When I managed to put that thought out of my head though, it was a pleasant sensation and I did feel extremely calm – which lasted until I fell over in the dining room at supper last night.

I was making my way through the tables to show Dr Pushpa a tiny ant bite on my finger when I slipped and crashed to the ground, bringing a chair down with me and making the most stupendous noise, so that every single person turned to stare. I lay on the floor for quite a while before anyone helped me up – I think I was such a horrible sight with my greasy un-made-up face, and oily clothes and hair (you are not allowed to wash your hair for twenty-four hours after an oil-dripping treatment), that no one felt like touching me with their bare hands.

Eventually AW and the doctor got me up and took me down to her office, where they left me to rest with a herb poultice on my spine while they went off to listen to the Catholic church choir which had come to entertain the guests. In all the drama I had forgotten it was Christmas Eve and as I lay there alone, with my back hurting, listening to the distant sound of 'Jingle Bells', I had a quiet cry. I had really begun to enjoy being here and was feeling sorry that we had only three days left, and now even those looked as if they were ruined.

26 December

Had a terrible night, but this morning Adrienne gave me some painkillers and with AW's help I managed to limp to church with him and the six others who'd put their name on the list for Christmas Day Mass, and hobble back again.

All diets were cancelled today and we could eat as much as we wanted of anything – plus there was roast turkey, the first meat we've seen for two weeks. AW and I, overseen by the Enforcer, have been really good about our diet, but it hasn't made much difference; Lesley, who recommended this place, lost a *stone*. On the other hand, we have given up smoking and I am going to try not to start again because I never want to go through the cold-turkey process again, ever.

13

Spouse Seize-Up

Somerset, 10 January

The last time I wrote my diary was Boxing Day in Sri Lanka.
The following morning, disaster struck. AW was down by
the pool when he slipped and, in an effort to regain his
balance, he twisted his body around and did something to his
back. He was in agony, could barely walk, and even lying
down was torture for him. The hotel people were very
concerned and told us about an Ayurvedic physiotherapist in
Colombo who might be able to help, and I arranged to stop
there on our way to the airport. We set off for our five-hour
drive in the hotel car padded with pillows for AW to lie on,
but even so it was painful for him – and for me as well – my
back problem didn't disappear when AW's started.

We found the Ayurvedic physio who lived in a house
completely cluttered with the sort of brass and glass and china
ornaments that you pray people will never give you. He told
us that the President was one of his patients ('He has a problem with his bottom') and he wrenched AW and me around
extremely painfully. I think it made everything worse. We
had hours to go before the plane left, and our driver took us
to wait in a seedy hotel by the airport, which plunged us into
even deeper gloom. Our lovely Ayurvedic spa by the sea
turned into a distant dream of paradise.

At the airport they put AW into a wheelchair, because he couldn't walk, and arranged for us both to be met with wheelchairs in London. I didn't know whether to scream with laughter or lie on the floor and sob – we've just spent two weeks in a *health resort*, and now we are being met with wheelchairs in London. It reminds me of the Irish joke about a man who goes to Spain on holiday and then dies on his return to Ireland. A mourner at his wake passes his open coffin, sees his suntanned face and says, 'Sure, that holiday did Kevin the world of good.'

At Gatwick a smartly dressed, good-looking man drove the nippy little vehicle that whizzed us through baggage collection and emigration. He told us that he used to work for Croydon Council on major projects, but when he retired he thought it would be fun to chauffeur the buggy for the old and disabled at the airport. He sounded as if he was enjoying this more than his real career.

The Ayurvedic physio in Colombo said AW had a torn muscle, so did our local doctor, so did Shepton Mallet hospital; they all said no treatment needed, it will get better on its own. When it didn't I arranged a scan which revealed AW had slipped two discs and might need an operation, but in the meantime they gave him an injection to take away the pain, which didn't work.

AW is miserable: he can't read, he can't work, he can't talk, and he is grumpy and angry. I think he is also going slightly mad. He keeps getting up at five in the morning, instead of seven, and the other day he lost his contact lenses and then found them in his eyes. I feel so sorry for him being in such pain and I don't know how to help. I have been invited to do a gig at the Jaipur Literature Festival in ten days' time and I don't know what to do about that either.

AW's retirement is coming up this year and if it's going to be anything like this, living in Somerset in the freezing cold with him in pain and in a terrible mood, I really think I may have to make a bid for freedom. I am trying hard to cling to the advice for a happy marriage I was given years ago: *be nice to each other*. Show your husband/wife you love them, even if you don't at that moment. I suddenly see how fragile a partnership is. I've been vaguely plotting our lives when AW stops work and how we will live cosily in Somerset together, travelling a bit, having the grandchildren at weekends – never thinking that at any moment either one of us could have a stroke, or become ill or disabled – or slip by a swimming pool – and suddenly, instead of the friend and companion you have lived with most of your life, you have a grumpy patient or, perhaps, nobody at all. I think a lot about my father who looked after our poor mother when she got Alzheimer's, it must have been so sad for him. I have never really thought about any of this before, but today is our thirty-sixth wedding anniversary, and I never imagined it would be like this.

28 January

AW said I should go to the Jaipur Festival – he actually seemed quite keen to get rid of me. So I set up a good support network in London for the week I was to be away: lots of food in the fridge/freezer; Hester and Claudia to oversee everything; and lists of friends who'd offered to come and keep him company, and then I left. As soon as I'd gone, he rang one of the friends and persuaded her to take him to the station to catch the train to Somerset where there was no food and nothing organised, and our neighbours had to look after him until Hester arrived on an emergency visit at the weekend.

Meanwhile, out in Jaipur I was having a lovely time but was racked with guilt. I got daily calls from Hester and Claudia reporting on AW's state. After five days they said, 'Mum you've got to come back, Dad's bonkers,' so I went home. (In Jaipur, people seemed to be fascinated by my lack of a husband: 'Is your husband dead?' they kept asking me, or, 'When did your husband die?')

AW was quite cross to see me home, and he'd drunk every single bottle of wine in the house. He wasn't at all interested in how my sessions at Jaipur had gone, and he didn't crack a smile when I told him I'd asked a waiter in Jaipur whether the curry he was serving was chicken and he said, 'No, madame, it is hen.' Nor that I had put my bag in the wash-basin on the plane, not realising that this would activate the tap so that everything in it was soaked.

London, 6 February

Something extraordinary has happened. I brought AW up to London to have another injection yesterday and he woke up this morning *pain free and totally sane and normal*. I just can't believe it and want to sprint round London screaming for joy. He can't even remember most of the past six weeks, which is probably just as well. He is planning to go back to work in Azerbaijan in ten days. What happened? I don't understand it, but it is like a miracle.

You are never allowed to be totally happy in this life, so today was the day I got a nasty email from a reader saying that there was not a single original word in *Dip Bag* and that I had stolen all *her* funny stories – 'with which I used to regale the dinner-party guests abroad'. She went on to say that she was '*not surprised*' to hear what Margaret Beckett had to say about us in the House of Commons. I was intrigued. I had no idea

Margaret Beckett (who had been Foreign Secretary for a short time) ever said anything about us.

When I looked into this, I learned a question had been asked in the House of Commons ages ago, about how and why permission was given by the Foreign Office for *Diplomatic Baggage* to be published, and that Margaret Beckett had replied that Brigid Keenan and her husband were 'not known to the British Foreign Office'. This is because AW works for the European Commission, but the reader took it to mean that he is only pretending to be a diplomat. (A bit like a friend of ours, Erica, who once said, 'I think you and AW live very quietly in Bournemouth where you make up outlandish stories about your lives. Then you come up to London "on leave" once or twice a year, and tell them to your friends.')

4 March

Just before leaving London to follow AW back to Azerbaijan, I got a message from Westminster Council to say that I was one of *only fifty people* in the whole borough to be selected to try a new phone system designed to help the elderly. The phone has a button on it that says I'M OKAY and you have to press this every morning and every evening. If you don't press it they ring you back, and if there is no reply they contact your relatives. I don't consider myself elderly, but I do know that I will forget to press the button every morning and that Hester and Claudia will be driven totally insane by calls from the council every day. I telephoned and told them I was going abroad, which is true.

We have been preparing our Palfest programme for this May. I am over the moon because I invited Michael Palin to come and – out of the blue – he said yes. It turns out that he has read Raja Shehadeh's prize-winning book *Palestinian Walks*, and is intrigued to know more.

Baku, 16 March

Since I was last in Baku a couple of months ago they have started building the World's Tallest Flagpole, and they've invented a new kind of fountain which doesn't just have lights that change colour in the water, but spews out *real* gobbets of fire.

Other changes: after the election last autumn there was a government reshuffle and our Minister friend is now an ex-Minister. He and his wife came to lunch two days ago and I was talking about the seven courses of lamb they served at their dinner in the dacha and how I can never find lamb in the market as delicious as theirs, and this morning there was a man at the door with half a sheep in a big box.

In the Fifties, middle class girls like me were often sent off to 'finish', i.e. have our social skills polished, instead of our brains at university. My finishing school didn't teach me butchery so Rovshan and I heaved it to City Mart where Ronaldo cut it up into joints for me.

17 March

St Patrick's Day today but no one thinks about that here, it's all preparations for the Nowruz spring festival. This is death to dicting as everyone gives everyone else boxes of baklava, which was invented in Azerbaijan. This is not baklava as we know it from Turkish or Arab shops in London, but home-made and much nuttier and less sweet and irresistible.

The weather is terrible: howling wind, rain, sleet, snow. People say this is normal – it is winter fighting off spring.

18 March

We have no clue as to when Brussels want AW to retire. It should normally be in June, but he has requested to stay on until September and no one has responded.

In the meantime there is a referendum being held in Azerbaijan today – it is to hear the voice of the people – ha ha ha – on the subject of whether the President's rule should have any time limit; at present he cannot serve more than two four-year terms and he is in his second one now. Everyone knows that the answer will be a resounding 'No' so he can stay in power for ever.

The Belgian Ambassador's wife, Phuong, from North Vietnam, came round today to learn how to make our cheesecake (she said she dreams of it!) and to teach us her spring rolls. It was good fun all cooking together.

20 March

We had the Mayor of Baku's Old City to lunch today. He is a very nice, sincere man and I don't know how he copes with his bosses' demands for new façades and coloured fountains that shoot out flames, etc.

I have started my cookery lessons with Tarana again and my obsession with food has come back worse than ever. I am driving AW (and myself) mad with uncertainty about menus. Before the mayor's lunch I wandered round for days asking anyone who'd listen, 'Should we have cheese soufflés, followed by salmon, or cold salmon followed by beef stroganoff, or should we have spinach roulade followed by moussaka, or should we have' . . . until AW exploded, made a decision (cold salmon with mayonnaise and chicken faisinjan), and wouldn't let me change it. I was so grateful because if my dithering had gone on much longer I would probably have had to be carried off in a straitjacket, still gibbering, 'Or should we have pork with . . .'

It didn't happen this time, but there's another disconcerting thing about menus: just when you've finally decided what to have, you realise that every course you've chosen looks exactly the same as the next one, i.e., they are all white and creamy, or red (beetroot, tomato sauce, strawberry sorbet) or they all have crumbs on them. AW says he is sick to death of all this talk about food, but he does wonder whether Napoleon ever ate beef Wellington.

20 March

The President has just been celebrating his victory in the referendum with a visit to the Old City. I watched him leaving from our balcony. As he got into his car all the officials around him started clapping. Clapping in ex-Soviet countries goes on for hours because in the old communist days no one dared be the person who stopped first, and they have got into the habit. In this case they were spared the exhaustion of clapping for forty-five minutes by the President's car sweeping away.

23 March

AW and I are just back from Lankaran where we went for a romantic weekend (AW says that at our age these should be called *rheumatic* weekends) to celebrate the festival of Nowruz. Lankaran is the southernmost part of Azerbaijan, down on the border with Iran. It's a lush, green area (they grow rice there) where, in the days of the oil barons, tankers used to load up with the rich soil and take it to arid

Baku for parks and gardens. The people who come from this area (including Rebecca and Tarana) are called Talish; they are an Iranian people who speak Farsi and cook Persian-type food – which is why Tarana can make *faisinjan* so well. It was lovely down there: we picnicked in a valley with a stream and old poplar trees; the people seem freer away from Baku (we met an old man in a village who laughed about the 'referendum' and said the President and his family were a bunch of mafia crooks) and the food was wonderful. Rovshan took us to tea with some friends of his who served huge platters of baklava, and the good part was that you couldn't refuse or it would have been an insult.

On the way home we photographed bus stops. Soviet bus stops tend to be artworks in themselves, and these were typical – each cement shelter was covered with mosaic to look like a Persian carpet. They won't be photogenic for long though, all the mosaic is peeling off. It's a pity they don't restore the bus stops instead of building the World's Tallest Flagpole.

Happy news! Claudia is having another baby, due in November – that's one thing to look forward to in retirement.

5 May

At dinner last night (Madhur Jaffrey's lamb and apricot pilaf, delicious, everyone had seconds) one of the women guests started a discussion about middle-aged European men running off with girls in the ex-Soviet Union and Eastern Europe, and the only middle-aged European man at the dinner (not counting AW) said that we women didn't understand, it wasn't about sex. 'These girls are crazy, magic; they don't care about the future – and this is what European men, bogged down in their jobs, find irresistible.'

We cynical women round the table agreed that 'crazy' and 'magic' were just other ways of saying *young*, and that the difference is that in Europe, young girls mostly don't even glance at middle-aged men because they don't need anything from them, whereas in places like Azerbaijan middle-aged European men are a ticket out of the country to a better future.

10 May

Today is Flower Day, when Azerbaijan celebrates the birth-day of Haydar Aliyev, the President's father and hero of the nation. There are rumours of a protest march– this is because *twelve people* – students and staff members – were killed by a rogue gunman in Baku's Oil Academy ten days ago, and there has been no official statement, no explanation, and no mourning period. The President has just ignored the whole thing, and it seems that now, for the first time, his people are upset with him for showing disrespect to the dead.

Later. The demo didn't have a chance to get off the ground because of the mass of armed 'security' blocking every road and preventing the protestors assembling. Several students have been arrested, including one of AW's friends.

11 May

The students have been released, but suddenly I sense a feel-ing of simmering resentment. I don't think I'd bet on this President dying in office at a great old age.

Almost lost my rag with Tarana today: I was trying to teach her Moroccan chicken pie but she kept turning away to chat to her daughter Sevil who'd dropped by, so I called Rebecca and said, 'Tell your mother I am giving up my time to teaching her so that she will never be out of work, but if she'd rather stop now, then just tell me.' There was a moment's shocked silence and then Tarana said she wanted to go on with the lessons and we all made friends again, and I felt a bit silly. Sometimes I think this is all a total waste of time and it would be a lot easier if I just cooked it all myself, but I really do want to see Rebecca and Tarana set up for life.

AW has sent lots of questions back to Brussels about his retirement – first and foremost, when is it supposed to be happening? Today he got a reply saying, 'Thank you for your questions, they will be answered within three months.' He wrote back: 'I am due to leave in six weeks; can't wait three months.' Since then, nothing.

This doesn't fill us with mad enthusiasm for our Europe Day party, which is coming up in three days' time. AW is on the verge of his annual panic about no guests turning up, and will soon be out in the streets asking passing strangers and tramps to attend. I have just realised that whether we retire in June or September this is the last Europe Day party we will ever have to host. *Hurrah!* It's the stress of it all, i.e., the wine suppliers have told AW that they have delivered the drinks for the party but no one seems to know where they've delivered them to – certainly not the EU office.

15 May

The wine was found, the party was a great success, and I enjoyed it – even though I realise I can't really wear high heels any more because my feet hurt too much.

My only gaffe was welcoming the Indian Ambassador and asking where he was from, as though I'd never seen him before. He said, 'I am the Indian Ambassador and I sat next to you at dinner at the Belgian Residence for three hours the other evening.' It's no use, I just can't remember faces, or names – or much of anything come to think of it.

14

Close Encounters with the Israeli Army

London, 17 May

I have just arrived back in London on my way to Palestine for our second Festival of Literature. We have a wonderful line-up of people, including Deborah Moggach, Michael Palin and Henning Mankell of Swedish detective Wallander fame. We will all meet up in Amman as we did last year and make our way to Israel by coach.

Just before I left Azerbaijan I taught Tarana how to make a Chinese stir-fry and she was going to do one for AW's lunch today. When I rang him to say I'd arrived safely, he said the stir-fry was delicious, but she'd served it with roast potatoes. Oh God . . .

Jerusalem, 23 May

We were held up at the crossing between Jordan and Israel for four and a half hours, just as we were last year, when the Israeli soldiers took all our guests with Arab names for 'questioning' while the rest of us waited with various degrees of patience. Of course, if you show signs of being cross or impatient they will make you wait longer, or possibly refuse you entry. At one stage I saw Carmen Callil stomping back through the terminal building towards the immigration officials, and I knew I had to stop her. 'Carmen,' I said, rushing up, 'where are you going?'

'I am just going to ask them what the *fuck* they think they are doing.' I dragged her back.

We arrived in Jerusalem with just enough time to change before our opening event. I sat next to Michael Palin on the coach from the border because he was my guest, though I hoped he wouldn't think I was stalking him. He has a reputation for being The Nicest Man in the World. We'll soon see.

We all walked together from the hotel down to the Palestine National Theatre for our opening event, but when we arrived there we found a group of Israeli soldiers in full body armour with guns, who told us all to leave. I went up to a group of them to ask what was going on, but they pretended they only spoke Arabic, and I forgot the First Rule of Living Abroad which is never ever have a row in a language you don't speak properly because you are bound to make a fool of yourself. They laughed at me.

None of the soldiers offered any explanation as to why they were throwing us all out and closing the theatre. They didn't need to: they had all the power and could just stand there with their guns, looking us in the eyes with a triumphant smirk, and there wasn't a darned thing any of us could do about it. We felt utterly impotent, but at least we had the luxury of being able to lose our tempers, which Palestinians can never do.

As we milled about, unsure what to do next, the French cultural attaché, one of the guests, announced that his office was down the road and we could hold our opening event in his garden. So once again, we all traipsed off together, performers and audience now, passing dozens of Israeli soldiers, and noticing that all the roads to the theatre had been blocked by armoured cars.

Henning Mankell spoke first and pulled the whole evening together. He was brilliant, and so were all the writers who spoke after him and, because we were all bonded together in adversity, it went more triumphantly than it would have done in the theatre.

I don't think I have ever been in a country in which people don't even try to disguise their unpleasantness with a veneer of politeness. In Israel they don't seem to be embarrassed to be rude and unpleasant. It is quite hard to take when you are used to living in Europe.

Ramallah, 24 June

Today we met up with Raja Shehadeh, author of *Palestinian Walks*. He took us on one in territory Palestinians are not supposed to enter, so we could have been arrested at any time. We walked up a stony hillside dotted with old olive trees and scrubby sweet-smelling herbs; it was hot and the slope was steep – more of a climb really – and we looked such a funny lot in our various outfits, none of them suitable for tramping round the Palestinian countryside. I walked with Deborah Moggach and Michael Palin. It was most peculiar being in the Holy Land with the star of *The Life of Brian*: I kept thinking everything was a stage set – there was even a huge hole in the ground and I wondered if we'd find an old hermit living in it, like the one in the film. Michael told us that when they filmed the scene of the crucifixion there were bicycle saddles nailed to the crosses so that the actors were supported. Even so, he said, it was extremely uncomfortable being up there for an hour at a time and they'd call out, 'Hurry up! Get a move on . . . We're being crucified here!'

25 May

We hear that the Scandinavian papers are full of outrage about Henning Mankell being thrown out of the theatre. I said to Michael Palin, 'You'd think the British would be outraged about *you* being thrown out,' and he said wistfully, 'Oh I don't know, I can just hear them on the *Today* programme, "Let's drop that piece about hedge-clipping, oh, and yes, let's cut Michael Palin on the West Bank."'

Today was one of the most exciting of my whole life. Our bus took us to the Freedom Theatre in the refugee camp in Jenin, where Henning Mankell and Michael Palin were going to do workshops for the young Palestinian actors there. The drama students had prepared two pieces for us to see. They acted them very well, but then Henning Mankell went on stage and showed them some simple ways of making their plays even better. (He has a theatre company in Mozambique.) After that Michael Palin got them to act with him. They all performed so well I got goose bumps.

This evening, instead of our usual literary panel discussion with different authors, the Palestinian-American hip-hop poet Suheir Hammad thrilled the crowd as she did last year. She is mesmerising. (You can watch her on YouTube.)

Bethlehem, 26 May

It took ages to get through the Qalandia checkpoint this morning leaving Ramallah for Bethlehem. The young Israeli soldiers made us fetch our luggage from the bus, open it up to be inspected, and then take it back to the bus again. And all the time we were doing this they were puffing away on cigarettes and deliberately blowing the smoke into our faces. I wanted to scream and punch them, but of course, you can't.

I haven't smoked for five months, but after this I very nearly had a cigarette myself – then my mates on the bus said that if I did, it would mean the Israelis had won, so I held firm.

Bethlehem, 27 May

Michael Palin has left – he's gone to the literary festival in St Malo (when he told me this yesterday I thought he said it was in *Somalia*). He has passed the test: he *is* The Nicest Man in the World, everyone on the trip agrees. We will miss him.

Today was an awful day. We went to Hebron where we found the situation even worse than last year. There is an Israeli tourist shop in the centre of town playing such deafeningly loud music that it drives everyone in the vicinity mad – apparently it goes on all day and night. As we strolled down the short stretch of road on which Palestinians are allowed to walk, I noticed a settler filming us. 'Hi!' I said to him in a friendly way. 'I see you are filming us and I just wondered who you are working for? Is it for television?' I never expected his reply.

'I am filming you for God [except he said *Gahd*]!' he shouted.

'Why on earth does God want you to film us?' I asked.

'Because God wants you to GO TO HELL!' he yelled. Then he put his face next to mine and spat, 'GO TO HELL!'

'You'll be in Hell before me,' I yelled back as I walked away, trembling with rage.

Jerusalem, 27 May

The writers did brilliant workshops at Hebron University yesterday but today everyone is taking time off to visit the mosques on the Holy Mount.

After last year's difficulties, Ahdaf had arranged this in advance so that when our group arrived at the gate we were met by an elderly Muslim cleric who issued us with scarves to put over our heads and skirts to put over our trousers before we went into the sacred places. We got dressed under the eyes of the Israeli soldiers guarding the gate. They watched us, waited until we were all ready, and then told us we could not go in. So we walked round to another entrance, the 'temporary' one near the Wailing Wall, where there are two checkpoints. We were stopped at the second one and forbidden to enter. No reason was given. We asked if we could talk to a senior officer. No one would answer us; they just remained silent. It's an effective technique I'd never thought of before.

I had lunch with a friend of AW's, the EC Representative in Jerusalem, and asked him, 'How do people stand it? How do they cope with this?'

'The only way to deal with life here,' he replied, 'is to detach – to separate yourself from it. Otherwise you would go mad.'

The Israelis closed our theatre again this evening, our last night. We thought they probably would, so we'd arranged to hold our final event – writers reading some of their favourite passages from books – in the British Consul's garden, and then we all had a celebratory dinner together.

Everyone told us we'd have a terrible time at Tel Aviv airport if they discovered we had been travelling in the West Bank, so the six of us going home to London together this morning were not only exhausted from our stressful days in Palestine, but quite scared about being questioned by the young women soldiers. As we stood in line, waiting our turn, I sighed and said, 'Oh I just can't *wait* to be back in London.' Then I panicked because that sounded as though I didn't like

Israel and the soldiers might keep me here for ever as a punishment. I tried to compensate by saying that I was homesick for my family but by now I was so nervous that this came out in a high girlish voice as 'I miss my little *babies*' – that and the idea of me having any babies at my age set us all laughing until tears poured down our faces, and all the more so because we knew we were getting up the noses of the guards – just like that unstoppable laughter that overwhelms you in church when you are a child and you know you must be quiet or you'll get into trouble.

15

Packing Up

I got back to Azerbaijan yesterday to find that Tarana has no teeth. When I gawped at the sight of her, she and Rebecca fell around laughing, and then told me that Tarana had had agonising pains in her gums for a few days, and then all her teeth fell out. What could that be? I can't think of anything except radiation sickness? (Nicole, head of the British Council here, always brings loads of food back from the UK with her because she is so scared of the pollution in Baku.)

While I was away the World's Tallest Flagpole in Baku was overtaken by one in some other country, and they have had to add six metres on to the height to keep the title.

12 June

Ages ago AW and I decided not to bother watching the American TV hit series *The Wire* because Hester said that we wouldn't understand a word anyone was saying, but we suddenly realised we could watch it *with subtitles* and so I have borrowed her boxed set and brought it back with me and we are now totally gripped and mentally living in Baltimore. (But I am also still half in Palestine which is obviously why last night I dreamed about McNulty meeting Yasser Arafat.)

15 June

AW and I have had to give up watching *The Wire* for the time being, we are getting too keyed up and involved and have begun to think that McNulty and Kima are our friends. Whenever problems or decisions have come up recently we've been only half joking when we've said, 'Hmm, we must talk to Kima about that, she'll know what to do.'

We still haven't heard about our departure day. Wouldn't it be awful if they suddenly said, 'You don't have an extension until September, you are leaving in ten days.'

Getting the table ready for a dinner party this evening I suddenly thought of Anna Wintour, the editor of American *Vogue*. She is English, but apparently once said to someone that she couldn't live in London, 'Because there is nowhere to wear one's clothes.' Looking ahead to our retirement, I realise that there will be nowhere back home to use one's six sets of salt and peppers, or one's enormous saucepans, or one's huge serving plates.

16 June

Betty Blair (editor of *Azerbaijan International*) and I went to look at the houses that are being pulled down in the kilometre-long redevelopment in the centre of town. We found an extraordinary oil baron's house with the grandest cut-stone façade and gracious high-ceilinged rooms with lovely plaster-work and frescos – but it is all going to be demolished in a couple of months. The house owners and tenants who are being evicted from this area are very upset because they are not being given enough money to be able to rent or buy anything else reasonably central; the only accommodation on offer for them seems to be in big apartment blocks way out of town.

On the way home, Betty and I looked at the 'Atlas House'. This is a famous building in Baku: it has four huge, stone figures of Atlas holding up its balconies, but now it has the forlorn look of a house that is about to be demolished. There is an empty lot on one side of it and another grand-but-dilapidated mansion on the other (the old Georgian Embassy), so someone is obviously going to develop the three plots together. So sad, as this is a pretty and untouched part of town.

My feet have been hurting so much recently that I looked up my symptoms on the Internet today and discovered I have something called *metatarsalgia* which sounds good, but just means painful feet. It's amazing how much better you feel, though, when there is a name for your symptoms; I suppose that's because it means you can't be the only person on earth suffering from them.

6 July

AW and I have been invited to attend a retirement course in Brussels, and I am now locked in a dispute with the European Commission. AW is having his ticket paid back to Belgium to do the course, but it seems I have to pay my own way from Azerbaijan. I wrote to AW's boss saying that wasn't fair because I am only in Azerbaijan because of AW's job, but he wrote back saying too bad, they have no contractual obligation to me. I am furious – *contractual obligation*! In the thirty-four years that I have been an EU spouse I have given lunches and dinner parties and receptions, I have decorated residences, I have supported and helped my husband (perhaps hindered him sometimes) and I have never asked for a single thing from the European Commission, and now this. I have written back saying all this. We'll see what happens.

Later. Have decided that I'll go anyway, and I can spend a few days with Hester and Claudia and their children in England on the way, but I am still seething, and there is a slight problem in that Tim Beddow, my photographer friend, is coming out to do pictures of the oil barons' houses and the palace at Sheki for magazine articles we have planned together, so I can't linger in Europe too long.

14 July

Today is Bastille Day, i.e., French National Day, which we celebrated beside the pool at the Hyatt Hotel, but, unlike the Greek Ambassador's reception last year, the weather was warm and there were no gale-force winds. I bumped into the Israeli Ambassador, who is leaving soon. I asked him where he was going and he looked me in the eye and said, 'I am going to *our* Jerusalem, the undivided, eternal, capital of Israel for three thousand years.'

I was shocked into silence for a second, and then said, 'How can you say that? What about the Palestinians in East Jerusalem?'

'We cannot do anything for people who attack our schools and kill our children,' he retorted.

'Hang on a minute,' I said, 'what are you talking about? You have just killed fourteen hundred people in Gaza.'

'I do not wish to continue with this conversation, madame,' he said.

And I said, '*Nor do I.*'

The man from the World Bank was listening to the beginning of this conversation but he slid away. Later he came up and told me how good and brave I was. I wanted to say, 'Yes, and you are a total coward,' but I'd had enough confrontation.

While we were all standing, listening to the French Ambassador's speech, I looked around and noticed among all the feet on my left, the highest-heeled shoes I have ever seen. I peered through the wall of people and saw that they belonged to the prettiest young woman at the party. I whispered to AW, 'Look to the left, there is the *most* beautiful girl.'

He whispered back, 'Yes, that's Samira, I know her.'

'What do you mean you *know her*?' I hissed furiously under my breath.

'Oh, I don't know,' said AW, still whispering, 'I met her at a party while you were away.'

He introduced me to her with a gloating look in his eye; she is charming; I am quite glad we are leaving.

16 July

I am tearing round Baku making appointments at the houses I'd like Tim Beddow to photograph for the article we are doing on the oil barons' palaces (the Nobel house, the Rothschilds' house, etc.). At one point today, trying to locate the man who has the key to an interesting apartment I've been told about, I found myself in a tiny basement shop where I suddenly noticed there were photographs of flying saucers pinned up: some taken in daylight, a couple at night with the lights of the saucer shining out. I'd never seen anything like them, and it turned out the shop owner had taken them himself – he had actually witnessed the saucers and was sure they were genuine. I want AW to look at them, but I am not sure I will ever find the shop again.

18 July

There's been a story going round Baku that the President paid USD$60,000 for two donkeys for his private zoo. AW's friend who was arrested two months ago has been arrested again – this time because he and a mate made a hilarious film that was shown on YouTube. One of them dressed up as a donkey and the other 'interviewed' him and in the course of this so-called press conference the interviewer asked the donkey what he thought about Azerbaijan, and the donkey replied, 'This is a great country; there is no limit to what a donkey can achieve here – why, a donkey can become President.' Now both men are in prison.

Brussels, 19 July

I've never really thought much about retirement before, but now everything seems to refer to it – coming through Heathrow (which I have just done on my way from Baku to Brussels) the first thing you see is a giant ad for Relianz – an elderly man sailing a boat in a manly way and looking rather smug because he has obviously bought the right insurance for his old age. I can't identify with any of these ads.

22 July

It's the first day of the retirement course. I feel quite excited about it – I have not been taught anything since driving lessons when I was seventeen. As AW and I walked to the building where the class is being held, we passed a sign to a 'Newcomers' Course'. It was so strange: the newcomers at the beginning of their careers, and us at the end of ours.

There are about thirty-five people in our class, most of them employees of the EC with only three other trailing wives like me, and one trailing husband. AW says we already look like old people in a home: the room is rather tacky with dusty artificial flowers, some bulbs in the ceiling are not working, and our plastic chairs are in a semi-circle round the teacher who is taking the place of the television in a retirement sitting room.

Our first lesson (health and nutrition) was given by a pretty young Irish woman. I was just thinking that she wasn't a very good speaker because she kept faltering, when she suddenly dropped out of sight behind the lectern: she had fainted. The poor girl recovered consciousness and was helped away and we oldies were sent off for a coffee break. Then someone else came and talked to us about pensions (and we learned that in France, out of 64 million people, there are 20,000 people over one hundred years old).

After the lunch break we had more on pensions and then a social-services speaker who told us that the EC will not repatriate our bodies if we die abroad. Then there was some practical information on how to hire crutches, find carers and nursing homes, etc. The teacher also gave advice on how to choose where to live in retirement – i.e., try and be near a good hospital, and don't move somewhere where you don't know anyone.

Oh God, it's all so depressing.

23 July

Today we had a talk on tax (don't die in Brussels because the death duties are so high), and then one on our legal rights, the best part of which was learning that we pensioners get a card to eat at the EC canteen any time. The canteen is excellent value and you could always pick up some cheap rolls or bread for supper. (My family were always smuggling food from breakfasts in hotels in France so that we wouldn't have to pay for lunch somewhere. I was telling this to a nice Irish woman in the coffee break and she said that she does this too – but once, on business in China, the staff searched her when she left the dining room and she was made to put back the croissants she had taken.) Last night we were all given a red mug with the EC Retirement Helpline telephone number on it. AW said he would have preferred a gold watch.

24 July

Our lesson today was on the social and psychological aspects of retirement, which took all morning and afternoon. The teacher kicked off by making a paper aeroplane and launching it into the audience and the person it landed on had to tell us all who he/she was, and what were his/her plans for retirement. Then that person had to launch the paper plane at someone else. AW groaned: he thought all this too trendy and said he was damned if he was going to tell anyone anything, but I was intrigued to know what the other people in our class are going to do with their lives.

It turns out we are ten different nationalities here, a very high proportion of whom want to retire in Brussels; lots of us are planning to play golf (not AW and me), and most of the others intend to learn something: archaeology, photography, medieval history, cooking, computer programming. (The man I empathised with thought he ought to spend his retirement sorting out a lifetime's photographs.) The thrust of this lesson was that we must seek structure in our new lives. It has always been our *jobs* that dictated that structure, now we have to find one for ourselves. He said retirement went in stages: Honeymoon Period, Meaninglessness, Reorientation, Acceptance, Stability. (Crikey, I hope we don't spend too long passing through Meaninglessness.) He cheered us up by telling us stories of people who became famous for things they did *after* retirement (writers and painters mostly). And he said that women found it all easier than men because it's essential to have a good social network, and they are better at networking. I'll say. AW has no social network whatsoever, but I have a good one so he can share mine.

The teacher also told us that when we are working we are too busy to process little health niggles in our minds, but when we retire we become more aware of our aches and pains and tend to think we are falling apart. 'Just remember,' he said, 'that if you wake up in the morning without any pain anywhere it means you are dead.' And he told us to live each day as if we are going to die tomorrow – 'because you might'.

At the end of this all-day class, our course was over, and one by one we left. It was sad, like the last day of school. We had all bonded and now we were off to face the grim reality of what we had been learning to cope with – having nothing to do.

Baku, 2 August

Am just back in Baku, and furious because AW, who returned a few days ago, has watched six episodes of *The Wire* without me. That's the problem with these boxed sets – they are just like those other ones of chocolates. 'It won't do any harm just to have *one* more,' you say about those, and 'It won't do any harm to watch just *five minutes* more,' you say about DVDs and the next thing is you've finished the box, and in the case of DVDs it's three in the morning.

It is less than a month now before AW reaches his EC 'use by' date, and there is so much to do, starting with going round Baku with Tim Beddow taking pictures. (He arrived two days ago and has gone to Sheki to photograph the painted palace there.) I am making a programme of things that have to be done every day – one of them is to go and have a bath in a hammam. This is because, in order to get Tim a free ticket out here, we have to do some stories for the BMed magazine and they want one on the old bathhouses or hammams of Baku.

4 August

A curious thing: the World's Tallest Flagpole has suddenly shrunk. What's going on? I asked AW. He thinks maybe they've discovered they've been defeated – even with the extra six metres they added a couple of months ago – and are going for the title of the World's Shortest Flagpole now.

I am still teaching Tarana in the mornings. We are doing Delia's pizzas and she seems to have a natural gift for making them. A year and a bit ago I was wondering whether to sacrifice writing and teach Tarana to cook European food instead – I am glad I did, she won't ever be out of work now and can take care of her family (her husband left her with their five children some years ago). I am going to give her the ice-cream maker and the blender and the mincer to help her along when I'm gone.

Later. Help! Tim's boiled egg was raw at breakfast this morning – we don't eat cooked breakfast and it never occurred to me that Tarana didn't know how to boil one – so today we are doing basic boiled, poached, fried and scrambled eggs. Maybe Rebecca will put on some weight if she eats eggs. We have never got to the bottom of her thinness.

9 August

In the 'protected' Old City street next to our house, they are putting balconies on houses that never had them before. (I have to say they look quite pretty.) AW says it is the balconisation of Baku. Ha ha. And to think that Baku Old City has just been taken *off* the UNESCO endangered city list. The city is becoming a sort of fake 'old' place, a Disneyworld version of itself. AW says I should stop fretting about it and that when the oil barons first put up their grand houses people probably complained about them pulling down medieval Baku: 'My dear, have you *seen* the monstrosity that those awful nouveau-riche Rothschilds are building?'

My boyfriend of more than forty years ago wants to be my friend on Facebook. *Friend!* This is the man who broke my heart and whose ankles I tried to hold on to as he left me. I wrote back saying, 'It may be too soon.'

I went for a pedicure today. It was a very modern salon with designer washbasins plumbed in *on the floor* – unlike the place I go to in London where they put your feet in a plastic washing-up bowl. The other customers were spectacularly slim and elegant young women: the combined cost of their handbags was probably more than AW earns, and their combined waist measurements probably didn't add up to mine.

Speaking of weight, AW and I passed an enormously fat woman on our evening promenade yesterday. 'Must be her glands,' said AW after she'd gone past. I'd totally forgotten about glands, no one talks about them any more, but in the fifties if a person was fat, everyone used to whisper, 'Poor dear, it must be his/her glands,' in a knowing way.

One thing I have learned in Baku is the importance of eyebrows. Azerbaijani girls are like Iranians, with perfect, dark, arched brows, which look really beautiful. Unfortunately, I plucked mine too much when I was young so I will never be able to achieve these.

I have persuaded Nicole of the British Council here, to come with me to try out our local hammam for my article for BMed. We are quite nervous about it.

14 August

Nicole and I packed towels, soap and swimsuits for the hammam and agreed that we were *definitely not* going to take off all our clothes.

In the tiny entrance hall of the ancient bathhouse we found three very large ladies sprawled on rickety old chairs smoking fags. As we stepped in, two of them leapt up and ushered us into a big room with stone pillars and a domed roof where there were about a dozen plump women in various stages of undress, chatting, patting on face masks and drinking tea – the tea-drinkers were resting their naked boobs on a table where a little boy of about three was *brrm-brrm*-ing a toy car round, weaving it in and out of the bosoms. Nicole and I wondered if he would be obsessed by breasts all his life.

Back in the sixties, when the first topless swimsuit arrived, someone invented the 'pencil test' to see if you had a good enough figure to wear one – you put a pencil under your breast, if it fell out, you could go topless, if it stayed there, you couldn't. The women in the hammam could have fitted yule logs under their breasts and they would not have fallen out. (Nicole knew of other 'pencil tests'. She comes from South Africa where, she said, in the bad old days of apartheid, the authorities would judge if people were 'coloured' by sticking a pencil into their hair – if it stayed put they were deemed to have 'African' hair. And in Turkey, apparently, if you put a pencil in your moustache and it stays there, it means you are a MAN.)

Anyway, back to the hammam. The two fierce women who had glued themselves to us in the hall turned out to be our self-appointed masseuses and now we had to negotiate their fees. Since the bath, plus scrub, plus massage, added up to only seven pounds we decided to have the lot. We pulled

on our swimsuits, put our clothes into an old wooden locker
we'd been allocated, and then followed the masseuses to
another huge domed room where, through the thick steam,
we could see a whole lot more extremely large naked females
washing themselves – it was an extraordinary sight, just like
an Orientalist painting done by Beryl Cook. Nicole and I
found ourselves surrounded by bulging breasts, buttocks,
stomachs; I felt positively skinny.

After a crowded sauna, the two masseuses – mine was
called Mila – made us climb up a metal ladder and jump into
an icy pool halfway up the wall: architecturally I couldn't
work this out at all, I think this part of the hammam was
quite a long way underground and maybe this was where a
natural spring came in. 'Oh God,' I prayed as I climbed up
the slippery ladder in my bare feet, 'please don't let me fall off
and break my neck.'

(When I told AW about it later, he said, 'Your obituary
would have read: "Brigid Keenan was born in India, and died
in a hammam in Baku".' Then he smirked and added, 'Oh,
Singer of the East . . .' – which is what is inscribed on the
tomb of the great traveller Sir Richard Burton in Mortlake. I
laughed till I cried.)

Now we were *ordered* to take off our swimsuits and lie face
down on stone benches where the masseuses (who'd also
taken off their clothes) got to work on us with gloves made
of knitted string. Each time I got to the exact point of thinking, 'I will have no skin left on my back/shoulder/arm,' Mila
would skilfully move to the next spot. As she leaned over to
massage me, parts of her body – breasts? stomach? I couldn't
tell – gently bounced on me; it felt rather warm and cosy. At
one point I put my hand up to scratch my neck and felt a
whole lot of rolled-up dead skin – yuk. I tried very hard not
to think of how much rolled-up dead skin must have fallen

273

on the floor of the hammam over the past 250-odd years, or of how much dead skin from other people was in the string glove she was using.

Just as all this was going through my mind, Mila threw a bucket of water over me which took my breath away, then she massaged me all over with shampoo, and, finally, went over my body with a rolling pin as if I was a giant lump of pastry (I suppose I am in a way). Another couple of buckets of water later, and then it was finished. I lay on the stone slab, pummelled and scrubbed to exhaustion and hardly able to get up. I no longer cared, as I walked back to our locker, that I didn't have any clothes on.

All the other women were obviously planning a long stay in the hammam and had brought food, drinks, oils and unguents to rub into their shiny clean bodies. I wanted to take a photograph of them all together because it was such a happy, warm, convivial scene, but of course they didn't want me to – except one who grabbed her enormous breasts in her hands as a joke and lifted them towards me saying, 'Yes! Please! Photo for Internet!'

Nicole and I drank our tea, stroked our silken skin, and decided we would definitely go back again, but we might bring our own string gloves next time.

16 August

Because it's summer and the diplomatic corps are mostly on holiday, we have had lots of time to watch *The Wire*, and tonight we finished the last episode. It is almost unbelievable that we won't see any of the characters again; they have become so real to us. It is like being bereaved – as if all our friends have suddenly gone over a cliff in a bus. Is this good for our emotions? In the old days people just knew their families and close friends or, at most, neighbours in their village. Now we get to 'know' and care about hundreds of characters who come in and out of our lives via television.

17 August

Our first empty evening since *The Wire*. Now we are desperately watching all those bits you never normally bother with: director's commentary, interviews with the stars . . . It's a bit like picking cigarette butts out of the dustbin when you are desperate for a fag and have run out. It's just as well it's over, actually, because the reality is that we have only fourteen days left here – not to mention to the end of AW's career.

I have only now begun to take in the fact that this is the last time in my life that I will live within hearing of the call to prayer from a mosque (my favourite sound), the last time we will ever have a driver, the last time I can sit drinking tea in tiny, womb-like carpet shops in the Old City, the last time we'll have a summer of blue skies every day. I realise I've made my final visit to a hammam with lots of friendly fat ladies (there is no time to go back), and this is the last time I will have a companion to cook with – I have come to love my mornings in the kitchen with Tarana. And it's also the last time I can be totally irresponsible: being an ex-pat means you never have to commit, it's, 'Oh I am so sorry I can't join whatever-it-is because I have to go back to Azerbaijan in a week,' and then, in Azerbaijan it's, 'Oh I am so sorry I can't join the fundraising coffee-morning group because I am going back to England in a few days.'

The World's Tallest Flagpole is growing again. Will it be finished, with its flag (apparently the size of a football pitch) flying before we go?

24 August

I took the photographs that I was permitted to take in the hammam over there today and our masseuses were thrilled. I also had to ask, for my peace of mind because I can't stop thinking about it, whether the water in the pool halfway up the wall is constantly changing, or is it the same water all day for all the many sweaty ladies. They said it is constantly changing. Phew.

In between teaching Tarana cooking this morning, I washed my hair and then tied it back because I had no time to curl it. AW came home for a rushed lunch and told me I looked like a buffalo because it had fallen into a middle parting with swags at the sides. I can see what he means.

I have had no reply to my letter to AW's boss in Brussels complaining about them not paying my airfare to the retirement course. I know from AW that there is a policy at the EC that all letters must be replied to within two weeks – so I have just written again saying that they obviously hold their officials' spouses in such low esteem that they don't even bother to apply this rule to *their* letters. I don't expect they will answer this one either. It makes me furious.

Patrick, the admin officer, rang this morning and asked me to meet him at an art gallery near our house to choose a painting the office can give AW as a leaving present. I picked a beautiful portrait of a Talish woman, which would remind AW of Tarana and Rebecca. He will be thrilled.

AW is demob happy: today he told one of his staff, who has always been difficult, that he is like a black cloud that sits in the office making everyone depressed. As a matter of fact I think we are both slightly unhinged at the moment. AW came across the random information that the rulers of Hunza-Nagar (ancient kingdoms in the Himalayas) were called Thums, and we have been making each other laugh by thinking up book titles: *Under the Thum*, a courtesan in the Kingdom of Hunza–Nagar tells her story; *Thums Up*, the life of a successful ruler of Hunza-Nagar; *Thums Down*, the fall of the house of Hunza-Nagar; *Thum Like it Hot*: how central heating came to the court of Hunza-Nagar, etc., etc.

25 August

At the retirement course they said 'wind down slowly before you leave work', but AW is in the office, flat out every day, to 6.30 or 7 p.m. Tomorrow is his official goodbye to the President (he is going to mention the two young men who are still in prison for the donkey film) and then he only has two days left at work.

There are lots of farewell parties being given for us – the one last night was quite eccentric as we didn't know any of the other guests. Our main one, being given by Eran, the office landlord and friend, is the day after tomorrow.

The packers are coming in five days' time. I have been trying to sell our carpets and some of our pictures and textiles because there is just no room for more stuff at home in England. The new people replacing us don't want any of our things, which is a pity because the room is so beautiful the way it is now, it seems a terrible shame to change it.

26 August

AW's farewell party in the office today. I cried all through it as the local people he has worked with here are so nice and kind and I know them all now, and I shall miss them dreadfully. They presented AW with the beautiful portrait from the art gallery and I could see he was extremely moved (he doesn't do crying, but would have if he did).

27 August, Four Days to Retirement

I think I am falling apart: such an awful thing happened today. I was sitting in my room, reading a book in my grubby old dressing gown (which was going to be washed today), when the doorbell went. It was 10.30 and I thought it must be something to do with packers. But no, Tarana knocked on my door and said someone had come to see me. I came out, hair not brushed, teeth not cleaned, bad breath, greasy face, and found two smart-looking American ladies waiting for me. I had no idea who they were and gaped at them in puzzlement – and then with horror I remembered that I had made an appointment to sign books for BP oil wives who'd been at a talk I gave weeks ago, and these must be them, bringing the books. When she'd got over her visible shock at seeing me like this, one of them took over. 'You go and get dressed,' she said, 'and we'll have a coffee while we wait for you.' The only good part is that I am leaving and never have to face either of these nice women ever again.

Speaking of that talk, someone there told me that BP wives are paid £3,000 a year to accompany their husbands abroad. I have just worked out that if the EC did the same I would have earned £99,000 by now. As it is, they don't even reply to my letters.

28 August, Three Days to Retirement

Eran's farewell party for us was perfect, we couldn't have had a better send-off. He and his wife have been so kind to us from the very first week I was here. I hope we stay in touch with them, but it's extraordinary how often, in this endlessly travelling life of ours, you swear eternal friendship to people and then get caught up in another life and never see them again.

29 August, Only Two Days to Retirement

Suddenly everything seems incredibly depressing and down-beat. We don't have any engagements this weekend because we thought we'd keep it free to organise ourselves. I have a toothache and the thought of having to pack all day tomorrow seems too exhausting to think about.

Still, I have made a list for my successor of everything that Tarana can cook and it comes to dozens of dishes, so she should be well pleased. The only slight worry is that my successor is Italian and I haven't taught Tarana any Italian dishes except pizza.

31 August, Our Last Day

The packers have been here all weekend, and everything of ours has gone. Our beautiful room looks rather empty and sad. To help us with unpacking in England, I asked the packers to write on the boxes what is inside. On the ones containing our bed linen they have written AMBASSADOR'S SHITS.

1 September, 00.30

Half an hour ago AW's office email address was terminated, and he no longer has access to anything on the computer to do with work. His mobile phone has been returned, he has ceased to exist as a European Commission official. His thirty-five-year-long career with them is over.

I am not saying this to AW, but I thought he might have received a phone call or a charming letter, or even an email from *someone* at the EC – Mr Barroso? his boss? – thanking him for all those years of loyal service, or at least some acknowledgement that he has retired today, but there has been nothing, not a single word. I am utterly shocked. AW seems unperturbed – I think he is just longing to be free.

2 September

Our plane left Baku in the middle of last night. The EC might not have cared about AW, but his office did – they *all* came to the airport to give him a grand send-off, including Tarana and Rebecca in floods of tears (no point in throwing water after us this time, as we will not be coming back).

This was a complete surprise, we'd got into the car with Patrick, our dear admin man, and Rovshan the driver, and set off for the airport – but at a secret rendezvous point on the way we suddenly realised we had been joined by a whole convoy of office vehicles. 'We look like an Azerbaijani wedding party,' said Patrick (who'd arranged it all) gleefully. It was a wonderful farewell – good enough to serve as an end-of-career one as well as a goodbye to friends in Azerbaijan. I don't think I stopped crying until we reached London.

Home is Where the Heart Isn't

France, 18–22 September

AW thought it would be a good idea to go to our house in France as soon as we got home, and in that way we could pretend AW was on holiday, and not facing the biggest Cinderella-backwards change from being a respected Person of Note in Azerbaijan to a Nobody in Somerset.

We drove down to the south, stopping at various *Logis de France*, which always reminds me of the time, years ago, when we were young and foolish and doing the same journey with my sister Tessa and her husband Malcolm. We stayed in a hotel which had a pleasant restaurant with big glass doors at the back on to a little parking area with trees. It was summer and very hot and I was tired and ate and drank too much and just before the end of the meal I knew I was going to be sick. 'Go outside, quick,' said AW, so I stumbled through the restaurant towards the blessed darkness of the car park – but as I entered it my body triggered the security lights so that the diners, who had all turned to see what was going on, were treated to the sight of me, spotlighted, throwing up. The absolutely worst part of this story is that I had to go back into the restaurant afterwards; I thought I might get a round of applause.

There is this new thing in France of vegetable foams and little glasses of some sort of froth or broth in between courses, but ever since I saw Dawn French and Jennifer Saunders being French chefs and creating the foam by spitting on the plates I've completely lost my appetite for these.

In one of the hotels we stayed in en route, a slip of paper in our room told us (in English) that we could order a 'cervical pillow' if we wanted one. After a moment of puzzlement I realised they meant a *neck* pillow and I should have told them about their translation, but I didn't feel up to discussing cervixes in French at reception.

While we were in France we got an email from Mark Elliott (author of the Azerbaijan guidebook) saying that he had just met the *British* manufacturer of Tallest Flagpoles in the World, who told him that it will be only a matter of months before someone else builds a higher flagpole than the one in Baku. What a brilliant idea for a business: with all these newly rich countries in the Gulf and in the ex-Soviet Union vying with each other for projects that will give them (so they think) prestige and fame, how could you go wrong – though there must be a limit to the height of a flagpole so when everyone has got the tallest what do you do next?

I have been wondering all the time we've been in France why AW is developing a deep mahogany Hollywood tan on his face that he has never had before – and then I discovered that he was wondering the same thing. The mystery was solved when he showed me the 'moisturiser' he was using every morning – it was a Dove self-tanning lotion that some-one had left behind in the bathroom.

Somerset, 22 September

Today is the first real day of AW's retirement. Got off to a bad start with AW asking what was for lunch. *Lunch?* I hadn't thought of lunch, I never really have it when I am at home in England on my own and now I realise we will be sitting down, just the two of us, for a proper meal every day. I don't know why this is different from having lunch together in Baku, but it is, somehow.

Retirement is traumatic. Suddenly you are at home all the time with your partner and with nothing particular to do for the rest of your life. You have no idea how you are going to fill your days; there is no real reason to get up in the morning. And worst of all you don't know who you are any more. We are all (especially men) defined by our jobs: we are diplomats, nurses, accountants, road cleaners, journalists, teachers, doctors, etc., but 'retired' means you aren't anything – and yet, apart from not going to work, you are exactly the same person as you were yesterday. When my hard-grafting dad retired at the age of seventy-one (he worked for the Greater London Council in London in the latter part of his life) he immediately got TB and the family all knew it was because he felt so guilty doing nothing he'd had to be ill as an excuse.

I said to AW that we must try to think up some interesting old-age projects, and he asked, Could he be mine?

I know about retirement because I retired thirty years ago when I left my job on the *Sunday Times* and joined AW who'd gone to Brussels to start a career with the European Commission. I'd never not worked since I was seventeen (or on three months' maternity leave as it was in those days) and I felt aimless and miserable – and I was lucky because we still had small children to get me out of bed in the mornings, and I eventually found work as a freelance writer.

I think retiring might be okay if there were no other people around watching and asking, 'What are you going to do?' or worse, 'How is it going? I expect you've had lots of offers?' when you haven't. (AW doesn't want to be a consultant, or an election monitor, so that's those out, plus he doesn't want a job that means living in London – these conditions seem to have scared off the head hunter he talked to, who was keen at first, but has been deathly silent lately.) A single friend once said to me that she wouldn't mind spending Christmas alone if there weren't people around knowing she was on her own and feeling sorry, or guilty or worried for her. Same thing with retirement: if there was no one else to see you not being offered directorships and so on, it wouldn't matter, you could potter around all day reading the books you'd never managed to catch up with during your busy working life. But no, there are all these friends watching and waiting and with expectations for you; AW and I can't talk about this at all, because I am one of them.

6 November

It's been pouring with rain and AW and I are trying to clear out the garage because our shipment from Azerbaijan is arriving in three days' time, plus the things that went back into storage in Brussels when AW left for Baku will be coming next month. I have to watch AW like a hawk because when I am not looking he throws away stuff I have been hoarding for years. At the back of the garage there was an old futon, left over from Hester's days as a student, which AW suddenly decided should go on the bonfire. I retrieved it and, next time our temporary gardener came to work, I asked him, 'Would you like a futon?'

He said, 'No thanks, I'd better not, I'm a bit fussy about my food. I think it was being an only child that did it . . .' I am still wondering what he thought I'd said.

The rain is relentless.

12 November

The Azerbaijan shipment arrived. The house is full of *stuff*. I just want to live in a whitewashed cell with a crucifix over my simple, white-covered bed. Even our larder (which has nothing to do with the things from Azerbaijan) is stuffed with old food: today I had to throw out four tins of anchovies which were five years past their sell-by date. I remember buying those anchovies as if it were yesterday; I was going to take them to Kazakhstan but forgot.

When I opened one of the AMBASSADOR'S SHITS boxes in the shipment from Baku, I found a whole lot of quite pretty but damaged lacy bedlinen I'd had made in India twenty years ago. I have no space for them now, so I took them to our local Mencap shop, but it was closed. As I was crossing the road back to my car thinking how annoying that was, I passed a woman who said, 'Those look pretty.'

'They're yours!' I said, and put them in her arms. She turned out to be visiting from South Africa and is going to take them back there, she was so pleased.

AW hasn't helped my mood. As the removals men left three days ago he said, 'Well, I suppose the next move is the one we won't have to pack for' – meaning death! We've already got to the stage when, each time we part, I wonder whether we'll see each other again, and if he is late in for lunch I hardly dare go into the garden for fear of seeing his legs sticking out from under a rhubarb leaf. (In which case, since AW has his hands, literally, on the controls, I will not be able to work the DVD player, nor record *Spiral* or *Borgen* or watch BBC iPlayer, and I will never again understand what anyone is saying because I don't know how to put on subtitles. Must get him to show me these things . . .) And, as AW pointed out the other day, there wouldn't be much point in having our fortunes told now. When I wrote *Diplomatic Baggage* I said that if I saw my own obituary in the paper I wouldn't feel that sad, but if I saw it now I'd think, 'Well, she had a good run for her money.'

London, 14 November

Some young friends of ours have just had a baby boy and emailed photos of the newborn. The baby has enormous purple private parts which make it quite embarrassing just looking at the pictures – am not sure what to write back. It reminds me that when we lived in Brussels we had friends who were nudists and how we used to dread being shown their holiday snaps because our eyes were always drawn to the bits of them we shouldn't be looking at and we never knew what to say.

17 November

Claudia's baby was born today safe and sound. He was delivered by Caesarean, and it was all a far cry from the awful thirty-six-hour labour of Maisie's birth. He is called Iolo, a Welsh name in honour of his other grandparents. (He doesn't seem to have quite the same bulging purple parts as the baby in the email pictures, which is a relief.)

21 November

It's a Big Birthday for me today. Claudia organised a family tea party and gave me a wonderful book of my life that she'd assembled with photographs and comments from friends and relatives. It was a complete surprise and I was deeply touched.

10 December

I have written the Christmas cards (why are there always three cards every year that never get posted because you don't know the addresses?). We have seventeen of the family for Christmas, so I am in the kitchen all the time now, frantically cooking to try and fill the freezer. AW says he is starving and could he please have a meal, but the answer is no: I've too much to do. Anyway he is a really good cook himself, especially when it comes to a fry-up.

AW has become a complete control freak: he tells me when to go to bed, how to chew gum (have taken to gum since giving up smoking), how to leave phone messages (mine are too long apparently), how I must not squeeze blackheads, etc., etc. Last week, while we were shopping in Castle Cary, I wandered into an antique shop and he shouted at me from the pavement, 'Come out of there! Come out now! We don't need antiques.' I thought he was going to say, 'Heel, girl, heel.'

He says I am suffering from Adult Deficiency Syndrome and that I talk too much; he walked past me telling someone a story a couple of days ago and said, 'Bor-ing.'

Going to Sainsbury's with him is a total nightmare. I say, 'I'll just go and get sugar,' and he says, 'Sugar? I'm sure we don't need sugar, we've only just bought sugar, sugar is so bad for you.' The same goes for every item and, last time, he refused to buy pickled onions – which he really loves – because they were £3.18. But that's nothing compared to his egg obsession: AW thinks they are sold too old in British supermarkets and why aren't they stamped with the day they were laid, as they are in Brussels. I completely agree, but I just want to finish the shopping.

Another thing about AW that drives me mad is that he never passes on messages so that, long after the event, people ring up with hurt voices and say did AW tell you that I had a stroke and was rushed to hospital and my family all flew in from New Zealand to say goodbye . . .? I just wondered because I didn't hear anything from you.'

Poor AW, he has spent his whole life in offices telling dozens and dozens of people what to do, and now he only has me to boss around. And to be fair, he says I am a control freak too. Claudia says we are just two old control freaks shut up together, bickering.

There was a piece in the paper the other day about what to do if your partner is grumpy. Their advice was to tickle each other or have a pillow fight, or tease your partner by spraying him/her with water when they are not expecting it. I can't actually imagine surviving the experience if I sprayed cold water on AW when he was not expecting it.

Al Gore and his wife split up after forty years of marriage, so I suppose this is always possible. But at least we do still have things to talk and argue about – and can hear each other (for the time being anyway) and are not yet like the elderly couple some friends of ours saw in a hotel dining room in Kenya: the man was quiet but the woman spoke occasionally through the meal, until, at the end, she suddenly said, 'Silly old fool, he can't hear a word I am saying.'

The reason I'm feeling a bit anti-AW today is because last night I dreamed that he made me go and play pan pipes all around Brussels and collect money – and they weren't even real pan pipes, but four recorders he'd tied together.

Somerset, 12 December

We heard from Baku today that Tarana has walked out of her job with my successor because she could not stand being shouted at for one more minute. I can't bear it. Tarana

– sweet mild Tarana – chucking in her job? All those hours she spent at the stove with me so that she would never be out of work, gone for nothing, because now she is. How could anyone be unkind to her? She was already a good cook and just needed a few more months of training by someone more efficient than me, to be able to cope with dinner parties. Rebecca says that if she can't get a job Tarana will go back to cooking for the priests, where I found her. She must be so upset and disappointed.

Other bad news from Baku came from my friend Betty who says they have pulled down the wonderful Atlas House for redevelopment as well as the attractive two-storey house opposite our flat. On the other hand, they have commissioned Zaha Hadid to design an extraordinary building there, so perhaps I shouldn't be so harsh.

3 January

The family are all gone now, which is sad but also a relief because Christmas is such hard work and I am not used to being with so many people after months of just Tarana and me.

What with the sadness about Tarana, and the endless rain, my spirits are low. When we lived abroad I used to think to myself that if things got too bad I could go home, but now I *am* home.

One of the problems is that AW and I don't have any kind of routine at all. We potter about in Somerset: I have been writing the articles for various magazines to go with the pictures Tim Beddow took in Baku, and AW is sorting out the garden, which has been neglected for years. We go up to London for a day or two almost every week to see friends, doctors (I've been going to an osteopath about my back, but it hasn't helped), exhibitions – and of course to visit our grandchildren, but we don't have any plan or a schedule, it is all completely random. Is this what they meant by 'Meaninglessness' on the retirement course?

The other day we took Malachy and little Jackson to the Army Museum where there is a soft-play area built like a big two-storey castle. After a very short time Malachy came out of the castle looking dejected and said that some big boys of five were being mean to him. I suggested that we go back in together, and was crawling down a cloth tunnel when I came across the boys lying in wait for Malachy. They got the fright of their lives seeing an elderly woman coming towards them on hands and knees, and they dispersed but then came back with reinforcements and cornered me in the tunnel and I literally had to fight my way out. It was like *Lord of the Flies*, slightly scary and so undignified.

Afterwards AW and I couldn't fold the pushchair (with buggy board) so we had to manoeuvre it, uncollapsed, into the front seat of the car. Then we tried to give Malachy and Jackson supper, but we didn't know how to operate the touch-control hob in their kitchen, nor how to get rid of the big notice in the middle of the TV screen telling us something was wrong (the boys seemed perfectly happy to watch CBeebies just round the edge) and then we couldn't figure out how to switch on the state-of-the-art taps in their bathroom and got drenched by the shower; and finally, next day, just when we were thinking all's well that ends well (and what a huge help we had been to Hester) she rang to say I had put the boys to bed in swimming nappies and so their sheets were soaking wet this morning and everything had to be washed.

All of which was only a degree worse than when we had the boys to stay down here not long ago. First, we forgot their suitcase in London and had to go to Sainsbury's and buy them each a whole wardrobe and then we found we'd left the key to our house in London and the man next door who keeps a spare was asleep and didn't wake up for two hours (which we spent in the playground in the rain). Mobiles don't work down here and he didn't hear us banging on the door.

I had always imagined my rosy-cheeked grandchildren playing nicely in the dappled sunlight in our garden – not in the drizzling rain trying to kill each other with the garden hoe. AW is not a lot of help, he says things like, 'Why can't you stop Jackson crying?' but he is extremely good at watching DVDs with them. I can't count the times he has seen *Ice Age 3*.

22 February

Claudia's little Maisie is very shy and has always avoided being embraced by me – but I thought there'd been a major breakthrough with her last weekend. When they arrived to stay she came running into the house and gave me a huge hug and even a peck on the cheek, and my heart was bursting with happiness until she said to her dad, 'I've kissed Dooda now, so can I have my chocolate?'

She has had an ear infection and told Claudia she thought there must be a hedgehog in her ear because it hurt so much.

6 March

It is a year and four months since I gave up smoking in Sri Lanka and though I am extremely proud of myself, I am also fed up because I have put on more than a stone in weight which I can't seem to shift and I am now a fat person. (One of the fattest women I know used to be slim, she told me, until she gave up smoking.) AW has put on weight too, so we are following a diet that Claudia discovered called From Pig to Twig (AW says in his case it is more like from Hog to Log), which is a slightly easier version of the Atkins one.

The other day in the car we passed a lorry with WASTE MANAGEMENT written on the side. 'That's what we are doing,' said AW, 'but in our case it's spelt WAIST management'.

7 March

Spent yesterday afternoon mending my tarantula. This could be the one item I'd save if the house caught fire. It's the corpse of an enormous one that AW squashed when we lived in Trinidad; I collected the body (it was big enough to get maggots on it while it was drying out) and keep it in a box to thrill the grandchildren but it is very fragile and every now and again I have to stick its legs back on.

24 March

We went to see our accountant about what to put in our wills and, curiously, managed to get through the whole conversation without ever using the *death* word. Instead the accountant talked about AW 'parking his car' and me 'stepping off the bus', so then we found ourselves picking up the challenge and talking about 'popping our clogs', and 'falling off our perch'. Apart from learning new euphemisms for death, nothing was achieved: we don't know how to divide our things between our daughters, so we are putting it on hold.

5 April

While we are on this efficiency kick, I thought perhaps we should get travel insurance for the year. I rang a company someone recommended and spoke to a man who asked whether AW or I had ever been seriously ill. 'No, no, not really,' I said, 'we are pretty healthy people.'

Then he said, 'Have either of you ever been hospitalised?'

I was just saying, 'No, no, we've never been . . .' when I suddenly remembered that AW has had a triple by-pass and I have twice had surgery for cancer, so I told him this and he said, please hang on a minute and then he came back and said our insurance had been refused.

This conversation reminded me of a time, back in the nineties, when AW had to have some medical procedure at a hospital in Bath which had a mirrored façade. We all went with him to boost his morale and, I suppose because we were all tense, we somehow found ourselves linking arms and doing the can-can together at our reflection, until a very embarrassed young woman came out of the building and said, 'I'm so sorry, we thought we should tell you that though that looks like a mirror, on the other side we can see through it and we've been watching you dancing.'

15 April

AW is recording *Gardeners' World*. I can't believe it has come to this.

My hair is falling out in handfuls: is there something wrong with it, or is this just the first step towards Old Lady's Hair, where you can see the pink scalp through? Oh God, I remember – it seems like just the other day – looking at elderly women and thinking, 'I am definitely never going to let my scalp show through my hair when I am old.' What I want to say now is that I would do anything not to have pink scalp showing, but it's probably going to happen, and it's not my fault.

By far the worst thing about getting older is forgetting names and stories at the very time you need them most. For now, I usually remember them again after a bit, but there is a delay, and so having a conversation with me these days is a bit like that *Two Ronnies* 'Mastermind' sketch when Ronnie Corbett will only answer the question before the current one. This means that when Ronnie Barker (the quizmaster) asks him, 'What is the name of the directory that lists members of the peerage?' Ronnie Corbett replies, 'The study of old fossils' (the previous question having been, 'What is palaeontology?').

22 April

I went into our local DVD rental shop today and unthink-ingly asked the woman behind the counter, 'Do you have *An Education*?' – meaning the film.

But she said, 'What do you mean, of course I have,' in a defensive voice – and then I realised how my question sounded, and explained, and we had a laugh.

30 April

Tim Beddow and I have been summoned to Syria by the President's wife, Asma al-Assad! Ever since I first saw her in Damascus when she asked us to do a book about the old building she has been given for her office, they have been restoring it and now, apparently, it's got to the stage where they think we should come and start our work. We are off to Damascus for a few days next month and they are paying our (economy) air tickets.

22 May

Am just back from our five-day trip to Damascus. I loved being there again among all the old familiar sights and smells. Tim and I stayed with our French friend, Jacques, who has a house in the Old City. We were collected every morning by a car sent from the President's office and taken to Mrs Assad's project, still a building site, where we interviewed people, took photographs and talked about the book. We never saw her though.

The house, a little palace really, is a very pretty building, rather like a small, classical, French chateau, and I've always loved it. Tim and I tried to photograph it for our book on Damascus but it was always bristling with guards and we could never get near it and had to use an old postcard instead.

Mrs Assad's book has turned into a much bigger project than first outlined to me – it is now a whole history of Syria, based on the house (where various Presidents, as well as the short-lived King Faisel, resided) and Tim's and my contribution is only a small part of it. We're not sure about the restoration; there is a great deal of white marble going in along with sound systems in every room, and it must be costing an absolute fortune. The garden designer and the architect are both British so I can talk to them about it later. Tim and I will have to go back to do the photographs when it is all finished next year.

24 May

I was ironing AW's trousers today and discovered the hem of one leg was *stapled* up. Poor AW: why didn't he ask me to stitch it for him, or perhaps Tarana did this in Azerbaijan?

Since the shipments arrived, our house looks like a storage depot so AW and I decided to send everything we don't need to the local sales. An auctioneer is coming to look round and tell us if we have anything valuable. You never know, both AW's grandparents and mine lived in the East and might have picked up some priceless treasure that we have in the back of a cupboard. We are rushing about dusting and washing things to make them look a bit less depressing and more valuable.

29 May

Auctioneer has been and gone. We don't have any treasures: our books are not first editions, any Chinese plates are cracked or too recent, our pictures are of the wrong views. And no one wants tea sets (I have four for some reason). But we're sending everything off to be sold anyway, just to clear some space.

2 June

There's just been a programme on telly about how Alfred Hitchcock hired Salvador Dalí to create the dream sequences for his film *Spellbound* in the 1940s. Dalí's dreams for the movie were, as you'd expect, surreal and very stylish, with disembodied eyes, a distorted wheel, a masked man, weird landscapes and so on – and I wondered if his own dreams were really like that, or banal and childish like mine: last week I dreamed that I had huge dandruff, like white corn-flakes, on my shoulders, and as if that wasn't disgusting enough, in another recent dream I was sitting in a plane across the aisle from AW who suddenly leaned over and said, 'There is a pile of poo under your seat, is it yours?' (It wasn't, but everyone on the plane thought it was.)

I went into the garden today to pick some of AW's first efforts at cabbage but it was just lace – slugs? caterpillars? (To be fair, most of the other things he is growing are quite impressive.)

12 June

The strangest thing: Tim Beddow and I have had a message from Mrs Assad's office saying, 'Our client no longer wishes to proceed with the project' – meaning the book is cancelled. Why? It's weird, and slightly disappointing. I was looking forward to doing it.

AW and I have lost quite a bit of weight on the Pig to Twig diet; in fact I went and bought some smart trousers in Jaeger to celebrate – and also because I have been wondering if there is an age at which you should no longer wear jeans?

19 June

While in London, I decided to get a box of chocolates and give them to Brian Haw, the protestor outside the House of Commons. I really admire him, camping out there in the wind and the rain for all these years. Claudia and my nephew William wanted to join me so we bought the chocs and then I drove boldly up to the tents in Parliament Square where I tried to stop, but the police went mad and were blowing whistles and coming after me so I thrust the chocolates into the hands of a man who was standing there, and said, 'We just want to say we all admire you so much.'

He looked surprised and said, '*Sank you. Danke.*' And we realised he was a German tourist.

'They're not for you!' Claudia yelled as I accelerated off. '*Give them to Mr Haw.*' The poor chap must have been totally baffled: first people drive up and hand him a box of chocolates, and then they all start screaming that he has to give them to someone else.

My other nephew, Perry, is living in Dublin and has been doing some research into my mother's Irish family and seems to have discovered that before they were Irish they were English Quakers and before that they were Moroccan Jewish clockmakers. No wonder we have never felt quite English. He has also found my grandfather's Dublin birth certificate, which means I could try and claim an Irish passport, which is what I desperately wanted to do at the time of the Iraq War so that I could return my British one to Tony Blair, but I have lost the momentum now and anyway I hear an Irish passport costs about 900 euros.

19 July

The strangest thing has just happened: Hester has been in New York on business, and had to go to a meeting at the German Mission to the UN a couple of days ago. As she was going through security she noticed one of the Filipino guards looking at her intently and suddenly realised it was Bing – our old butler from Syria. They fell into each other's arms and then rang us up using Hester's mobile. In Somerset AW answered the phone and thought he must have slipped into a time warp when he heard Bing's voice calmly wishing him Good Afternoon as though he'd seen him an hour ago instead of fifteen years. What a wonderful world.

22 July

An astonishing hoard of more than 52,000 ancient coins (from AD 253 to 305) was found earlier this year by a man with a metal detector in a field outside Frome, and today they were displayed at Frome Library.

The whole idea of buried hoards is so thrilling – I am now fantasising about AW and I taking up treasure-seeking in our old age with metal detectors welded to our Zimmer frames.

London, 30 July

Claudia and Aled and I took all the children to the park in Pimlico this afternoon. On the way there, Malachy needed to do a pee so I took him to the gutter between two parked cars – at which point a young man came up and said loudly, 'Do you think this is appropriate behaviour?'

'Yes,' I replied, 'this is a three-year-old child who wants to go to the toilet, what is the alternative, tell him to pee his pants?'

'Yes,' said the man, 'this behaviour is entirely inappropriate in public.'

'Okay,' I said, 'let's call the police so that you can make a complaint.'

Then it turned out that he *was* a policeman in plain clothes. He walked away in the end, leaving me trembling with rage – it isn't as if there isn't dog poo all over the place, much dirtier and more unpleasant than a little boy's wee.

Somerset, 9 August

Things are settling down. We still don't have a proper routine, but we are getting there: AW has enrolled on an Iranian language course at the School of Oriental and African Studies in September. He spent part of his childhood in Iran and did Farsi (and Arabic) at university and now he'd like to brush it up. This means we will spend several days each week in London and that means that we will *have* to develop some sort of timetable, in order to buy the train tickets if nothing else.

16 August

In a Frome antique shop today I saw a wooden castle with four towers and a keep and a ramp up which you marched your soldiers, exactly like the one we had when we were children. It's pretty unnerving when the things you've grown up with are in antique shops or, worse, museums. A couple of weeks ago I saw a copy of *The Butterfly Fairy* in the window of an antiquarian bookseller off Shaftesbury Avenue. This is a picture book that my sister Tessa and I loved when we were small so I dashed in to ask the price and it was £280! Couldn't wait to ring Tessa to find out if she's still got it, and she has, but it has all fallen to bits so it's worthless, like everything we have.

The main event this weekend was that Claudia found *a worm in her cod loin*. I'd cooked the cod in butter and lemon, delicious, and never noticed a thing – but there it was, a horrible pinky creature in between lovely white flakes of fish. I stormed into Sainsbury's and they said unapologetically, 'Oh yes, there are worms in cod sometimes . . . and in salmon.' Now we can never eat fish and chips again because of what might be hidden away under the batter.

2 September

We have just had our village fete, which always has a hay-bale throwing competition. I swear they only include this so they are able to announce, 'Can we have all the tossers in the field please?' – the same way they have a category in the dog show that involves requesting all the bitches to line up.

The event everyone loves (it must touch some deep-down cave person in us all) is the tug-of-war; this year it was between the pub goers and the rest of the village. It's extraordinary how all our familiar local blokes suddenly turn into handsome, testosterone-filled gods as they heave on the rope, ferociously digging their heels in, thigh muscles bulging . . .

I say the blokes are familiar, but in fact, our village is changing – the dour farmer has given up animals and built expensive houses in his yard, the railway signalman expert on the queens of England has died and lots of posh people are moving in: we have about six old-Etonians now and increasing numbers of big 4x4s, and any minute it is going to replace Chipping Norton as the *chic*-est place in the UK.

London, 19 September

Good news from Baku: the young men who were sent to prison for making the YouTube film about the donkey have been released. But bad news from my friend Betty who says that the hideous flame-shaped towers the President's wife is building grow taller by the day.

I went to Mass in the Pimlico Catholic church today – it was heaving with people as usual (anyone who thinks that religion is struggling in Britain should take a look there). The priest had asked the children to bring 'something that God has created', so they'd brought plants, rabbits, dogs, guinea pigs, hamsters, a rat – and one small boy dragged an even smaller one down the aisle and then shouted out, 'I brung my bruvver.'

I sobbed all the way through the service with happiness. As a matter of fact, I notice that I *am* happier. I found myself walking along in Pimlico yesterday singing 'Oh Happy Day' out loud. It's not that I've been feeling *that* unhappy, but everything has seemed difficult and a bit depressing, and I've been feeling flat and lethargic and nothing has seemed particularly joyful – but all of a sudden it does.

And then I realised what has happened: it is almost precisely twelve months since AW retired and we returned from our travels. It has always taken me about a year to settle into each new posting and coming home was no different. England has been just another new country in which to find my way.

Epilogue

So there we were, AW and I, settled into our retirement (we'd moved from Meaninglessness, through Reorientation and Acceptance to Stability), inching slowly towards that final departure when no packing up will be necessary (and trying not to think about the ways in which that will happen), happy and contented and hoping to stay the same for the next decade or so. I had given up writing my diary since there wasn't that much to report (though I had noted how many old British men seemed to be getting into trouble: a seventy-six-year-old crashed a plane into someone's garden, a seventy-four-year-old was caught smuggling tons of hashish into Egypt, and an eighty-one-year-old was arrested for grooming girls. Where did they get the energy?).

I was just beginning to understand why my mother always said that her cosiest decades were her sixties and seventies . . . And then suddenly we found ourselves in an *annus horribilis* – and not because of our own health problems, but those of our beloved daughter Hester. In her early twenties she had developed epilepsy, which was found to be caused by tiny tumours in her brain and now she was told that she must have these removed. She underwent a long, difficult and dangerous operation in the bravest possible way and now her epileptic seizures have stopped; she is back at work and is continuing to mend. Thank you God (and the National Health Service).

Three months into that worry, Aled, our son-in-law who was just thirty-six, had a serious heart attack on holiday in France with Claudia and their children and ended up spending the best part of a week in intensive care – but he too survived and is fitter now than he has ever been.

And just before all that, Jackson was helicoptered to Bristol burns unit when he tipped hot tea over himself, and my precious sister had to have a double mastectomy . . .

In the meantime the Syrian revolution had broken out. At first we believed that Bashar al-Assad would see sense and give the people what they wanted: more freedom and less harassment by the secret police. If he had done so he would have become the hero of Syria, but he didn't and instead has locked the country into a hideously destructive civil war in which hundreds of thousands of people have been killed, injured, tortured or 'disappeared', and millions made refugees. (I can't believe that his wife, the bright young woman I met in Damascus, is complicit in all this, but she certainly seems to be.)

When we lived in Syria, AW and I could never discuss politics with our friends – they were far too afraid, but we felt that most of them secretly wished for the regime to be toppled and we did too. Now many of them have fled to Paris or to the US, losing everything they had in Damascus, and the ones who have to remain there still cannot say what they feel on the phone. God knows how this will end, all we can do is contribute to refugee relief and pray.

Still reeling from the emotional battering of the past twelve months, we suddenly heard some wonderfully cheering news: our dear Rebecca in Azerbaijan had married Herman, the kind man in church who introduced us to her family, and then, to make us smile some more, one of the Wikileaks turned out to be about the Azerbaijan President's wife – US embassy cables revealed that she seems to have a problem showing 'a full range of facial expression', probably due to having had 'substantial cosmetic surgery'. And then, out of the blue, AW was asked to do a job – he didn't really want it: he didn't feel like abandoning the book on date palms he had started writing, or his garden, and going to London, but he was persuaded, and has joined a wonderful charity supplying medical aid to Palestinians. He is pleased with life.

And, at the end of the day (and not counting my secret dread of our endings), so am I.

Acknowledgements

I thank Alexandra Pringle, my guardian angel at Bloomsbury, and her colleagues, Alexa von Hirschberg and Kate Johnson, and David Godwin my agent, and I thank my daughter Claudia again for reading this book in its first draft and cutting out the most embarrassing bits.